The Islands in the Sun Cookbook

Culinary Treasures of the Italian Isles

ALSO BY MARLENA SPIELER

Flavors of Mexico

Sun-Drenched Cuisine

Hot & Spicy

Naturally Good

From Pantry to Table

The Classic Book of Home Cooking (with Mary Berry)

Mexican Snacks

Mexican Main Courses

The Classic Barbeque and Grill Cookbook

The Flavor of California

Vegetarian Pasta

The
Islands in the Sun
Cookbook

CULINARY TREASURES
OF THE ITALIAN ISLES

by
Marlena Spieler

Lowell House
Los Angeles

Contemporary Books
Chicago

Library of Congress Cataloging-in-Publication Data

Spieler, Marlena
    Islands in the sun / by Marlena Spieler.
        p. cm.
    Includes index.
    ISBN 1-56565-450-1
    1. Cookery, Italian.   2. Cookery, Mediterranean.   I. Title.
TX723.S69 1995
641.5945—dc20
                                                 95-50267
                                               CIP

Requests for such permissions should be addressed to:
Lowell House
2029 Century Park East, Suite 3290
Los Angeles, CA 90067

Lowell House books can be purchased at special discounts when ordered in bulk
for premiums and special sales. Contact Department JH at the address above.

Publisher: Jack Artenstein
General Manager, Lowell House Adult: Bud Sperry
Managing Editor: Maria Magallanes
Text design: Laurie Young

Manufactured in the United States of America
10 9 8 7 6 5 4 3 2 1

ACKNOWLEDGMENTS

Thank you: Gretchen Spieler; Janice Gallagher for both her patience and editing excellence, as well as friendship; Paul Richardson of Ibiza, Spain, for sharing his enthusiasm for Sardinian culinary ways; Michael Green of London, Liguria, and the Italian isles, for his generous sharing of recipes, travel notes, and suggestions; Amanda and Tim Hemmeter for their vineyard lunches and much more; Jerome Freeman and Sheila Hannon, Jon Harford, Sandy Waks, Kamala Friedman, Paula Aspin, Rachel Edelson, Esther Novack, and John Chendo, my colleagues at the *San Francisco Chronicle;* and to my family, whose appetite for the delicacies of Italy is robust indeed: my parents, Caroline and Izzy Smith, my aunt and uncle Estelle and Sy Opper, and my grandmother Sophia Dubowsky (Bachi).

Contents

PREFACE

From the moment I stepped off the rowboat onto the damp sand on the tiny isle of Panarea, I was utterly captivated.

Each time I visited Italy I checked the ferry and hydrofoil schedules and was quickly off to the nearest island, eager for discovery and adventure; soon the idea for this book began swimming in my mind. It became apparent that Italy's islands were a second Italy, the foods of the islands the same but different (Sardinian and Sicilian food being their own regional cuisines). The islands seemed like an amplification of Italy; the cuisine as well.

Though my own heritage is from Eastern, not Southern, Europe, and I do not live in Italy, from where I could observe day-to-day life, I nonetheless embrace the Italian islands with greed and passion.

My greed is for sniffing, tasting, and cooking, and discovering as much as I can about the way people eat and how to prepare the most delicious dishes I come across. My passion is to share it all.

As a respectful foreign visitor whose heart is full of appreciation and delight with the foods and ways of the Italian people, I offer this book. The recipes are a mixture of traditional and contemporary, learned as I tasted my way through the islands from restaurants, trattorie, strangers on trains, and little old ladies in the markets. I got recipes from the man selling garlic in the street and another from the sea-urchin seller in Erice, and sometimes, alone in the kitchen with a table full of marvelous fresh ingredients, I made them up.

The recipes I offer typify to me the foods of the islands: strong flavors and bright colors, simplicity of preparation yet often with a twist distinct from the traditions of the mainland, an individuality that comes from living an isolated sea-life.

Out of necessity, there were many dishes I could not include. In addition, my own gastronomic prejudices curtailed recipes such as pig's blood ravioli (eaten for dessert), horse in tomato sauce with basil, and sheep's head (a grisly though delicious dish). In addition, if dishes are quite famous and available in other books, I have not included them unless they are unusual or distinctive versions.

The book also reflects my own background: American, specifically Californian, rather than Italian—lots of recipes for little vegetable dishes, poultry, and olive oil. Though lard is often used for frying in Sicily, I specify olive or vegetable oil.

I hope that what this book lacks in academic authenticity, it makes up for in enthusiastic, vibrantly good food.

To Leah and Alan

INTRODUCTION
ISLANDS IN THE SUN

Visit an Italian island: quirky, eccentric, maybe crazy; you will never feel the same again.

To me, the Italian islands *are* Italy, only more beautiful, more ugly, and more crazy. Sometimes they buzz with something akin to a frenzy; at other times, they are infused with an eerie calm.

Italy's islands are filled with contrasts and contradictions. There are dusty towns lacking even rudimentary sidewalks; industrial wastelands that seem like post-civilization villages; rough mountain towns that are raw and somber, lacking the lyricism one expects to find in Italy.

Yet the islands are often breathtakingly beautiful. Cities, towns and villages, churches, and ruins and castles dot the hillsides. The contrast of international jet set with villages where nothing has changed in centuries is beguiling. The islands mean opposites: wild terrain and gentle land-scapes, manicured villas and humble stone huts, luxury lifestyles and primitive living, simple meals of bread and wine as well as dishes of great finesse. You never know exactly what you are in for.

On the islands I have found an almost intoxicating, end-of-the-world atmosphere where everyday life is put aside and a sense that the rest of the world, including the rest of Italy, doesn't really exist.

Unlike the Greek islands which are a central focus of Greek life, the Italian islands are viewed as peripheral to real life, like precious trinkets scattered in the sea, existing solely for vacation pleasure. With the exception of the two largest islands, Sicily and Sardinia (which may be two of the wildest, maddest, craziest places on earth), the islands are lovely destinations to escape the dulling brutality of everyday life in the cities. Small, personal islands are an antidote to the anonymity of mainland and mainstream travel.

How can one resist warm summer nights, sun-baked afternoons, little tables set on the cobblestones under the cloudless sky, laden with edible riches?

I hope that this book will provide a travelogue of the landscape, agriculture, and history of the islands, and ultimately enrich your appreciation of this land and its cuisine.

The Flavor of the Islands

There is no one unified island cuisine as there is no one unified Italian cuisine. With the dramatic exceptions of the traditional cuisines of the two largest islands, Sicily and Sardinia, the islanders tend to eat the specialties of the mainland regions they lie closest to. Yet these foods reflect the local flavor and individual personality of the islands themselves.

The unifying factor of the islands' cuisine is the shared heritage of the ever-present sea. The sea has been the catalyst for island life, overriding the centuries of foreign and mainland influence.

Isolation from the mainland has provided a rich environment for the growth of eccentricity. The very word *isolated* comes from the Italian word *isola,* meaning island. Island dwellers have an attitude and independence that mainlanders never do. The peaceful sense of isolation paired with the charm of Italy's cultural heritage is a heady combination. And, there is an intimacy with the people you won't find elsewhere. Until the next boat arrives—and that can be quite a while on the smaller islands—you are a member of the community.

Islands have an almost erotic, sensual feeling. Surrounded by water and the primal rhythm of waves lapping on the shore, one almost has the feeling of a lover's embrace. Sailing to an island, one feels as if one is approaching the beginning of life itself as it gradually comes into focus: the volcanic cliffs, green foliage, or desert vistas. As the boat lands, it feels like a new life is about to begin.

The cuisine of the islands is different from that of the mainland, dependent on foods grown locally, traditions and gastronomic habits that might veer toward the eccentric, all put together with typical island independence and sensuality. Innovation of necessity and whim imprints the cuisine, and while all the islands serve up lush fresh foods from the sea, many island specialties feature beans and legumes readily available during seasons when nothing else is.

The Italian islands are connected historically, culturally, and gastronomically to the other Mediterranean islands such as Corsica, Corfu, the Balearics, Malta, and Crete. Pirates had their way with most of the islands, causing endless pillaging and ruin; invaders and conquerors trampled through the islands as well. Traveling from one island to another, one country to another, we find recurring influences: Greek and Carthaginian, Roman, Arab, Spanish, French. Ports throughout Italy are little pockets of North Africa, Spain, France, and Greece. And so we find little dishes from Spain appearing in a corner of Sardinia, French dishes in Elba, Greek flavors savored in parts of Sicily, Arab flavors dominating other regions; everywhere we find eggplant and olive oil and garlic, tomatoes and crusty bread, fruits dripping with sunshine, and fish hauled in pristinely fresh from the sea.

A BRIEF HISTORICAL TOUR AND TRAVELOGUE

With the exception of Sicily and Sardinia, most of the main islands lie widely scattered and grouped together into eight separate areas: Tuscan Archipelago (which includes Elba), Tremiti, Pontine, Bay of Naples, Aeolian, Egadi, Pelagie, and Stagnone. They are connected to the mainland by ferryboats, taxi boats, hydrofoils, yachts, bridges, planes, and helicopters, depending on the island.

Though they often share grand histories of political power from the days when the Mediterranean was a bustling traders' highway, the importance of the Italian islands has been declining since the days of Phoenician traders and ancient prosperity. Invaders may have left behind a legacy of cruelty, but they also left a rich variety of food specialties.

Many of the islands are surrounded by spectacular cliffs, jagged rocks, twisted volcanic outcroppings sea-eroded by the salty winds. Not all are the sites of villages and towns. Three are prison islands, and others, such as Montecristo, are wildlife preserves. Numerous tiny islands are personally owned—Rudolf Nureyev owned two. There are large islands with strong cultures that differ distinctly from one town or village to another, and there are tourist attractions such as Capri that are known as playgrounds of the notorious, rich, and famous.

Some islands, like Panarea, are isolated in the midst of what seems like an endless sea. Others fringe the mainland so closely they are joined not by ferry but by bridge. There are tiny little islands like specks in the sea lying off the coast of bigger islands, and there are towns built on little groups of islands linked by footbridges. Sicily and Sardinia seem more like small continents than islands.

In addition, there are islands that were once a part of Italy's various kingdoms but now belong to other nations. Corsica presently belongs to France, and its language and cuisine display hints of Italian as well as French influence. The Greek island of Corfu, lying between Brindisi and Albania, was once a part of Venice and then was part of Yugoslavia.

The typical Italian island town consists of tall, green-shuttered houses painted in hues of brick, dusty pink, ochre, and yellow or washed in white, all clustered around a tiny harbor. Yet, many of the islands, like Giglio, Capraia, Capri, and parts of Sicily, are more Greek in style, with hilltop towns overlooking the harbor. Elsewhere, in places such as Favignana, Ustica, Portoferraio, and Elba, the towns are more urban with a modest downtown centered on a main piazza just off the port itself.

Despite their differences, all the islands share an indefinable similarity among their foods. Much of the island soil is volcanic, rocky, and, in general, poor. Thus, island fare is often frugal, but at the same time enlivened with an inventiveness born of sensuality and artistic flair.

Sicily and Sardinia

Sicily and Sardinia, Italy's two largest islands, are like nations apart from the Italian mainland—in fact, separate from the rest of the world. Each has its own cultural and gastronomical character, the people clinging to the traditions of their tables, with many foods prepared remarkably like they were three thousand years ago.

It could be said that the very flavor-essence of what we think of today as Italian food originated in these regions. The Greek conquerors imparted their culinary techniques to the Sicilians, and the Phoenician invaders left behind their gastronomical expertise in Sardinia. Over the millennia, wars and invasions, traders and commerce have added layers of Arabian, African, Etruscan, Roman, and Spanish cookery styles to both islands. Added to the pot is the local produce, fish from the surrounding sea, fresh milky cheeses from the sheep and goats that wander the rough terrain.

Poverty has also shaped the cuisine of both islands. The people of these often barren lands have frequently subsisted on bread and/or pasta, seasoned with whatever wild herbs, vegetables, fish, and game they were able to hunt and forage for. From this *cucina di povera*, or food of poverty, a staggering array of imaginative bread and pasta dishes has emerged.

Sicily

With its bitter history of conquests, pestilence, and famine, Sicily is a land of extremes. The island has been been dominated by Greeks, Phoenicians, Romans, Arabs, Normans, French, and Spaniards, each adding their own flavor to the food of the island. In fact, Sicily has been invaded by so many foreign forces during the course of history, its tourist board's official slogan is: Invade Sicily, Everyone Else Has.

Having known more than its fair share of hardships and suffering, Sicily consoles itself with celebrations. Sicilians throw themselves into holidays wholeheartedly and ostentatiously. Each holiday has its own food traditions, and one of the most touching is the *pasta reale*, or marzipan, which is prepared for Sicily's winter holiday, *i morti,* the day of the dead.

For the season of *i morti,* almond paste is formed into lifelike shapes, as luscious in taste as they are startling in their super-realism. These delicacies can be as confusing as they are grand: Is that really a window filled with sausages, salami, and cheeses? Imagine marzipan sandwiches, cakes of soap and tubes of toothpaste, take-away pizzas in paper cartons, fried eggs on a plate, even a whole fishmonger's display, or a greengrocer's with fruits and vegetables (complete with bruises and an insect or two). Marzipan flowers might convince you that a window is really a florist's; and a display of fettucine, spaghetti, plump ravioli, and round tortellini could easily fool you into thinking it was the real thing instead of sweet almond paste.

Sicily has a passion for *fuori tavola,* little snacks or anything eaten anyplace other than properly, at a table. The Casbah-like streets of the marketplace, *la vucciria,* in Palermo—officially Europe's loudest city—is the place to fully indulge in street food. The din of voices and noise is overlaid with the strong scent of spices, pungent salami, salty dried fish. The fishmongers' displays are lavish and abundant, silvery scales shimmering in dappled sunlight, eyes fresh and shining.

Walk through the stalls and inevitably you will be offered samples from the great piles of olives, sweet chewy dried fruits, and fresh cheeses that are so local, they are never seen anywhere else. Buy a stick or two of meaty kabobs or any of the fried foods ubiquitous to Palermo: whole artichokes and eggplants, florets of broccoli or cauliflower, tiny octopus or squid, fritters of zucchini and peppers, stuffed squash flowers. Bite into an *arancia,* a round golden fritter that looks like an orange but consists of fried risotto stuffed with savory meat and peas or melted cheese.

Pasta alla Norma (eggplant pasta) vies with *pasta con le sarde* (pasta and sardines) as the Sicilian national pasta, both served in a myriad of versions throughout the island. Elaborate pasta molds, layered with tomatoes, meatballs, and cheeses, encased in either more pasta or a crisp crust, are celebration fare, proudly prepared for holidays and family festivities.

As for other pastas, Sundays and holidays you'll find great hunks of meat simmering in tomatoey sauce; the sauce is served splashed onto hearty shapes of pasta such as macaroni or bucatini, while the meat is eaten as a separate course.

Everywhere on Sicily you'll find fresh, fresh fish, prepared in savory ways—with olives, tomatoes, raisins and nuts, garlic, herbs, lemon, oranges, artichokes, and lots and lots of olive oil.

Dinner usually ends with fruit, but for celebratory feasts, desserts and pastries are extravagant. The sweet tooth of Arab cuisine is overlaid with the finesse of French, the zest of Spanish, and the peaceful richness of the convents that prepared sweets not only for religious celebrations, but also to earn a little extra cash. Many still do.

Sicilian towns and regions differ widely in character. Siracusa is on the eastern side of the island where Greek ruins are scattered throughout the town. Its people have Greek features and a reputation for being calmer than other Sicilians. Erice, set high on a cliff overlooking the sea, is also notably calm, and famous for both its seafood and almond paste sweets.

As for the teeming city of Palermo, I refer you to the following post-card from my friend Rachel Edelson describing the Felliniesque, half-grotesque and half-delightful exerience of her visit:

> Palermo stikes me as a movie set . . . disintegrating baroque architecture, slathered in grime, laundry hanging outside the most elegant of buildings. Bits of paper litter the streets in profusion; luxuriant, large flower stalls at every fourth street corner. Too beautiful, too ugly, too intense!
>
> The hospitality was so relentless we longed to escape, desserts so sweet we thought we might scream for the nearly unbearable richness of them, and everything heavy on the garlic and oil—which I love. I ate a dish of orange slices, sardines, eggplant cubes, carrots, and beef tendons and it tasted as wonderful as it sounded strange.

Sardinia

Sardinia is a land of great contrasts, both geographical and economical. Poverty sits side by side with prosperity; rolling hills and plains climb into craggy mountains, all surrounded by 1,500 kilometers of coast. The poor eat well in Sardinia as the best foods to be found are often the cheapest, though the rich enjoy a wealth of exquisite seafood.

While Sardinia has felt the brunt of many invaders—Phoenicians, Arabs, Spanish, Piedmontese—they never ventured beyond the coast and thus the interior remains staunchly unconquered. The Sardinian interior remains rooted in traditions that have existed since classical and preclassical times. Flocks of sheep cover the landscape, tended to by shepherds wearing the *mastruca,* or ancient goatskin coat.

The coast has its traditions, too. Fishermen still use wooden hooks and tridents, undeterred by the yachts that berth nearby. The Sardinian table abounds with the foods of the sea, often prepared very simply: lobster, eel, swordfish, mullet, and tuna, made into such specialties as spicy fish soup, *burida;* kassola (a souplike seafood casserole); *scabecciu,* or pickled fish much like the Spanish escabeche. Lobster is adored: split, bathed with olive oil and lemon, topped with crumbs and roasted, or served simply with tomatoes or a scattering of fresh fava beans. Sardinian fish are exported all over Europe—and yes, the island did give its name to the little fish that swim abundantly in the surrounding seas.

While fish is abundant, Sardinian cookery boasts a wealth of meat dishes, especially wild animals. Hunting is a favorite sport for the wealthy and a necessity for the poor. A favorite way of cooking meat in Sardinia is *su carraxiu:* The meat is buried in a hole in which hot coals have burned, then a fire is set on top of the earth mound. It is said that this method arose during the days of animal rustling, as those who had stolen the animal didn't want the cooking aromas to give them away.

Often restaurants in the Sardinian countryside specialize in either *su carraxiu* or fire-roasted meats, offering a selection of antipasti such as boar-meat salami, and pastas with local meats and vegetables or coastal seafoods. A wonderful organization is the *agroturisme* enterprise, a network of farmhouses whose farmers prepare local dishes for paying guests using ingredients grown, hunted, fished, or foraged by themselves.

Just off the road outside Alghero, we stopped at Zia Maria, an unassuming restaurant. It was an immense meal, beginning with antipasti that included shredded roast piglet (with parsley, garlic, and olive oil); eggplant in vinaigrette; wild boar braised in sweet white wine; bread rubbed with garlic, tomatoes, and olive oil; *carta di musica* (Sardinian flatbread) or *pane carasau* (*carta di musica* toasted and sprinkled with salt and oil); marinated artichoke hearts; roasted red peppers; olives; marinated sardines; thinly sliced fennel-scented salami; and more. Bowls of the local pasta, *malloreddus*, were brought to our table, scented with saffron and awash in a spicy tomato sauce; then succulent roast lamb, surrounded by lots of fresh raw fennel chunks, with no dressing at all, deliciously refreshing to nibble on between bites of the rich roast lamb. We drank a homemade red wine, so light it was almost a rosé, and ended the meal with sips of fiery grappa, also made on the farm.

Sardinia is said to have learned its pasta cookery from the Genoese. In addition to the sizes and shapes eaten throughout the rest of the country, specialties include: *makkarrones a ferrittu*, rectangles of pasta draped around knitting needles and left to dry; *culigiones*, ravioli stuffed with spinach and saffron, or made with a potato dough and flavored with onions and mint; *sa fregula*, a couscouslike pasta that originated in ancient Rome; and saffron-flavored dumplings known as both *succu tundu* and Malloreddus (page 90).

Bread is a crucial food on the Sardinian table. Fresh chunky bread is eaten with everything, while stale bread is layered into great rustic casseroles with soup, cheese, and sausage or vegetables. There is also a crisp, flat crackerlike bread, known as *carta di musica* for the cracks on its surface that look much like the lines that form musical staffs. It lasts for months and at its humblest and most sustaining is carried into the fields by the hungry shepherds and herdsmen to eat with their midday meal.

A surprising Sardinian food is yogurt. While yogurt has been eaten in Western Europe only since the early 1900s, Sardinia has enjoyed this tangy fermented milk food since the Roman Empire when there were colonies of Italians and Sardinians in Bulgaria. While the rest of Italy didn't take to it, Sardinia embraced it, no doubt because of the large amount of sheep that graze on its hillsides. Yogurt is therefore a part of Sardinian cuisine, mixed with cheeses and vegetables in ravioli, cannelloni, or dumplings. And, incidentally, traces of Sardinian culture can be found in parts of Bulgaria today.

The Tuscan Archipelago

Scattered in an arc shape in the Tyrrhenian Sea off the coast of Tuscany, the Tuscan Archipelago includes Italy's third largest island, Elba.

Covered with forests, the archipelago is geographically much like Corsica with its abundance of pink granite and pine-covered mountains. Elba is a homey rather than glamorous resort, popular with European families and not as impossibly crowded as other seaside resorts at the height of summer.

Because Elba was invaded and settled by Sicilians, Etruscans, Romans, Moors, Spanish, Pisans, and finally the French (under Napoleon), Elban cookery has a rich overlay of flavors and twists. And Elban soil has a high iron content that is said to give the food that grows there a special flavor. Viticulture proliferates with excellent Elban wines.

Specialties of Elba include *puttentaio,* a ratatouillelike vegetable stew that includes potatoes, favored in the town of Portoferraio. Capoliveri boasts a fish soup with decidedly Spanish origins, *la spurrida.*

Zucchini ripiene, stuffed with a savory meat filling, then fried until crisp, is eaten throughout the islands, as well as a myriad of dishes that combine seafood with pasta and rice. These include *pasta da marina*, with octopus, cuttlefish, clams, and a white wine sauce; and *riso nero,* rice cooked with cuttlefish. Napoleon's favorite dish, by the way, is said to have been Seppie coi Carciofi, squid and artichokes, still a specialty of the island (see page 127).

Tiny Gorgona and Pianosa are both destinations for involuntary residents only: those who are remanded to the Italian penal system. You can catch a glimpse of these islands from the Elba-Livorno ferry, but there is little to see. Once covered with vineyards, monasteries, and farms, they were raided to abandonment by pirates and the land laid to waste.

The isle of Montecristo was made famous by Alexander Dumas's novel. Once a royal playground, it is now a nature reserve that allows no visitors except at the ferry dock and immediate environs.

Giglio and Gianuttri lie farther south. Giglio is known as *dove di mangia bene*, "the place where one eats well." Sadly, barren patches where green forests once stood show the tragedy of what happens to beautiful locations that succumb to the lure of easy tourist bucks, and it will be difficult to eat well if no food grows.

Tiny Gianuttri, unlike most of the other Italian islands, was never plagued by pirates, so it lacks outside culinary influences. No doubt the pirates left the island to itself because it had little water, agriculture, or other things of value.

The Ponziane Islands

Le Isole Ponziane, the little islands that lie in the Gulf of Gaeta, have remained peaceful and charming. Two, Ponza and Ventotene, are inhabited; three, Zannone, Palmarola, and Santo Stefano, are virtually abandoned. They are submerged volcanic structures, rising from the baby blue ocean under equally blue skies, where the sea breezes blow in to cool the suffocating heat of summer.

It is a three-hour sail from the mainland to Ponza, the island that many say is the most beautiful of all the Italian isles. Visiting Ponza is like visiting the Capri of forty to fifty years ago: beautiful, enticing, and utterly Italian. Few cars clutter the streets and the town overlooks the sea and odd rock formations. Cats roam the streets, acting as though all has been built for them alone, and vineyards cover the hills that surround the little town.

The scent of garlic wafts everywhere, and the food is as strong, generous, and lusty as its people. A lentil soup, *lenticchie alla Ponzese*, is favored along with *coniglio alla cacciatore* (rabbit with tomatoes, onions, and mushrooms) and all seafood, including fat local lobsters.

Ventotene is a beautiful little island. Lentils and fava beans are the main crops, asparagus a close third. Then there is Zannone, a nature reserve and home of wild sheep and exotic flora and fauna. Palmarola harbors a few hearty souls, while Santa Stefano is little more than a big rock jutting out of the sea.

Islands in the Bay of Naples

The islands in the Bay of Naples—Capri, Ischia, and Procida—shimmer in the sea as idyllic Italian islands, the destination for hedonistic holidays, the locale par excellence for sun-sex-and-pasta seekers.

Capri was made famous by Emperor Tiberius and his orgies. Young people of both sexes dressed—and undressed—as little Pans and nymphs and frolicked in the gentle countryside, earning the island the title, "Island of Pleasure." Since then it has done its best to live up to its reputation, and has been known as a destination for artists, writers, and heirs and heiresses.

Capri reclaimed its status as a tourist destination with the discovery of the Grotto Azurro, or Blue Grotto. This brought boats filled with tourists aching for a glimpse of the sea cavern bathed in that ethereal blue light. Filippo Marinetti and the Futurists came to Capri to compose the diet that would fuel Italy to strength (pasta was forbidden; unusual foods and provocative colors were emphasized).

When at last it seemed as if Capri could get no wilder, it sank to a sort of middle-class resort spot. But despite its commercial success it retains its taste of *la dolce vita,* the sweet life. Capri remains charming, with an insouciant air of having seen it all. Touristic development is restricted to a small space and the rest of the island is rich with flora, nearly eight hundred species of plants, and a dreamy sun-drenched beauty.

Food in Capri tends to be as full-flavored as its lifestyle. Tomatoes, basil, and olive oil appear with everything, either unadorned as the famous salad, *insalata di Caprese,* or saucing pasta, seafood, chicken, even eggs. Aqua Pazza (see page 40), translated as "crazy water," is a Caprese soup of tomatoes and water or fish stock.

Ischia, a calm island covered with vineyards and filled with mud baths and hot springs, is four times the size of Capri and a welcome destination when the latter becomes claustrophobic and circuslike.

It was the first Greek colony in Western Europe, an outpost along the Mediterranean trade routes, dating back to the eighth century. A hundred years later the Romans occupied it, built baths, and planted vineyards on the slopes of Monte Epomeo. By the end of World War II, Ischia was discovered by artists and writers fleeing the overly popular, tourist-infested Capri. The social set soon followed, seeking the pleasures of the mud baths and springs, adding a certain elegance and sophistication to what remains a simple, quiet, and exquisitely beautiful island.

The towns on Ischia vary from tiny Sant' Angelo, reminiscent of a Greek island, to Ischia Porto, the island's capital. And the people are not overwhelmed by the tourists; streets are lined with trees, shops, and cafes, townspeople strolling through the warm evenings on their way to enjoy an *aperitivo* or to supper at their local trattoria, where they might dine on *zuppe di datteri e cozze* (sea dates and mussels in broth).

Procida, though close to Naples and Ischia, has been bypassed in the development of tourism. A Neopolitan resort in the late eighteenth and nineteenth centuries, it remains unspoiled and charming, a little island covered with lemon groves, vineyards, and fields of artichokes. You might find dishes scented with lemons and their leaves, meat or game stewed with wine, or tender artichokes prepared in a number of ways.

A little islet, Vivara, connected by bridge to Procida, is wild with the hares that are stewed into the special rabbit dishes of Procida.

Seafood, fruits, and vegetables join these rabbit dishes in the cuisine of the three islands, all reflecting Neopolitan flair and international influence. Traditional dishes include spaghetti with sea urchins, stuffed eggplants and peppers, and *antipasto di mare*—whatever is freshest from the briny blue sea.

The Tremiti Islands

The four main Tremiti Islands—San Domino, San Nicola, Caprara, and Pianosa—lie twenty miles off the coast in the Adriatic Sea. They are the only major Italian islands in the Adriatic; other islands there that once belonged to the various Italian kingdoms now belong to Slovenia and to Greece.

The Tremiti Islands, historically at the mercy of invaders and conquerors, pirates, and other intruders, as well as the site of a penal colony up to the days of the Fascists, are today a summer holiday destination. Almost everyone makes a living from tourism. Blue sea, cool fragrant pine trees, cliffs, beaches, and rocky seaside make this little archipelago a terribly pretty place.

San Domino and San Nicola are the primary tourist islands; Pianosa is flat and uninhabited, and Caprara is inhabited mainly by wild rabbits. The latter is still covered with the capers (*capperaia*) that grow wild there and give the island its name.

Troccoli is the local homemade pasta. Seafood features prominently in other island specialties: *spaghetti alla pirata* (with seafood), fish soups such as the famous *brodetto de pesce*, and eggs scrambled with sea urchins.

The Aeolian Islands

Also known as the Lipari Islands, these comprise Lipari, Vulcano, Salina, Panarea, Filicudi, Alicudi, and Stromboli, surrounded by numerous islets. Rising sharply from deep clear water off the coast of Sicily, they are stark and rocky, looking like petrified sirens.

All are volcanic, swept by the wind, surrounded by the violent Tyrrhenian Sea. Their beauty is otherworldly, with rock formations of sharp and strange shapes and colors, soft rolling green hillsides yet great land expanses of white—the pumice of Lipari—or black—the volcano of Stromboli. The highest peak of each island is nearly always shrouded in mist, adding to the sense of mystery.

Until only three or so decades ago, life on the Aeolian Islands was one of struggle and destitution, where people eked out a meager living in the pumice mines, fished from small boats in rough seas, or coaxed a bit of fruit from reluctant vines. Locals have migrated in large numbers, not only to the mainland but also to foreign lands, and at the same time mainlanders have sought refuge in the Lipari Islands, a region of great simplicity and charm.

Lipari, like many of the other islands of the region, is known for its caper bushes, as well as lush, sweet Malvasia wine. Potato focaccio flavored with rosemary and spread with olive paste; tomato and basil bruschetta; and dishes using salted, pressed ricotta cheese (much like feta) are specialties. A local soup is prepared with tomatoes, olive oil, wild mint or oregano, a poached egg, and a bit of diced, salted, and pressed ricotta. Tuna is a favored fish, prepared in a wide variety of ways, especially grilled, then marinated with hot peppers.

Vulcano, an island with five volcanoes, is a strange palette of unusual earth colors: ochres, yellows, oranges, whites, and brick-reds, with pungent, sometimes unpleasant odors rising from the earth. Wildflowers grow in profusion and hot mineral pools dot the island, sometimes bubbling steamily into the sea, while tiny geysers shoot water and mud into the air.

Salina is a fertile green island, its two volcanoes appearing as simple rounded hills, its coastline smooth. Agriculture, rather than tourism, is the economic base of Salina. Capers in huge amounts are exported; grapes are made into Malvasia.

Filicudi is abundant with ferns and palm trees. Volcanic formations rise from the sea off its coast; grottoes and sea-caves dot the island. There are two little villages on the island, with a restaurant or two.

Alicudi is one of the most remote islands in the Mediterranean, a two-square-mile, green, sloping terraced hillside poking up from the sea. There is one village, and the few outsiders who visit come for the excellent fishing, especially lobsters.

Panarea is even smaller: 1.3 square miles, surrounded by numerous islets, known in ancient times as Euonymos, meaning "of good luck."

There is no pier to dock at; when you sail to Panarea your ferry or hydrofoil is met by a rowboat, which will then take you to the area you request. Panarea's coastline is lined with rocky cliffs, the sea often steaming from the hot springs that lie beneath the surface (which were worshiped as gods in ancient times). Wine and olives are specialties of Panarea, and capers are grown on the islet of Basiluzzo.

Stromboli is famous for its black sandy beaches and its volcano's nightly fireworks. The climb is *molto pericoloso*—dangerous and anxiety-provoking—but the rewards are spectacular: The earth rumbles menacingly, a cascade of sparks and embers shoot into the night sky like a red-hot fountain, mist gathers at the top of the mountain contributing to the weird, unreal, extraordinarily beautiful experience. The island was immortalized in Roberto Rossellini's movie of the same name, a name that grew synonymous with scandal as its star Ingrid Bergman left her family for the love of Rossellini.

Ustica

Ustica was first inhabited about 2000 B.C. by people with close ties to both Sicily and the Aeolian Islands. Its name comes from the Roman word *ustum,* meaning "burnt," referring to the charred appearance of the volcanic rocks.

Today the three-square-mile island is a center for underwater activities, beautiful scenery, wildflowers, and little wooded areas. The coastline is wild, scattered with grottoes and tourist hotels; most of the island's residents live in the port and town. Besides the local fish and wines, quail dishes are a specialty.

The Egadi Islands

The three Egadi Islands—Favignana, Levanzo, and Marettimo—lie off the northwest coast of Sicily. In between are the Formiche islets of Formica and Marorone.

Caves show drawings of bulls, dancing figures, deer, and donkeys. The earlier drawings of 12,000 years ago are graceful and fluid of line; the later drawings of Neolithic times are much less sophisticated, almost crude.

In the busy path of Phoenician trading, these islands were at the center of battles and ruled first by Phoenicia, then by Rome. Little is known of the islands' history after the fall of Rome. Genoese traveling merchants stopped there, as did the Spanish, who sold the Egadis to Genoa. The Bourbons then turned Favignana into a penal colony. With the unification of Italy the Egadi Islands joined Garibaldi's forces.

As with most of the islands, young people have been emigrating in order to earn a living; with the advent of modern tourism, however, many are now able to stay home and operate businesses that cater to the tourist trade.

The islands are rich with fish, especially tuna, and the ritual tuna killing festival, or *Mattanza*, is one of the great traditions of the island, despite the fact that modern ways of catching tuna are much more efficient. The pageant and splendor of the festival dates back to the tenth century. These days, with the canning factory in the town of Favignana shut down, the amount of tuna in the sea ever-decreasing, and increased animal-rights sensitivities, the *Mattanza* is becoming a thing of the past. Still, in May and June the festival takes place. This bloody mass killing is not for the faint-hearted.

Favignana is the largest and most populated of the islands, Levanzo the tiniest at 2.2 square miles. Levanzo is an extraordinarily peaceful little place, with dairy cattle, a bit of fishing, and a small community of extremely friendly people.

Marettimo is a place of rock formations and grottoes, with a fishing village unchanged for centuries. The people of Marettimo have little to do with Favignana or Sicily, and are uninterested in tourism.

The Stagnone Islands

Part of the commune (much like a borough) of Marsala, the three Stagnone Islands—Isola Lungha, Isola San Pantalea, and Isola Santa

Maria—are largely uninhabited except for a caretaker or two. Isola Lungha is a regional park dotted with salt flats and lagoons.

Pantelleria

Closer to Tunisia than to Sicily, Pantelleria is isolated and fascinating. It is an agricultural community where ecology students from all over Europe come to observe the local ways of managing natural resources.

Grapes and capers are main crops, and while there are some tourists, they haven't yet intruded on the culture of the island. From the Phoenicians, Romans, Byzantines, and Arabs, Pantelleria is layered with a rich strata of cultures and influences. Special foods of the region include wine made from raisins, tumma cheese, fish and vegetable couscous, *pesto pantesco* rich with tomatoes as well as basil, and *ravioli amari*, filled with ricotta and mint.

The Pelagie Islands

The islands of Lampedusa, Linosa, and Lampione make up the Pelagie archipelago.

Gastronomic specialties of Lampedusa include *pagghiata di pisci*, a paellalike dish of rice and fish; spaghetti with sardines; and grilled tuna.

Linosa lies about 30 miles north of Lampedusa. The little volcanic island is one of the hottest locations in summertime Italy, its three extinct volcanoes obscuring any cooling breezes that might be blowing their way. A tiny agricultural island, with its main road no longer than two miles, Linosa has its own distinctive style of orange and white cottages, their doors and windows slashed with brown or crimson, set dramatically against the dark backdrop of volcanic landscape and deep blue sky.

Lampione is an islet of about one square mile, devoid of vegetation but blessed with waters that are rich in fish. The island is a stop for fishermen, who might whip up a lusty fish stew for their midday meal.

And the Others . . .

All along the Italian seacoast lie a smattering of little islands, some no more than rocks, many with a building or two rising from the sea. The Lido is the long island that lies off the coast of Venice; Murano, Burano, and Torcello are the islands in the lagoon famous for their glass and crafts; Grado is known for its spa. The seafoods, rice, and bitter greens of the Venice/Treviso area are eaten here as well.

On Italy's east coast, near Ferrara, lies Comacchio, a small town built on thirteen islands joined by bridges over canals. Eel is the most favored dish, grilled or simmered in tomato sauce, and young eel are especially prized.

And it is not just the sea that is studded with islands. Italy's lakes have islands, too, perfect for day trips, consisting of gardens, forests, and little restaurants with their own specialties. Throughout Umbria, Piedmonte—indeed, anywhere in Italy that you find lakes—chances are you'll find islands resting in their waters.

Antipasti

APPETIZERS

Meals in the islands often begin with brightly colored, vibrantly flavored antipasti eaten outdoors, under the shade of a lemon tree or beneath a grapevine trellis. Whether rustic foods in near-primitive surroundings or sophisticated flavors in a chic decor, it all tastes so much more delectable when eaten in the open air.

In the islands, as in the rest of Italy, antipasti act as the doorway to the meal. They usher the diner into the mood and rhythm of the meal. They might be strongly flavored salads, simply prepared seafood, or thick slices of rough bread rubbed with garlic and topped with savory spreads. What they all have in common is an informality, full of flavor and simplicity.

Following is a selection of antipasti, some traditional, others inspired by traditional flavors made with what I had on hand.

I Olive
OLIVES

ONE of the delights of the antipasto table is the array of ceramic bowls filled with glistening olives. Whether green or black, large or small, dried in salt, preserved in oil, or bobbing up and down in tangy brine, the olive tastes essentially of the Mediterranean and is an intrinsic part of any antipasto. Indeed, a crock of olives, a loaf of bread, and a plate of herbs make one of the most evocative, satisfying antipasti imaginable.

Marinating olives adds even more flavor and is a delightful way to add a personal taste: lemon, hot peppers, herbs, sun-dried tomatoes, and aromatics all enhance the briny olive, as does garlic. When home canning olives, however, take care that you don't keep the olives in a tightly sealed jar with garlic and olive oil for longer than two weeks since chopped raw garlic breeds botulism.

Olive Verde con Pomodori Secchi
GREEN OLIVES WITH SUN-DRIED TOMATOES

The combination of tangy green olives and sweet-savory sun-dried tomatoes is zesty and full of flavor. I adore the way the tomatoes are chopped into an uneven sort of paste: some in chunks, some more saucy. It gives a lively flavor and interesting texture. Serve with goat or sheep cheese and bread, along with a small basket of fresh young vegetables.

$1/4$ to $1/2$ cup marinated sun-dried tomatoes

3 cloves garlic, finely chopped

Large pinch thyme

2 cups green olives, pitted (any green olive is fine: Italian, Spanish, Californian)

1. Whirl sun-dried tomatoes with a bit of their marinade in blender or processor on and off until you have a chunky paste: You want some of the tomatoes to remain whole or in halves, the rest in a saucy pastelike mixture.
2. Combine tomatoes with garlic, thyme, and olives, adding a bit more of the marinade if needed. Serve right away, or leave to marinate. Keep chilled until an hour or so before serving, then bring to room temperature.

Olive Verde e Finocchio in Salsa Verde
GREEN OLIVES AND FENNEL IN PARSLEY-GARLIC SAUCE

This makes a lovely green garlic-scented sauce to cloak the olives and fennel in. You'll probably find yourself dipping your bread in as well.

4 to 5 cloves garlic, finely chopped

4 to 5 tablespoons chopped parsley, preferably flat-leaf Italian

Large pinch fennel seeds

2 tablespoons olive oil

1 fresh fennel bulb, diced

2 cups green olives

2 teaspoons sherry or red wine vinegar, or to taste

Combine garlic with parsley, fennel seeds, and olive oil. Mix well, then toss with fennel bulb and olives. Add sherry or vinegar and chill until ready to serve.

Olive Neri Picante
SPICY BLACK OLIVES

Oil-cured black olives have a dark, intense flavor that is enhanced by a provocative spicing of hot peppers. Serve a little bowlful with a plate of highly seasoned salami-type sausages, a wedge of pungent cheese resting on a bed of herby greens, a loaf of rough country bread, and a flask of red wine.

1 cup oil-cured black olives

1/2 to 1 teaspoon red pepper flakes, or to taste

2 tablespoons olive oil

Juice of half a lemon (optional)

Combine ingredients.

Variation: Add garlic to taste.

SWEET, ripe tomato salads are an intrinsic part of Italian summer meals, especially on the islands where the tomatoes are local, vine-ripened, and often astonishingly good. They may be sprinkled only with a little salt and olive oil or dressed more lavishly, with aromatics, herbs, and a splash of vinegar.

In my home we greedily dip our bread into the delicious pink-tinged juices left behind. Sometimes we decide to forgo the rest of the meal, and as the salad disappears, I cut up more and more tomatoes and toss them into the bowl. We eat and eat until we are happily sated.

Pomodori con Salsa Basilica
TOMATOES WITH BASIL DRESSING
Sardinia

Serves 4 to 6

I ate this salad in Sardinia, made from the brilliantly flavorful little island tomatoes. The dressing was made by our Ligurian cook and is reminiscent of her specialty, pesto: green, fragrant, and garlicky. Serve it right away, however, as the vinegar in the dressing turns the basil gray within a half hour or so.

8 to 12 ripe tomatoes, sliced

Salt and pepper

Pinch of sugar

2 to 3 cloves garlic, chopped

2 to 3 tablespoons balsamic or red wine vinegar

3 tablespoons pesto

1. Arrange tomatoes on a plate and sprinkle with salt, sugar, pepper, and garlic. Drizzle with olive oil and vinegar.
2. Dot with pesto before serving.

Shortcut: When I have good, bright green, strongly flavored pesto and sweet ripe tomatoes available, I shortcut this salad: Drizzle a bit of olive oil and good red wine or balsamic vinegar over the tomatoes, then dot with pesto.

Insalata di Pomodori
TOMATO SALAD WITH ROSEMARY AND FRESH MINT
Sardinia

Serves 4 to 6

Like most Mediterranean islands, parts of Sardinia are covered with hill-sides of fresh rosemary. Though I know of no local traditions combining the two, we picked handfuls on our walks, then chopped the herbal spiky leaves and tossed them into our daily tomato salads, along with tender leaves of sweet, fresh mint.

8 to 12 ripe tomatoes, sliced or cut into wedges

1 to 2 tablespoons thinly sliced fresh mint leaves, or 1 teaspoon crumbled dried mint

1/2 to 1 teaspoon chopped fresh rosemary leaves

Sprinkle of salt, pepper, and sugar

Balsamic (or red wine) vinegar and olive oil to taste

Sprinkle tomatoes with mint and rosemary, then salt, pepper, sugar, vinegar, and olive oil. Serve right away at room temperature or chill up to 2 hours until ready to serve.

Pane e Caponata

BREAD SALAD
Lipari

A classic salad of stale bread and juicy tomatoes, splashed with olive oil and vinegar, this is much like the *panzanella* of Tuscany and the other bread salads found throughout the Mediterranean. It makes a pleasing lunch dish on a languid day, followed by grilled seafood and a fresh, cooling wine.

The following recipe is loosely based on a description given to me by an Italian boat captain particularly passionate on the subject. While the traditional way with bread salads is to first soak the bread in water, then squeeze it dry before dressing, the captain said "No!" and I agree with him. This can make too watery a dish. Instead, toss everything onto the dry bread directly, adding tomato juice to the olive oil, vinegar, and other dressing ingredients, with extra vegetables as well, to provide even more savory juices for the bread to absorb.

$2/3$ pound stale French bread such as sourdough (do not use baguettes—they have too much crust)

10 garlic cloves, chopped

10 medium-sized ripe tomatoes, diced

1 small to medium-sized red onion, chopped

1 medium-sized red bell pepper, diced

$1/2$ cup tomato juice, or as needed

$1/2$ to $2/3$ cup olive oil

$1/4$ to $1/3$ cup red wine vinegar

Salt and pepper

$1/2$ cup pitted and halved Italian or Greek-style black olives

1 medium-sized celery stalk, diced

$1/2$ cup chopped fresh basil

$1/2$ cup coarsely chopped parsley

1. Cut stale bread into cubes. If bread is not quite stale, spread cubes on cookie sheet and dry in a 250–300°F oven for 30 minutes.
2. Toss bread cubes with garlic, tomatoes, onion, red pepper, and

tomato juice. Dress with olive oil and vinegar, adding more if needed, then season with salt and pepper and add olives, celery, basil, and parsley. Taste and adjust seasoning.

3. Let sit covered until ready to serve, or chill if it is longer than 3 hours. (Bread salads can be very tasty the next day, but extra juices should be poured off if needed, and the flavor oomphed up with extra seasonings.)

Pomodori al Forno
TOMATOES BAKED WITH HERBS
Sicily

Serves 4 to 6

Ah, such delicious simplicity: tomato halves, strewn with herbs and splashed with olive oil, then baked until soft and yielding. While such dishes are eaten in various guises throughout the Mediterranean, to me they taste like the essence of Sicily.

Enough ripe but firm tomatoes to fill the bottom of an earthenware casserole when halved

About ¼ cup coarsely chopped fresh basil or parsley

About ¼ cup coarsely chopped fresh mint leaves

3 to 5 green onions, thinly sliced

3 to 5 cloves garlic, chopped

3 to 4 tablespoons olive oil, or to taste

Salt

1 teaspoon balsamic vinegar, or to taste

1. Cut tomatoes into halves crosswise. Arrange cut side up in casserole.
2. Arrange the basil or parsley, mint, and green onions around the tomatoes, then sprinkle the tomatoes with garlic, olive oil, salt to taste, and balsamic vinegar.

3. Bake in 350°F oven for 45 minutes or until tomatoes are tender but not mushy. Remove from oven and let cool. Enjoy with crusty bread.

Insalata di Pere e Parmigiana
PEARS, PARMESAN, BASIL, AND MINT WITH BITTER GREENS
Lido, Venetia

Serves 4

This marvelous salad of contrasting flavors and textures combines the bitter greens the Venice and Treviso area is so well known for, along with pungent salty cheese from nearby Parma, and sweet fruit and herbs. It is particularly good served with sautéed chicken or grilled meats, the meaty juices adding their savor.

About 4 cups mixed bitter greens: frisee, radicchio, baby lettuces, etc.

3 tablespoons olive oil, or as desired

1 tablespoon red wine vinegar, or as desired

Salt and coarsely ground black pepper

¹/₄ cup each thinly sliced fresh basil and mint leaves

1 ripe pear, thinly sliced or diced

About 2 ounces pungent cheese such as Romano or pecorino, cut into shavings

Toss greens with olive oil and vinegar, and salt and pepper to taste. Arrange on a serving platter and strew the top with mint, basil, pear, and cheese shavings. Serve at once.

Insalata di Pomodori con Maize e Basilica
Tomatoes, Zucchini, Sweet Corn, and Fresh Basil
Sardinia

Serves 4

The little salad is at its most memorable when made with the best of summer's harvest: corn freshly picked and sweet, tiny zucchini that have not yet grown bitter and astringent, and ripe, juicy tomatoes.

4 ears of sweet young corn on the cob (I especially like white kernels)

1 pound zucchini (about 4 small to medium or about 16 baby-sized zucchini)

8 ripe medium-sized or 12 smaller tomatoes, cut into wedges

3 tablespoons olive oil

1 tablespoon red wine vinegar or balsamic vinegar

Salt and pepper

1/4 small to medium-sized onion, finely chopped

1 clove garlic, finely chopped

About 2 ounces pecorino or Parmesan cheese, thinly shaved

2 to 3 tablespoons thinly sliced fresh basil leaves

1. Shuck the corn and discard the husks, saving a handful of the cornsilk to add to the cooking water (though it will be discarded, it amplifies the corn flavor).
2. Cook corn, along with handful of cornsilk, covered, in rapidly boiling water until corn is just tender. For fresh corn, this should take only a few minutes. Do not overcook. Remove corn from water to cool, then strain cooking water and use for preparing soup another time.
3. Cut the kernels off the cooled cobs, using either a sharp knife or a special tool for cutting corn. Set kernels aside and discard cobs.
4. Meanwhile, tend to the zucchini: If using medium-sized ones, cut into bite-sized pieces. If using baby-sized ones, leave whole. Cook zucchini in a small amount of boiling water until just tender.

Drain (I always reserve cooking liquid for soups) and let cool.

5. Arrange corn and zucchini on a plate along with the tomato wedges. Dress with olive oil and vinegar, and season with salt and pepper. Sprinkle with onion, garlic, cheese shavings, and basil, then serve.

SARDINIA

THE TOMATOES OF SARDINIA, GROWN IN THE SANDY SOIL OF SANTA MARGHERITA, ABOUT TWENTY MILES DOWN THE COAST FROM CAGLIARI, ARE FAMOUS THROUGHOUT ITALY. THEY ARE NOT THE MOST BEAUTIFUL, SOMETIMES MARKED WITH SPLOTCHES OF GREEN OR POCKED WITH LITTLE DENTS. ONE COULD CALL THEM PUNY, AS THEY ARE HALFWAY IN SIZE BETWEEN AN ORDINARY TOMATO AND A CHERRY TOMATO. BUT THEIR SMALL SIZE BELIES THEIR BIG FLAVOR: BITE THROUGH THE FIRM SKIN AND ITS SWEET-TANGY FLESH NEARLY EXPLODES IN YOUR MOUTH.

THESE TOMATOES TASTE LIKE ESSENCE OF TOMATO; THEY ARE PROUDLY EATEN IN A WIDE VARIETY OF SALADS, SAUCES, SOUPS, AND STEWS, OR WITHOUT EMBELLISHMENT AT ALL, OUT OF HAND.

Bietole Agrodolce
SWEET-SOUR BEETS WITH ONIONS, GARLIC, AND MINT
Sicily

Serves 4 to 6

Earthy-tasting beets are particularly good prepared in Sicilian "agrodolce" style—sweet and sour. The balance of sweet and the pleasant shock of sour, along with the aromatics of onion, garlic, and mint, reflect Greek and Arabic heritage.

Serve with crusty bread and a selection of several other salads: ripe tomatoes and goat cheese, marinated seafood, a simple plate of black olives.

4 medium-sized beets

2 medium-sized yellow or white onions, chopped

4 to 5 cloves garlic, chopped

3 tablespoons olive oil

2 tablespoons lemon juice

2 tablespoons sugar, or to taste

Salt and black pepper

2 teaspoons chopped fresh mint, or about $1/4$ teaspoon dried mint (to taste)

1. Steam or boil beets until just tender, then remove from pan and let cool.
2. When cool enough to handle, slip off their skins and cut the beets into large dice or small chunks. (Alternatively, add diced raw beets to the sautéing onion and garlic in the following step. Allow a much longer cooking time, however—about 30 minutes, taking care to check the beets and add extra liquid if they show signs of burning.)
3. Lightly sauté onions and half the garlic in the olive oil until softened, then add the beets, lemon juice, sugar, salt and pepper, and half the mint.
4. Simmer, covered, for 10 minutes or so. Add remaining garlic and adjust seasoning. Return to heat for another 5 to 10 minutes, then let cool. Serve at room temperature, sprinkled with remaining mint.

Funghi con Vinaigretta e Formaggio

MUSHROOMS WITH MUSTARD VINAIGRETTE AND
SHAVINGS OF PARMESAN

Capri, Ischia, Procida

Serves 4 to 6

These pert, sharply dressed, thinly sliced raw mushrooms are delicious with crusty bread or grilled meat or poultry, or as an appetizer paired with marinated fresh mozzarella.

2 to 3 cloves garlic, finely chopped

1 to 2 tablespoons Dijon-type mustard

1 tablespoon balsamic vinegar, or to taste

4 tablespoons olive oil

Salt and pepper

¾ pound fresh mushrooms, thinly sliced

1 tablespoon finely chopped parsley

2 to 3 ounces coarsely shredded or shaved cheese such as Parmesan, pecorino Romano, or aged asiago

Combine garlic, mustard, vinegar, and olive oil. Season with salt and pepper, then toss with mushrooms and parsley. May be eaten right away, or left to chill and marinate. Before serving, sprinkle with the shredded or shaved cheese.

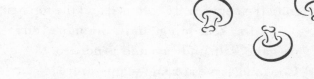

Peperoni
BAKED MULTICOLORED PEPPERS
Sardinia, Sicily

Serves 6

With flamboyant flavor, a brilliant flash of color, and an aroma scented with garlic, these peppers are delectable as an appetizer, relish, or sandwich filling. I like serving briny black olives and a soft goat cheese with this.

The addition of raisins is both Sardinian and Sicilian. They add their fruity sweetness to the savory peppers while a little extra vinegar gives an Arabic sweet-sour flavor.

2 medium-sized red bell peppers, seeded and cut into pieces 1½ to 2 inches wide

2 medium-sized green bell peppers, seeded and cut into pieces 1½ to 2 inches wide

2 medium-sized yellow bell peppers, seeded and cut into pieces 1½ to 2 inches wide

6 cloves garlic, chopped

1 ripe tomato, diced

2 tablespoons tomato paste

3 tablespoons raisins

3 tablespoons olive oil

1 to 2 tablespoons red wine vinegar

1 to 2 teaspoons sugar

Generous pinch oregano

Salt and cayenne pepper to taste

1 to 2 tablespoons chopped parsley

1. Combine all ingredients except the parsley in a baking dish and spread evenly.
2. Bake in a 400°F oven for about 40 minutes, turning once or twice, until the peppers are softened and the top lightly browned in spots.
3. Taste for seasoning and add more olive oil, vinegar, sugar, oregano, salt, and cayenne as needed.
4. Cool and serve at room temperature, sprinkled with parsley.

Sicilian Variation: Add a handful of slivered almonds and a tiny dash of almond extract.

Fave en Umido
FAVA BEANS STEWED IN TOMATOES
Elba

Serves 4

Fresh fava beans, freed from their tough outer skin, are light and fresh, and very good stewed in a zesty Mediterranean tomato sauce. The addition of a little stock is not really authentic since in Italy the fresh ingredients have so much more flavor than supermarket ones at home do. If your tomato paste is full of vine-ripened wonderful flavor, omit the stock.

1 onion, chopped

2 to 3 cloves garlic, coarsely chopped or sliced

3 tablespoons olive oil

2 tablespoons chopped parsley (preferably flat-leaf Italian)

2 to 3 teaspoons torn or chopped fresh basil leaves

1 teaspoon chopped fresh mint (optional)

1 to 1½ cups young green fava beans, cooked and peeled

2 to 3 tablespoons tomato paste

½ cup chicken or vegetable stock

Pinch sugar if needed

Salt and pepper if needed

1. Lightly sauté onion and garlic in olive oil until softened. Then add parsley, basil, mint, and cooked, peeled fava beans. Cook a few minutes, then stir in the tomato paste and stock. Continue to cook until sauce is thickened. Add more liquid if needed.
2. Season with sugar, salt, and pepper to taste.

Insalata di Patate

POTATOES WITH OLIVE OIL, GREEN ONIONS, AND LEMON

Throughout the Islands

Serves 4

Creamy tender new potatoes, still tasting of the earth they were dug from, tossed with a little green onion–scented olive oil, a squeeze of lemon, and a sprinkling of fresh oregano make the quintessential Italian potato salad. White onion or garlic may be used in place of the green onions, and other herbs can be added at will: chives, parsley, or borage, which is favored throughout the islands, especially Sicily (a handful of salad greens and little blue borage blossoms make a splendid garnish).

This makes a spunky antipasto or light lunch, combined with other little salads such as Bietole Agrodolce (page 12), and thin slices of a cured or smoked fish or the salted fish roe beloved throughout the islands, bottargu.

3 pounds small to medium-sized young and tender potatoes, well-scrubbed

Salt and coarsely ground pepper

About ¼ cup olive oil, or to taste

1 bunch green onions, thinly sliced, or 1 small white onion, chopped

1 teaspoon chopped fresh oregano or marjoram, or to taste

Juice of ½ lemon, or to taste

1. Cook potatoes in rapidly boiling salted water until cooked about halfway through. Remove from heat and let sit in the hot water for about 30 minutes to let the heat slowly finish cooking them.

2. When the potatoes are tender, drain and cut into halves or chunks. Toss with remaining ingredients and season to taste. Serve at room temperature.

Lenticchie con Aglio
LENTILS IN OLIVE OIL WITH HOT PEPPER, GARLIC, AND PARSLEY
Tremiti Islands

Serves 4

This simple little antipasto of bay leaf–scented lentils dressed in olive oil, hot pepper, and garlic is a dish whose vivacity belies its humble ingredients and ease of preparation. The strong flavors are typical of the region.

Though one thinks of fish and sun-drenched garden vegetables when it comes to Italian island food, in fact beans and lentils are a staple of all the islands, especially during seasons when fresh food is scarce.

Serve with chunks of crusty bread and several other little salads: thinly sliced cucumbers, roasted peppers, tangy goat cheeses.

½ cup brown lentils	2 cloves garlic, chopped
3 to 4 bay leaves	Salt
1½ cups water	1 tablespoon coarsely chopped parsley
Cayenne pepper	
4 tablespoons olive oil, or more as desired	

1. Place lentils and bay leaves in a saucepan and add water. Bring to a boil and cook for 20 minutes or so or until half-tender (you want the lentils to retain their shape and not become mushy and overcooked). If mixture becomes too dry, add a little more water.
2. When lentils are half-tender, remove from heat and cover. You want to have just enough extra liquid in the pan so that the lentils can expand a bit as they finish cooking. Let sit until they reach room temperature.
3. Drain (reserving any liquid for soups), remove bay leaves, and place lentils on plate. Toss with cayenne pepper, olive oil, garlic, and salt, then sprinkle with parsley and serve.

Insalata di Mare
SEAFOOD SALAD

Serves 4 to 6

You'll find such simple mixtures of seafood, eaten at room temperature, with little more than a cloak of olive oil and lemon, throughout Italy's seafronts and islands. Sometimes the salads will include potatoes, as this one does; others include white, brown, or green beans. Still others feature only the luxury of seafood. Often, too, *insalata di mare* will be served with homemade mayonnaise; I prefer one flavored with pounded raw garlic, much like aïoli.

An interesting nuance of flavor is given by soaking the mussels and clams in bay leaf and lemon-scented water overnight, and cooking the shrimp in lemon water by an almost Asian steeping method rather than a quick boil.

1 to 2 pounds mussels, in their shells

1 to 2 pounds clams, in their shells

2 to 3 bay leaves

2 to 3 lemons, 1 halved, the other 1 or 2 juiced

8 ounces raw shrimp, shells left on

8 ounces cleaned squid, the bodies cut into rings, the tentacles into bite-sized lengths

About 1½ pounds waxy potatoes (5 to 8 small to medium-sized ones)

8 ounces very fresh thin green beans, trimmed

Meat from 6 cooked crab legs or 2 lobster tails, cracked and picked

⅓ cup olive oil

Salt and pepper

2 to 3 tablespoons chopped parsley (preferably flat-leaf Italian) and fresh oregano or marjoram, to taste

1. Place mussels and clams in pot with bay leaves, one lemon half, and generous water to cover. Leave overnight in cool place or refrigerator to clean the sea critters of their sand and grit and to subtly flavor their flesh. The next day remove shellfish and place in pan with just enough water to cover. Cook covered over high heat for about 10 minutes, or until shells pop open. Discard any that remain shut. Let cool.

2. Remove mussels and clams from their shells and set aside.

3. Place shrimp in pan with remaining lemon half and water to cover. Bring to a boil, then remove from heat, cover, and let steep until water is cool. Shrimp should be pink and cooked through but very tender. Drain and discard lemon half. Remove shells.

4. Place squid in pan of water and bring to a boil, then remove from heat and let sit, covered, until the water is cooled and the squid cooked through.

5. Meanwhile, cook potatoes until just tender. Drain and let cool until they can be easily handled. Cut into halves or bite-sized chunks and set aside.

6. Steam or boil green beans until just tender, about 5 minutes. Drain and rinse in cool water, then cool.

7. Combine mussels, clams, shrimp, squid, potatoes, green beans, and crab or lobster. Dress with olive oil and lemon juice, season with salt and pepper, and sprinkle with parsley and oregano or marjoram.

Fagioli Borlotti
BROWN BEANS WITH ONIONS, GARLIC, AND OLIVE OIL
Tremiti Islands

Serves 4 to 6

Borlotti beans have a certain meaty, rough, and distinctive flavor (see Special Ingredients, page 258). Earthy and unpretentious, they are good in pastas and risotti, or added to a stew or soup, but are at their best cooked simply, as in the following dish. Season with a bit of onion and garlic, a drizzle of olive oil, and just enough lemon juice to add a tang.

2 cups cooked borlotti beans (either cooked dried beans or canned and drained), rinsed well with cold running water

1 onion, finely chopped

2 cloves garlic, chopped

Salt and pepper

2 tablespoons olive oil, or more if desired

1/2 teaspoon lemon juice

Combine beans with remaining ingredients. Let sit for at least an hour before serving.

Variation: Con Rosmarino
Sprinkle the beans with 1/2 teaspoon or so of chopped fresh rosemary.

Melanzane all'Usticese

TINY EGGPLANTS IN SWEET-SOUR DRESSING

Ustica

Serves 4

This sweet-sour marinated eggplant dish comes from the little island of Ustica, off the coast of Palermo. While it is at its best with the tiny Italian eggplants that look enchanting and keep their shape as they cook, the dish is also delicious using either ordinary eggplants or oblong Asian ones, cut into chunks about 3 inches in length.

1 pound baby eggplants, no larger than an adult thumb

About 2 tablespoons chopped dried mint, or 4 tablespoons chopped fresh mint

6 to 10 cloves garlic, slivered

3 tablespoons olive oil

1 red bell pepper, diced (optional)

3 to 5 tablespoons red wine vinegar, or as needed

2 tablespoons water

2 to 3 teaspoons sugar

Salt and pepper

1. Wash the tiny eggplants and leave their stems on. Make a cut in each and insert first a bit of dried (or fresh) mint and then a sliver of garlic.

2. Brown the eggplant in olive oil along with the diced red pepper, then reduce heat and add half the vinegar, the water, sugar, and salt and pepper to taste. Cook over low heat, covered, for 15 to 20 minutes. Eggplant should be very tender but keep their shape and garlic stuffing. The sauce they are cooking in should be sweet-sour and flavorful.

3. Season with remaining vinegar to taste and let cool until ready to serve.

Sicilian Citrus Salads

SALADS of citrus fruit abound in Sicily, stunning in their tart-sweet simplicity, often combined with fragrant mint or pungent onion and dressed with rich olive oil.

Blood oranges, tangy juice oranges, slices of breathtakingly sour lemon all find their way into salads or are simply dressed in olive oil and set out on plates to accompany any meal, for a fresh contrast with the richness of the other dishes.

Citrus salads balance bitter greens, pungent olives, spicy onions, and chiles. They make a refreshing base for richer toppings: herring, celery, shrimp, olives of all sorts, anchovies, cold boiled beef, bitter greens, sardines. Indeed, with typical Sicilian generosity there is no end to the toppings these salads might come embellished with.

While they might be a surprise to tastes not acclimated to them, citrus salads are quintessentially Sicilian, full of Mediterranean flavor, and one of the most refreshing dishes one could eat, especially when the sun scorches and the air hangs hot and sultry.

Insalata di Arancia, Peperoni, e Spinaci
ORANGE, ROASTED RED PEPPER, AND SPINACH SALAD
Sicily

Serves 4

This salad is as beautiful as a Fauvist palette or a sunset over a green hillside: streaks of scarlet atop cubes of bright orange, all surrounded by dark green spinach. Slice the oranges if dicing them is difficult and you end up with more juice and pulp than you do fruit. Using a sharp knife makes all the difference.

Serve as an antipasto along with a plate of salami or large Mediterranean anchovies and thin shreds of celery, followed by roast chicken and a plate of fruit and cheese for dessert.

½ bunch spinach or 1 package frozen spinach (about 12 to 16 ounces)

2 oranges, peeled, seeded, and diced; or 3 tangerines, peeled, seeded, and diced

1 roasted red bell pepper, peeled and cut into short strips

½ white or yellow onion, chopped

Olive oil to taste

Juice of about ¼ lemon, or to taste

Cayenne pepper or coarse black pepper

Pinch dried mint or chopped fresh parsley or basil

1. Cook spinach until al dente and bright green (if frozen, cook covered, directly from the freezer, turning every so often so that it cooks evenly). Rinse and dry well, squeezing out excess liquid. Set aside.

2. Combine oranges, red pepper, and onion. Drizzle with lemon juice, olive oil, and cayenne or black pepper to taste. Chill for at least 30 minutes.

3. When ready to serve, sprinkle orange and pepper mixture with mint, then garnish with spinach. Drizzle with extra olive oil if desired, then serve.

Insalata di Arancia, Limone, Olive, Finocchio, e Aglio
ORANGE AND LEMON SALAD WITH OLIVES,
FRESH FENNEL, AND GARLIC
Sicily

Serves 4

Garlic—strong, fragrant, and distinctive—is surprisingly delicious in orange salads. In fact, the simplest recipe was given to me by an old fisherman: Slice an orange, sprinkle with garlic, drizzle with olive oil, and eat very cold. He liked it alongside most fish and seafood dishes, he said. With a nudge, nudge, wink, wink, he added, "Very healthy, good for everything."

3 to 4 ripe flavorful oranges, peeled, pith and seeds removed

1 lemon, peeled, pith and seeds removed

1 to 2 cloves garlic, finely chopped

½ bulb fresh fennel, including some of the fragrant wispy leaves, chopped

3 tablespoons olive oil

5 to 8 black oil-cured olives

1. Slice oranges and lemon thinly. Arrange slices on a large plate or platter and sprinkle with garlic, fennel, and olive oil. Chill until very cold.
2. Arrange olives over the top and serve.

Insalata di Arancia con i Fiori
ORANGE AND BASIL SALAD WITH BORAGE FLOWERS
Sicily

Serves 4 to 6

The little cucumber-scented leaves of borage are eaten in Sicily, scattered atop salads and beany stews, such as the traditional rustic *maccu,* a hefty potage of fava and often other beans as well.

The flowers, too, are tossed into salads, where their blue blossoms are as charming as their fresh scent.

3 to 4 oranges, peeled, with pith and seeds removed

1 onion, peeled and thinly sliced

Handful of basil leaves, thinly sliced or coarsely chopped

Olive oil

Black pepper

Squeeze of lemon juice

Handful of borage blossoms (if not available, substitute $1/4$ European cucumber, chopped; it won't look as beautiful but will add a similar flavor)

1. Slice oranges and arrange on a plate along with onion slices. Sprinkle with basil.
2. Dress with olive oil, black pepper, and lemon juice. Chill until ready to serve.
3. Just before serving, scatter with borage blossoms; if these are not available, scatter with diced cucumber and a handful of other edible blossoms such as purple chive blossoms or nasturtium petals.

Caponata
SWEET-SOUR SPICED EGGPLANT SPREAD
Sicily

Serves 4 to 6

Caponata, caponatina, or *capunata,* depending on the dialect, is the classic Sicilian sweet-and-sour mixture of eggplant, tomatoes, capers, celery, and olives. Often this feisty-flavored mixture is garnished with a variety of ingredients: tuna, hard-cooked egg, or a strong-flavored fish roe such as bottargu. Delicate seafood such as lobster, baby octopus, shrimp, or mussels may be added for visual appeal, since *caponata* looks a bit like lumpy brown sludge, not as pretty as it is tasty.

The provocative, almost shocking sweet-sour flavor reflects Arabian influence on Sicilian flavors. You'll probably have to tinker with the sugar and vinegar balance; it should be distinctively sweet and sour and the amount of sugar you need will depend on the acidity of the vinegar you use.

This is at its best the day after you make it, when its juices have had a chance to mingle and its sweet-sour onslaught is slightly tamed.

1 medium-sized eggplant

Salt if needed

Olive oil for browning (begin with about 1/4 cup, use more if needed)

1/2 head celery, diced

1 medium to large onion, thinly sliced

1/2 cup tomato paste

4 to 5 teaspoons sugar, or to taste

1/2 to 2/3 cup red or white wine vinegar, or to taste

2 tablespoons capers

1/2 cup sliced or halved green olives (either pitted or pimiento-stuffed)

Coarsely ground black pepper

1/4 to 1/2 cup coarsely chopped parsley

1 to 2 cloves garlic, chopped

1. Dice eggplant. Taste it—if bitter, sprinkle generously with salt and let sit to draw out the bitter juices. Rinse and dry.
2. Sauté eggplant in about 3 tablespoons olive oil until tender and browned. Remove from pan.
3. Add remaining tablespoon of oil to pan and brown celery, then return eggplant to pan along with sliced onion, tomato paste, sugar, and vinegar. Cook 5 to 10 minutes to mellow out the harshness of the vinegar. Add several tablespoons of water if mixture becomes too thick and threatens to burn.
4. Add capers, green olives, black pepper, half the parsley, and the garlic. Taste for sweet-sour balance and adjust if necessary. Let cool, then serve sprinkled with remaining parsley.

Zucchini al'Scapice

SAUTÉED AND VINEGARED ZUCCHINI

Sicily

Serves 4

Tart with vinegar, rich with olive oil, reeking deliciously of garlic, and flavored with either fresh mint leaves or sage, Zucchini al'Scapice is typical of Sicilian vegetable antipasti.

4 small to medium-sized zucchini, thinly sliced lengthwise or at an angle

8 cloves garlic, chopped

¼ cup olive oil

2 tablespoons red wine vinegar

3 tablespoons thinly sliced fresh mint leaves

Salt and pepper

1. Sauté zucchini with half the garlic in the olive oil until zucchini is slightly golden-flecked but still crisp. Do not let the garlic brown or it will become bitter.
2. Remove from pan and toss with remaining garlic, vinegar, mint, and salt and pepper to taste.
3. Serve at cool room temperature.

Variation: Zucca al'Scapice

Winter pumpkin is delicious sautéed, then simmered until sweet and sour. Follow the recipe above, substituting about 1½ pounds peeled and sliced pumpkin for the zucchini. Substitute 1 sliced onion for half of the garlic as well, and add a few spoonfuls of sugar, to taste, as the pumpkin simmers in the vinegar.

Salumi
Prosciutto, Bresaola, Salami, and Other Cured Meats

Cured meats such as silken pink prosciutto or thinly sliced air-cured beef, bresaola, and salamilike sausages make a typical Italian start to a meal. Each region has its own specialty—for instance, the outstanding boar salami of Sardinia. These meats are good served in small amounts, their savory flavors paired either with a few other antipasti or contrasted with sweet fruit.

In Tuscany a plate of *salumi* will be accompanied by several hot, crisp crostini, and I never tire of wondering exactly what I will be served when I order *salumi* or *antipasto della casa*.

Antipasto della Casa
An Appetizer of Rustic Elegance from a Mountaintop Trattoria
Tuscan Archipelago

Serves 4

Serve this extravagant platter of luxurious foods with their rustic flavor accompanied by flavorful, coarse country bread.

Truffle oil may be used instead of the olive oil and truffles, or in place of the olive oil and in addition to the truffles. Too much of a good thing? Never!

4 ounces prosciutto, thinly sliced

4 ounces smoked turkey or goose breast, thinly sliced

1 to 2 fresh porcini mushrooms, thinly sliced

Olive oil, strong and fragrant

1/2 fresh black truffle, or a few fragrant truffle shavings

Arrange the prosciutto and smoked turkey or goose on a plate, along with the sliced porcini. When ready to serve, drizzle with olive oil and dust with as much fresh truffle as you can afford.

Bresaola e Menta
AIR-DRIED BEEF SCATTERED WITH SWEET FRESH MINT

Serves 4 to 6

Air-dried beef is much like prosciutto, but prepared from beef rather than pork. The fragrance of sweet mint enhances the savory meat and makes an exquisite antipasto, light yet satisfying. We enjoyed it sitting at a long cloth-covered table, set out under the fruit trees as the day cooled into evening.

Accompany with crusty bread, but no butter to obscure the simple, strong flavors.

4 to 8 ounces air-dried beef, thinly sliced	**Several tablespoons thinly sliced fresh mint leaves**
Olive oil to taste	**Lemon wedges**

Arrange beef on plate and drizzle with olive oil. Sprinkle with mint leaves and serve with lemon wedges.

Bresaola con Formaggio di Caprina e Rughetta
AIR-DRIED BEEF WITH DELICATE GOAT CHEESE
AND ROCKET LEAVES

Serves 4

Bresaola makes a delicious pairing with delicate goat cheese and pungent leaves of arugula. Serve the strong, tangy flavors with chunks of bland crusty bread.

4 ounces bresaola, thinly sliced

2 to 3 ounces mild goat cheese

1 to 2 tablespoons olive oil

1 clove garlic, finely chopped

Pinch thyme leaves, either fresh or dried

Handful of young rocket leaves (arugula)

1. Arrange bresaola on plates or platter.
2. Combine goat cheese with olive oil, garlic, and thyme, mixing well until creamy and lightly whipped.
3. Serve each portion of bresaola garnished with a dollop of goat cheese mixture and rocket leaves.

Prosciutto e Mango
PROSCIUTTO AND MANGO

Sicily

Serves 4 to 6

Prosciutto and melon is a classic, and you find exquisite melons in the islands, fruits with so much perfume and flavor that you remember them long after the season has faded away. Such melons are made to enjoy with prosciutto, but when they are not in season, unripe melons offer only disappointment, not worthy of sharing a plate with the delicious pink slices of ham.

In Sicily I've often eaten prosciutto with mango or pineapple, their sweet-tart fruitiness offsetting the saline richness of the dry, salt-cured ham. For such a dish you need the best mangoes you can find, and the best prosciutto, imported from Italy.

I like to serve this with a few leaves of young arugula or mache.

2 to 3 ripe, sweet, juicy mangoes

8 ounces thinly sliced prosciutto

Garnish: Arugula or mache leaves (optional)

Peel and slice mangoes, then arrange on platter. Drape the prosciutto around the mangoes in an appealing manner, then garnish with the leaves. Serve immediately, or lightly chilled.

Variation: Serve prosciutto with slices of lush, juicy-sweet pineapple.

Six More of My Favorite Fruit and Salumi Pairings

Is there a more seductive way to begin a meal than with the Italian tradition of combining thinly sliced cured meats and slices of fresh, sweet fruit? It doesn't fill you up but stimulates your senses: Sweet and tart contrast with salty and spicy; juicy fruit balances the dry, almost chewy texture of the meat.

It's a very sociable antipasto as well, since the fruit and cured meats may be nibbled on elegantly for a long time, each diner enjoying the company of the others at the table and the pleasure of the day. It requires no preparation other than laying on a plate, tastes equally good in elegant surroundings or outdoors, and can be toted to a beautiful picnic spot along with a bottle of wine and a loaf of bread.

While melon and prosciutto is the traditional starter throughout Italy, and different regions enjoy variations, in the islands I have enjoyed wilder combinations, especially in Sicily: mango, papaya, pineapple—fruits that reflect the islands' closeness to North Africa.

- Three melons and prosciutto: as pretty as it is delicious. Arrange thin slices of three differently colored melons, coral, pale orange, and light green, alongside sliced pink prosciutto.

- Fresh figs: the fat flesh split in two, served open on a plate surrounded by spicy, garlicky dry salami.

- Ripe pears: very sweet and fragrant, with prosciutto and mortadella.

- Kiwi: pale green slices, with orange persimmon (the Japanese firm type are easiest to serve this way) paired with pink prosciutto.

- Papaya: orange-colored and tasting of the tropics, with slices of meaty, chewy coppa (a cured meat, rolled into a sausage shaped like salami).

- Summer-sweet nectarines with coppa, garnished with a few sprigs of sweet fragrant basil.

Formaggio all'Argentera
BROWNED AND MELTED CHEESE WITH GARLIC-VINEGAR SAUCE
Sicily

Serves 2

This is a typical peasant dish, eaten with crusty country bread, perhaps prepared over an outdoor fire as a snack in the field during the *vendemmia*, the picking of the wine grapes.

The dish is authentically made with aged caciocavallo cheese, which is hard to get and, to be honest, not my personal favorite. I make this with most any kind of flavorful cheese: asiago, Monterey Jack, Parmesan, Italian Fontina, or a combination of cheeses. The Cypriot cheese halloumi is particularly good.

Sometimes I sprinkle it with chopped parsley or chives.

8 ounces cheese, cut into two "steaks" or large slabs (if using a mixture, layer the cheese in smaller, thinner pieces)

2 cloves garlic, thinly sliced

1 teaspoon crumbled dried oregano

Several grindings of black pepper

3 to 4 tablespoons red wine vinegar

1. Heat a heavy frying pan and place the cheese in it, then reduce the heat to medium-high. Cook on one side for about 3 minutes or until lightly browned, then turn cheese over with a spatula and brown the other side.
2. Halfway through the second side, add the garlic, oregano, and pepper, and continue to cook. When cheese is finished, add the vinegar, cook a few minutes longer. Serve with the pan juices, accompanied with a chunk of bread.

Mozzarella Marinati

MARINATED FRESH MOZZARELLA

Serves 4 to 6

Mozzarella at its very freshest is delicious on its own, served with just a sprinkling of salt and a drizzle of olive oil to enhance its character.

At its not so freshest or to keep it for up to a week, bathe it in a marinade of garlic, olive oil, herbs, and hot pepper. It both flavors and preserves the cheese balls for a slightly longer time. They will keep deliciously in the refrigerator up to a week, growing even more delicious as they absorb the flavors.

It makes a smashing antipasto with either fresh or sun-dried tomatoes and any fresh herb you fancy: basil, oregano, thyme, marjoram. Any leftovers could be tossed into a dish of pasta or an omelet.

1 pound bocconcini (fresh, small mozzarella balls) or larger fresh mozzarella ball(s), cut into bite-sized pieces

3 to 5 cloves garlic, chopped

2 to 3 tablespoons thinly sliced fresh basil leaves, or several pinches crumbled dried oregano or basil

Several pinches red pepper flakes

3 tablespoons olive oil

Salt and pepper

2 teaspoons balsamic vinegar

1. Combine bocconcini or cut-up mozzarella with other ingredients. If bocconcini are too large for one-bite eating, cut into bite-sized pieces before marinating.
2. Marinate at least overnight in refrigerator. They improve with marinating, up to a week or 10 days, when the cheese will deteriorate.

Formaggio al Salsa Verde
FRESH CHEESE IN GREEN HERBAL SAUCE
Isola di San Pietro

Serves 4

Just off the southwestern coast of Sardinia lies the little island of San Pietro, where I was surprised to find a pocket of Ligurian (Genoese) culture. The strong dialect is distinctly Ligurian, as is the peasant costume, and the houses bear Saracean influence with their kitchens on the top floor. The food is scented with the distinct character of Genoa, especially fresh herbs. Yet the island is nearly on the doorstep of Africa.

Long ago the prince of the island, besieged by pirates, made an offer to the Ligurian fishermen to inhabit the island and thus protect it from intruders.

Today the Ligurian influence remains distinctly in the island's cookery, as this dish of creamy goat cheese topped with a tangy, herbal green sauce reflects.

1 slice country bread, cut into little pieces

About ¼ cup red wine vinegar

3 cloves garlic, chopped

1 cup coarsely chopped parsley

1 ripe tomato, chopped

1 to 2 tablespoons chopped fresh herbs such as marjoram, oregano, or thyme

2 to 3 anchovies, chopped

Black pepper

½ cup olive oil, or enough to make a creamy, emulsified sauce

6 to 8 ounces tangy fresh goat cheese (if cheese is dry and/or crumbly or powdery, beat in a little sour cream, crème fraîche, or olive oil)

1. Place bread in bowl and cover with red wine vinegar and half the garlic. Let sit until bread absorbs the vinegar.
2. Whirl in blender until creamy, then add remaining garlic, parsley, tomato, herbs, anchovies, and black pepper to taste. When smooth, with the machine still running, slowly add the olive oil until it forms a smooth emulsion.

3. Taste for seasoning, adding more vinegar, olive oil, or pepper if necessary (you will probably not need salt since the anchovies and cheese are salty).
4. Place cheese on plate or in shallow bowl and spread with the salsa.

Variation: The tangy green salsa makes a zesty little dipping sauce to serve with *calamari fritti,* crisp-fried squid. Cut the cleaned squid into strips, then toss with seasoned flour and fry quickly, crisply, in hot vegetable oil. You might want to lighten the green salsa with a few spoonfuls of mayonnaise for a creamier mixture.

Formaggio alla Griglia con Limone
GRILLED CHEESE ON LEMON LEAVES
Capri, Ischia, Procida

Serves about 4 as an appetizer

A slab of mild cheese, laid onto a lemon leaf (be sure to use unsprayed leaves), then grilled or pan-broiled until the cheese melts, delights in its simplicity. This dish is typical of the Amalfi coast and its islands where lemon groves cover the hillsides and their fruit are plentiful with tangy flavor and perfumes. The leaves, too, impart a lemony, spicy edge. You might also find meatballs wrapped in the glossy green leaves, then grilled, or skewers of seafood served on a leaf-lined plate.

When the cheese melts onto the leaves, the leaves brown and dry while protecting the cheese and imparting a subtle flavor. Peel the dried, slightly curled leaves off before you fork up the rich, melted cheese. I like to serve thinly sliced vinaigrette-dressed tomatoes alongside.

About 8 ounces mozzarella cheese, sliced into 8 pieces (use aged, rather than fresh, creamy cheese, for this; it melts better and is considerably cheaper)

8 unsprayed lemon leaves

Place a slice of cheese on each lemon leaf, then place in a heavy frying pan. Heat over medium heat, covered, until cheese melts. Serve immediately.

Minestre, Brodo, e Zuppe

SOUPS, BROTHS, AND FISH SOUP-STEWS

Throughout the rustic island countryside, soup, or *minestra*, remains a nurturing everyday meal. Scraps of bones, trimmings of vegetables, a handful of sausage or prosciutto, a scattering of pasta: These simple soups are as delicious as they are frugal and practical. A nourishing potful is the sustenance of everyday family fare, either as a first course for the larger, midday meal, or on its own for a light supper. My favorites are the light soups based on vegetables and broth, flavored with fragrant herbs, and there are quite a few in this chapter.

Minestrone, of course, is the epitome of a *minestra*, a hearty soup filled with vegetables, beans, and pasta. At celebration feasts, however, you'll likely be served a first course of clear broth, or *brodo*, perhaps with a scattering of pasta or a flotilla of stringy egg-drops thickened with bread crumbs or Parmesan cheese. The finely clarified broth may be simmered from beef, veal, chicken, pigeon, or other game.

Along the seacoasts, both on the mainland and the islands, *zuppe*, or fish soups, are a mainstay of the diet. On the little boats and in the villages, in trattorie and in homes, a wealth of soups are made from fish: spicy, savory, often ladled over garlic-rubbed bread, more of a hearty stew than a polite bowl of broth (for heftier, main-course fish soups, see the fish and seafood chapter).

While the other soups and stews are similar to dishes on the mainland, there is a soup casserole peculiar to Sardinia. This dish, called *zuppa*, takes stale bread and layers it with cheese, vegetables, sausages, bacon, or leftover meats, moistened with hot broth and baked until sizzling. The bread soaks up the savory soup and the cheese melts enticingly. It is peasant fare: frugal and filling and unlikely to be found in restaurants, but rather in a shepherd's hut in the Sardinian interior.

Minestra di Zucchini

ZUCCHINI SOUP WITH PASTA AND FRESH HERBS

Capri

Serves 4 to 6

Trattoria fare, this soup was chalked up on the board moments after being picked in the garden and spooned up by myself not long after.

Enjoy as a first course, followed by Pollo con Salsa di Olive (page 134).

1 quart chicken or vegetable stock

1/2 cup dry white wine

1 teaspoon chopped fresh rosemary leaves

1 teaspoon chopped fresh marjoram leaves

1 pound young tender zucchini, cut into large bite-sized chunks

Salt and pepper

3 ounces large pasta, such as rigatoni, seashells, elbows, etc.

3 cloves garlic, chopped

2 tablespoons olive oil

Pinch hot pepper flakes

2 to 3 tablespoons thinly shredded fresh basil leaves

Freshly grated Romano or pecorino cheese, to taste

1. Place stock, wine, rosemary, marjoram, and zucchini in a saucepan and bring to a boil. Reduce heat and let cook, covered, until zucchini is very tender, about 15 to 20 minutes. Season with salt and pepper to taste.
2. Meanwhile, cook pasta until al dente, then drain.
3. Heat garlic in olive oil until fragrant and slightly golden; sprinkle in hot pepper flakes.
4. When zucchini is tender, add sautéed garlic to the soup.
5. Serve the soup in bowls, each ladled over several spoonfuls of the pasta. Sprinkle generously with fresh basil and grated cheese.

Aqua Pazza

TOMATO BROTH

Capri

Serves 4

Aqua Pazza is a Caprese tomato broth, light and vivacious, served over crisp garlic croutés or a bit of very thin pasta. While Aqua Pazza (which, by the way, literally translates as "crazy water") is usually made with water, I've used fish stock here for a soup with more substance. Chicken or vegetable stock would be equally good.

This is an excellent broth to use as a base for poaching shellfish, or to spoon over a bowlful of grilled fish and shellfish.

1 quart fish stock; or 2 cups chicken stock plus 1 cup each clam juice and white wine

2 medium onions, thinly sliced lengthwise

10 garlic cloves, 6 left unpeeled

1 bay leaf

1 cup diced ripe tomatoes such as cherry tomatoes (canned are fine, including juices)

2 marinated sun-dried tomatoes, diced

3 tablespoons chopped parsley, preferably flat-leaf Italian

1/4 teaspoon red pepper flakes

Cooked thin pasta or 4 garlic crostini (see page 46)

1. Combine stock with onions, unpeeled garlic cloves, and bay leaf. Bring to a boil, then reduce heat and simmer until garlic cloves are tender. Spoon out and push the garlic flesh through its skin; return garlic flesh to the pot and discard the skin.
2. Finely chop remaining garlic and add it to the broth, along with the diced tomatoes, sun-dried tomatoes, parsley, and red pepper flakes. Continue to cook another 5 to 8 minutes or just long enough for broth to be full-flavored.
3. Serve right away, ladled over either cooked thin pasta or garlic crostini.

Pappa col Pomodoro e Basilica

TOMATO AND BASIL SOUP WITH BREAD

Tuscan Archipelago

Serves 4

This traditional country dish of bread cooked with tomatoes and broth is savory yet humble. Basil, garlic, and Parmesan cheese give it lavish flavor.

Pappa can be hefty, mostly bread, or it can be like this one: light and lively, the bread only a thickening for the zesty tomato and basil soup.

1 onion, chopped

4 to 5 cloves garlic, chopped

2 tablespoons olive oil, plus a little extra for drizzling

2 pounds ripe tomatoes, or 2 cups chopped canned tomatoes

1 cup tomato sauce, or 3 tablespoons tomato paste

2 cups chicken broth

¼ cup coarsely chopped basil leaves

2 slices stale country bread whole-wheat or unbleached sourdough bread, crumbled into small pieces

4 tablespoons freshly grated Parmesan cheese

Salt and pepper

Pesto (optional)

1. Lightly sauté onion and garlic in the olive oil until softened, then add tomatoes and cook over medium heat for about 10 minutes.
2. Add tomato sauce or tomato paste, chicken broth, and half the basil. Simmer for about 30 minutes, then whirl in a blender until smooth.
3. Return soup to pot. Add crumbled bread and simmer 5 minutes, then add remaining basil and Parmesan cheese. Season with salt and pepper, then ladle into bowls, garnished with extra Parmesan cheese, a drizzle of olive oil, and a dollop of pesto if desired.

Pasta Mista in Brodo alla Zenzaro

GINGER-SCENTED TOMATO BROTH WITH MIXED RAVIOLI

Ischia

Serves 4 to 6

This delightful soup is simple to prepare and charming in its sophisticated simplicity: a light tomato-scented broth perfumed with ginger, enlivened with a little green onion. Though ginger is not a common flavoring in Italy, it appears occasionally, usually in Umbria. Somehow it made its way into this soup. Almost Asian in its simplicity, it makes the perfect bowlful in which to float a handful of savory stuffed pastas.

This makes an elegant first course, followed by herb-studded roast lamb and a salad of little greens or a selection of grilled fish and vegetables. Accompany with crusty bread. For dessert: a light, rich cheese with a plate of berries served with berry sauce (page 238).

3 cups chicken broth

1 1/2 cups diced tomatoes (canned are fine)

1/2 cup tomato juice

3 cloves garlic, chopped

1/2 to 1 teaspoon chopped fresh ginger

3 green onions, thinly sliced

Black pepper

Dash of Tabasco sauce

8 ounces mixed ravioli and tortellini, preferably one-half meat-filled and one-half spinach or other vegetable

2 teaspoons olive oil

1. Combine broth, tomatoes, tomato juice, garlic, and ginger and bring to a boil. Cook a minute or two, then remove from heat. Add green onions and cover. Season with black pepper or Tabasco sauce.
2. Cook pasta in rapidly boiling salted water until al dente, then drain.
3. Place several pasta in each bowl, then ladle the soup over. Drizzle a little olive oil on each portion, then serve.

Minestrone di Ceci e Spinaci

CHICK-PEA AND SPINACH MINESTRONE

Sardinia

Serves 4

In Sardinia wild greens would be added to this soup in place of the spinach: nettles, dandelions, purslane, or whatever might be gathered in the fields. Commercially grown dandelions are often available in the United States, as are leafy green endive and other greens, but these can be quite strongly flavored. If you use other greens in place of some or all of the spinach in this recipe, blanch them first.

The Sardinian touch of *pasta mista*, a combination of pasta shapes tossed into soups, gives a rich and varied texture. The pasta mixtures are sold in the marketplaces, no doubt a result of the shopkeepers' combining the last bits of pastas from their bins. To make your own, simply combine a selection of several differing shapes about the same size. I usually save a little bit from the end of each bag, letting the mixture grow more interesting with each inclusion.

Traditionally, this dish is seasoned with large crystal sea salt, for the particularly saline flavor it imparts.

1 medium onion, chopped

3 cloves garlic, chopped

2 tablespoons olive oil

6 ounces diced pancetta or similar salted rather than smoked meat

2 cups cooked chick-peas

1 cup tomato sauce or puree

3 cups broth of choice

Several pinches dried oregano to taste

1 bunch spinach or beet-tops, cleaned of all grit and cut up (frozen are fine)

About $1/2$ cup mixed small pasta shapes

Salt and pepper

1. Sauté onion and garlic in the olive oil until softened, then add pancetta and chick-peas and cook until chick-peas are cloaked in the fragrant mixture.

2. Pour in tomato sauce or puree, broth, oregano, and spinach (or beet tops) and cook over medium-high heat until spinach is tender and chick-peas have taken on the flavor of their surroundings.

3. Meanwhile, cook the mixed pasta shapes in rapidly boiling salted water until almost tender. Drain.

4. Add pasta to the soup and heat through, letting the pasta heat until al dente. Season with salt and pepper. Serve immediately.

Variation: Minestrone di Ceci con Zafferano
CHICK-PEA AND SPINACH SOUP WITH SAFFRON
Prepare as above, but during the last few minutes of cooking add a generous pinch of saffron dissolved in a tablespoon or two of hot water. Traditionally the tomato is omitted when you add saffron, but the combination of the two is nice.

Variation: Minestrone di Lenticchie
LENTIL AND SPINACH SOUP
Typical Sardinian mountain fare: In place of chick-peas, cook a cup or so of brown lentils in the broth. Add spinach or greens once the lentils are tender.

Minestra al'Lipari
TOMATO BROTH WITH POACHED EGG, CHEESE, AND HERBS
Lipari

Serves 4

Lipari, the largest of the Aeolian isles, lies gently in the emerald sea. Its volcanic hills are covered with wild geraniums; mint and fennel scent the air while grapevines grow wildly.

Along the winding road, past stone houses half-obscured by the green leafy growth, two women with their hair tied up in brightly colored peasant scarves rode donkeys to the olive grove up the hill. I came upon them later, when I was lost on a long walk and they were beating on the trees to shake the ripe olives loose onto a cloth below.

Appearing inscrutable and closed to strangers as they passed me on the road, in the olive grove their faces were softer and more open. As they directed me back down the hill I helped them gather their olives, and they described this local specialty of eggs poached in tomato broth with oregano or wild mint. They used water instead of broth, and included diced pecorino cheese; I've made it with no cheese at all, or with halloumi cheese since fresh pecorino is not easily available.

2 cloves garlic, chopped	4 eggs
2 tablespoons olive oil	1/8 to 1/4 teaspoon (or to taste) dried oregano, or 2 teaspoons chopped fresh oregano; or a mixture of chopped fresh peppermint and parsley
2 cups broth of choice	
1 cup diced ripe tomatoes (either canned or peeled fresh)	

1. Lightly sauté garlic in the olive oil until it smells fragrant but does not brown.
2. Add broth and cook over high heat 1 to 2 minutes, then add tomatoes. Lower heat to simmer.
3. Meanwhile, crack each egg into a cup or bowl and slide individually into the simmering soup. Sprinkle with oregano or mint and parsley. Cover and cook until eggs reach desired doneness, firm on the outside, soft and runny within. This should take about 3 minutes.
4. Remove each poached egg to a bowl and ladle the hot soup over it. The amount of soup will be small. Serve right away.

Variation: Divide 2 to 3 ounces of white cheese such as halloumi or fresh pecorino into 4 bowls and ladle the hot soup and poached egg over it. The cheese will warm and soften but not melt completely.

Zuppa di Datteri, Vongole, o Cozze

CLAMS, SEA-DATES, OR MUSSELS IN BROTH TOPPED
WITH GARLIC CROSTINI

Ischia, Capri, and Procida

Serves 4 to 6

This classic is made from sautéed aromatics, a splash of white wine, and a handful of briny sea creatures. In the unlikely event that you find datteri, the brown bivalves that look much like a large date but in fact are much like mussels, use them. Otherwise, use either mussels or clams.

1 medium onion, chopped

1 small carrot, chopped

4 to 5 cloves garlic: 2 to 3 chopped, and 2 cut into halves for rubbing the bread

1 medium stalk celery (including leaves), chopped

1 to 2 teaspoons chopped fresh rosemary

1 to 2 teaspoons chopped flat-leaf Italian parsley

$1/4$ to $1/2$ fresh hot pepper such as jalapeño or several pinches dried red pepper flakes

2 to 3 tablespoons olive oil, plus extra for the bread

2 to 3 tablespoons tomato paste

2 cups fish stock or clam juice

1 to 2 cups dry white wine

$2^{1}/2$ pounds datteri, mussels, or clams, well washed and soaked for $1/2$ hour

4 to 8 slices country bread

1. Lightly sauté onion, carrot, chopped garlic, celery, rosemary, parsley, and hot pepper in olive oil until softened. Add tomato paste, fish stock, or clam juice, and white wine and bring to a boil, then cook over high heat until it reduces in volume a bit and intensifies in flavor.

2. Add seafood to the broth, reduce heat, cover, and simmer for about 10 to 15 minutes or until the seafood shells open. Discard any that do not open.

3. Meanwhile, make garlic crostini: Brush bread slices with olive oil and broil or bake in a hot oven until golden and crisp. Repeat

on the other side. Remove from heat and rub the toast with cut garlic slices.

4. Place a slice of garlic bread in each bowl, then as soon as the seafood is ready, ladle it over the toast. Serve immediately.

SARDINIAN BREAD CASSEROLE-SOUPS

IT is an ancient custom in Sardinia to save every scrap of bread. To throw away even a crust smacks of sacrilege on this island that has frequently known famine.

Having dried bread on hand has given rise to a variety of bread-based casserole dishes, in which bread and aromatic broth are layered with cheese, then baked to bubbling.

This rustic bread and cheese casserole may be flavored with all manner of ingredients, including herbs that grow wild on the hillsides, little bits of pancetta or prosciutto, or bits of leftover vegetables.

Much like the French onion soup or similar soups ladled over thick country bread in other regions of Italy, these hearty casseroles are at their best when prepared with very aromatic yet light broths. Whatever broth you use—chicken, beef, lamb, pigeon, bacon, vegetable, and so forth—will flavor the entire dish. I use the cooking liquid from vegetables, sometimes adding the braising juices from meats or the delicious bits from deglazing a pan. Sometimes I simply simmer a handful of herbs in a saucepan with water and a bouillon cube.

This rustic casserole can be eaten as a first course in small portions. In larger portions it makes a fine one-dish supper, accompanied by a salad or plate of raw vegetables and cold meats or fish.

Zuppa Gallurese (Suppa Kuata o Gadduresa)

CASSEROLE OF BREAD, CHEESE, AND HERBS

Gallura, Sardinia

Serves 4

This layered casserole of bread, cheese, and broth is a specialty of Gallura in Sardinia. It is traditionally made with savory animal fat and drippings left over from roasting meats or poultry, and/or bits of pancetta or prosciutto. I use olive oil instead, and while it is slightly different, it is very good.

Serve this rustic dish with a leafy green salad and very tender simmered chick-peas garnished with grilled sausages. Serve sweet juicy melon for dessert, with a glass of brandy, and thimbles of dark black coffee to finish.

1/2 loaf stale bread, cut into thick slices

8 ounces mild cheese such as Jack, coarsely grated

8 ounces fresh pecorino or feta cheese, crumbled

1/2 cup freshly grated Parmesan, or more to taste

Generous amount of chopped fresh herbs: rosemary, sage, green onions or shallots, chopped garlic, basil, parsley

3 cups strong homemade broth (more if needed)

1/4 cup olive oil or to taste

1. Layer bread in casserole with the cheeses and sprinkling of herbs, reserving enough of both to top the casserole with.
2. Pour broth over the bread, sprinkle with remaining cheese, then splash with the olive oil.
3. Bake at 375°F about an hour or until top is cheesy and crusty and the bread has absorbed the liquid and formed a casserolelike dish. Serve immediately, sprinkled with the remaining chopped fresh herbs.

Mazzamurru
CASSEROLE OF BREAD, TOMATOES, ONION, AND CHEESE
Cagliari, Sardinia

Serves 4 to 6

This *zuppa* from the Sardinian town of Cagliari is layered with tomatoes and cheese, with flavors much like a pizza. Serve for supper, along with a crisp salad of tender green beans, mixed lettuces, chopped shallots, and perhaps a few oil-cured black olives.

6 ounces tomato paste, preferably rich and flavorful

2 pounds ripe flavorful tomatoes, thinly sliced

3 to 5 cloves garlic, chopped

Salt and pepper

Whole fresh basil leaves, to taste

1 pound stale bread, sliced

6 to 8 ounces mild creamy cheese such as Jack or mozzarella

4 ounces grated strongly flavored cheese such as aged asiago, Jack, Parmesan, or pecorino Sardo

1 cup broth of choice, or as needed

1/4 cup olive oil, or to taste

1. On the bottom of a casserole, smear a little of the tomato paste, then add a layer of sliced tomatoes. Sprinkle with a little garlic, salt, pepper, basil, then a layer of bread.
2. Top with the cheeses, more tomato paste, tomatoes, garlic, basil, and so on, ending with a layer of cheeses.
3. Drizzle broth over the top, then the olive oil. Bake 25 to 35 minutes in a 375°F oven until crusty brown on top, the bread softened and the tomatoes cooked through inside. Serve immediately.

Pasta, Risotto, e Polenta

Pasta, Rice, and Polenta

In the islands that are scattered throughout the sea around Italy, it is the first courses, or *primi piatti*—pasta, rice, sometimes polenta or soup—that flavor the entire meal. This first course must be zesty and provocative enough to cajole us into the repast: a feast for the eyes and nose as well as the stomach.

The first course means more than pure nourishment; it is a time to unwind from the rigors of the rest of the day—sitting around the table, forking up the pasta, spooning up the risotto, slowly savoring life itself.

Practicality dictates that the first course be filling enough so that the second course of meat, fish, or poultry needs only the most modest of portions.

Pasta has long been synonymous with Italian food, especially on the islands where the easily stored dried pasta may be quickly cooked and prepared with whatever is freshest in the garden, on offer in the market, or hauled up from the sea. Local habits and tastes of the islands imprint their own distinctive personalities on even the simplest of dishes.

With around 700 varieties of dried pasta—at my last tally—even if one were to use the same basic saucing ingredients, you could have pasta twice daily for a year without repeating the same dish. With such a huge number of pastas, it is difficult to recommend the exact type of pasta for each dish: A good guideline is that fine, thin pastas are best with lighter, zestier sauces, while heavier pastas can take on a heftier saucing. When a specific pasta is authentic or traditionally used, I try to indicate it.

Stuffed and flavored pastas are favored, especially in Sardinia, where fillings range from spinach, mashed potatoes, and cheese to eggplant. Baked pastas are particularly Sicilian, great hefty casseroles that can always stretch to feed unexpected guests.

Rice, especially plump Arborio rice, is stirred into a creamy risotto or sometimes cooked simply and served with a lively or rich sauce.

Polenta, that warming golden porridge of cornmeal, is a favorite in the Sardinian mountains, where it is served up with rustic sauces of game, platters of browned sausages, or spread out into a firm mass, then sliced and grilled. Sometimes it is seasoned with chopped vegetables or sun-dried tomatoes, or enriched with creamy ricotta cheese and butter, then topped with a rich, meaty ragu.

Couscous is eaten in both Sicily and Sardinia, a culinary souvenir of Arab rule. Known as *cuscusu* in Sicily, it is eaten with spicy fish stews, while in Sardinia it is eaten with vegetable stews, and its close cousin — *sa fregula* — is eaten and eaten and eaten: spooned into soups; served with fried onions, garlic, cheese, and parsley; or with spicy sauces and grilled fish.

What Type Pasta with Which Sauce?

THROUGHOUT the regions and islands of Italy, tradition governs not only what pasta is most often served, but also which pasta goes with which sauce.

Most of these dicta, which on the surface might seem a bit stringent, are based on common sense: A creamy sauce clings best to fine, delicate pastas; nuggets of savory morsels are best with a pasta that has little nooks for them to get deliciously stuck in; and hefty sauces are best with big, hefty pastas.

On the other hand, while tubular pastas are considered the proper choice for dishes with hearty vegetables like broccoli or cauliflower, I prefer supple, chewy spaghetti. Like so many other choices in life, the best pasta for the sauce is the one that suits your palate and taste.

Capellini o Spaghettini all'Estiva
CAPELLINI OR SPAGHETTINI WITH GREEN BEAN–
TOMATO SAUCE, OLIVES, AND BASIL
Panarea

Serves 4

The little Aeolian island of Panarea charms completely: covered in lush greens and pink bougainvillea, edged in black rocks and aqua sea with whitewashed stone houses that are more Mediterranean, Greek, even Arab rather than Italian, with tiny square windows, painted shockingly bright green or blazing hot pink. There are no cars (though there are little three-wheeled carts of a sort). The little streets are not lit by electric lights, nor are the shops; when night descends, the entire island is lit by lanterns, the light soft and magical.

It is an island of contrast between its natural rusticity and invading international tourism. In the summer the island is overrun with the rich and the beautiful who flock with their latest styles, the girls lying bikini-bottomed on the beach, digging painted toenails into the sand and awaiting their next adventure, or if that doesn't look too promising, their next meal.

The following pasta is quintessential summer food: lusty and garlicky, studded with olives and green beans, fragrant with basil.

5 cloves garlic, coarsely chopped	Salt and pepper
3 tablespoons olive oil	12 ounces thin spaghetti
1 cup green beans, cut into 2-inch lengths	10 Kalamata or other black olives, pitted and quartered
2 cups chopped ripe tomatoes (canned are fine)	Handful of coarsely chopped fresh basil leaves and/or fresh marjoram leaves
Pinch sugar if needed	

1. Sauté garlic in olive oil until softened but not browned, then add green beans and tomatoes. Cook over medium-high heat until saucelike, then season with sugar, salt, and pepper as needed.
2. Cook pasta until al dente, then drain and toss with sauce, olives, and basil/marjoram. Serve immediately.

Capellini alla Spiaggia

PASTA FOR A BEACH PICNIC: ANGEL-HAIR PASTA WITH AN
UNCOOKED SAUCE OF GARLIC, HERBS, AND RAW TOMATOES

Serves 4 to 6

Delicate strands of pasta are cloaked in an uncooked saladlike sauce of garlic, herbs, and raw tomatoes. The tanginess of the dressing comple- ments the simple flavors of the pasta. This makes a perfect summer supper, but I have named it after a marvelous meal we ate on a beach on a not very chic stretch of Sardinian seafront.

We made an open fire and rigged a barbecue out of an old metal barrel or cannister. Over this we boiled the pasta as we grilled kabobs of sword- fish skewered with chunks of bread.

8 cloves garlic, coarsely chopped

**¹/₄ to ¹/₂ cup olive oil, plus
1 tablespoon for dressing
tomatoes**

**¹/₂ to 1 cup chopped fresh herbs
such as basil, parsley,
marjoram, chives, mint,
rosemary, sage, or thyme**

**1 pound ripe tomatoes, diced
(preferably very flavorful,
multicolored tomatoes)**

Dash balsamic vinegar

1 pound capellini

Salt and black pepper

1. Heat 6 of the garlic cloves in ¹/₄ to ¹/₂ cup olive oil until fragrant, then toss in the herbs. Remove from heat.
2. Combine tomatoes with reserved garlic, reserved tablespoon olive oil, and balsamic vinegar. Set aside.
3. Cook pasta in rapidly boiling salted water until al dente, then drain and toss with the herb mixture. Season with salt and pepper.
4. Serve garnished with the tomato mixture.

Vermicelli al Pomodori
VERMICELLI WITH GARLICKY TOMATO SAUCE
Capri

Serves 4 to 6

Few foods satisfy so deliciously as simple tomatoey pasta dishes at their best. This is one of my favorite versions: strong with garlic and hot pepper, with flavor as lusty as the reputation of the hedonistic island itself.

Sautéing the garlic in the oil, then removing it and using the garlic-flavored oil, gives a certain elegance and smoothness to the flavoring (I like to scatter the reserved golden sautéed garlic over the top of the pasta, though not everyone I have fed this to agrees).

I like this best with dried vermicelli or fettucine, the type of flat noodle that is chewy when al dente. It is a dish best eaten as a late supper, in a bowl rather than a plate, when you're tired and need a pick-me-up both for the body and soul.

8 to 10 cloves garlic, halved or sliced

2 tablespoons butter

2 tablespoons olive oil

3 cups diced tomatoes (canned are fine)

½ teaspoon sugar, or to taste, to balance the acidity of the tomatoes

Salt and pepper

12 to 16 ounces vermicelli, fettucine, or other dried narrow flat pasta

Freshly grated Parmesan, Locatelli Romano, or pecorino Sardo

Optional garnishes: Generous shake of red pepper flakes or cayenne pepper; or thinly sliced fresh basil leaves

1. Heat garlic in butter and olive oil over medium heat until garlic becomes golden. Remove garlic from butter/oil and set aside.
2. Drain the tomatoes and save the juice (reserve any extra juice for soups or sauces). Add the diced tomatoes and about 2 tablespoons of their juice to the fragrant oil and cook over high heat until thick, adding more juice if needed for a strong, thick mixture.

Season with sugar, salt, and pepper. Set aside and keep warm.

3. Cook vermicelli in rapidly boiling salted water until al dente. Drain and toss with hot sauce. Serve immediately, sprinkled with grated cheese and garnished with either the reserved fried garlic, hot pepper flakes, or fresh basil.

Variation: In Caltagirone, Sicily, we ate *Occhi di Lupo.* Translated as "eye of the wolf," these squat, short shell-shaped macaroni are eaten with the above sauce, minus its hot pepper, and strewn with a blanket of torn fresh basil leaves.

SUN-DRIED TOMATOES

DURING TOMATO SEASON IN SICILY YOU'LL FIND TOMATOES DRYING EVERYWHERE: LAID OUT ON BOARDS, AGAINST STONE WALLS, EVEN ON OLD BEDSPRINGS. SMALL ONES ARE LEFT WHOLE, TIED BY THEIR STALKS INTO BUNCHES AND HUNG FROM THE LATTICEWORK OF A PERGOLA OR FROM THE RAFTERS OF A HOUSE.

Pasta e Fagioli
THREE-BEAN PASTA WITH TOMATO SAUCE AND PECORINO CHEESE
Tuscan Archipelago

Serves 4

Tuscans are known as *mangiafagioli,* or bean eaters, because of their penchant for legumes. On the islands beans are even more important, because food is often scarce, or limited in variety because of difficult growing conditions and the need to import foodstuffs.

This simple and homey dish can be varied at will: diced fennel sausage, bacon, or pancetta added; wine or broth used for half the liquid; hot peppers, or a green vegetable such as broccoli or spinach, added.

1 onion, chopped

4 to 6 cloves garlic, chopped

3 tablespoons olive oil, more if needed

½ cup each: cooked and drained borlotti beans, chick-peas, and red kidney or white cannellini beans

2 cups tomato passata (or sauce, or puree)

1 cup vegetable, beef, or chicken broth

Salt and black or red pepper

Pinch of sugar if needed

Oregano leaves to taste

12 ounces macaroni of choice: shells, elbows (preferably something hearty, with little hollows to trap sauce)

Generous amount freshly grated pecorino cheese

1. Sauté onion and half the garlic in olive oil until onion is softened, then add the beans and cook together a few minutes for the flavors to infuse.
2. Pour in tomato passata and broth, then bring to a boil and cook over high heat about 10 minutes or long enough to reduce in volume and intensify in flavor. Season with salt, pepper, a pinch of sugar if needed, and oregano to taste. Keep warm.
3. Cook pasta in rapidly boiling salted water until al dente, then drain and toss with sauce and sprinkle with cheese.

Maccheroncini con le Fave Fresche

SMALL MACARONI WITH FAVA BEANS

Sardinia

Serves 4

Sardinians are very fond of young tender fava beans, especially in the region around Alghero, where the flavor of the table often seems more Catalan than Italian. Until recently everyone still spoke the Catalan language; the street signs of the old port are bilingual even now.

Here the little springtime beans are cloaked in garlic and hot pepper and simmered in broth, then tossed with al dente pasta. Any number of additions might find their way into your bowl: diced mozzarella, pitted black oil-cured olives, chopped anchovies.

Serve as a first course, followed by a simple dish of meat braised with red, yellow, and green peppers; or for those with a hearty constitution, fork up this spicy dish as a midnight supper.

5 to 8 cloves garlic, chopped

3 tablespoons or more olive oil

1 cup fresh or frozen blanched favas, peeled of both their fuzzy outer skins and (if fresh) their inner skins; or 1 cup baby lima beans (frozen are fine)

1/8 teaspoon red pepper flakes, or to taste

1/2 to 2/3 cup chicken or vegetable broth

2/3 to 1 pound small macaroni

Fresh grated Parmesan or similar cheese

1. Heat garlic in olive oil until fragrant, then lightly sauté favas or limas in this mixture. Sprinkle with red pepper flakes, then add broth and boil down until only 3 to 4 tablespoons liquid remains.
2. Meanwhile, cook the pasta in rapidly boiling salted water until al dente. Drain.
3. Serve the pasta tossed with fava beans and sauce, sprinkled with cheese to taste.

Variation: Conchiglie con le Fave e Mortadella

PASTA SHELLS WITH FRESH FAVAS AND MORTADELLA

Use shell-shaped pasta in the above basic recipe, and add about 2 ounces sautéed diced or julienned mortadella just before you toss the favas with the pasta.

Variation: Pasta con le Fave Fresche e Cozze

PASTA WITH FAVAS AND MUSSELS

The briny flavor of mussels balances nicely with the earthy little beans. Add a generous handful of mussels—5 or so per person—to the sautéing favas and cook, covered, until mussels pop open. Remove lid and boil liquid down until reduced and flavorful.

Variation: Culigiones con le Fave, Menta, e Cippolini Verdi

SARDINIAN RAVIOLI WITH FAVA BEANS, FRESH MINT, AND GREEN ONIONS

Use cheese-filled pasta such as homemade culigiones (page 91) or store-bought ricotta-filled ravioli in place of spaghetti. Serve sprinkled with lots of chopped fresh mint and green onions.

Spaghettini con Zucchini

THIN SPAGHETTI WITH CRISP ZUCCHINI AND SPICY TOMATOES

Sicily

Serves 4

"Pasta e zucchini: cucina povera," the couple on the train said, as they went on to describe the traditional poor people's food of their home in Sicily. We were sharing a compartment on a train heading north to chic Milan, where their son and daughter-in-law were living. Halfway through the trip the conductor, too, stopped in and began to contribute his recipes for pasta with zucchini. The combinations are endless, we all agreed, and our discussions kept up for hours while the couple shared their provisions with me: bread, olives, a cucumber, ripe tomatoes, some runny and deliciously smelly cheese.

We discussed the methods of preparation: batter-fried zucchini coins or diced chunks; grated cheese and beaten egg or hot peppers and garlic, or lots of olive oil and garlic. We discussed crisply cooked zucchini versus the tender stewed vegetable, short pasta in a soupy zucchini sauce or al dente pasta strands with crunchy little zucchini matchsticks. By the time we had reached the topic of zucchini blossoms, our train had pulled into the station.

8 cloves garlic, sliced

3 tablespoons olive oil

3 small to medium-sized zucchini, thinly cut into coinlike slices

1½ cups diced ripe tomatoes or canned tomatoes, well-drained (save the juice for sauce or other use)

½ cup tomato passata plus the juices drained from tomatoes (about ¾ cup total)

Salt and cayenne pepper or hot pepper flakes

Pinch sugar

12 ounces spaghettini

Several fresh basil leaves, thinly sliced (optional)

1. Heat garlic slices in olive oil for a few moments, then add zucchini and lightly brown (garlic slices may be removed at this point as they have already flavored the oil. Or you can leave them in, as I prefer). Add well-drained tomatoes and cook over medium-high heat for a few moments, then transfer to another pan and cover.

2. Into the sautéing pan, pour tomato passata and reserved juices and cook down over high heat until thickened and very flavorful. Season with salt, cayenne pepper, or hot pepper flakes, and sugar (to balance any acidic edge). You should have enough cayenne pepper or hot pepper flakes to announce their presence—enough

for the whole dish to have a spicy piquancy. Pour hot sauce over reserved vegetables and keep warm.

3. Meanwhile, cook spaghettini in rapidly boiling salted water until al dente, then drain and toss with sauce. Taste for seasoning, adding salt and/or cayenne or hot pepper flakes to taste.

4. Serve immediately, garnished with a sprinkling of basil.

Variation: Add, to taste, creamy fresh ricotta or ricotta salata, or even diced feta, when serving.

Pappardelle con Broccoli di Rabe e Formaggio di Capra
FLAT WIDE PASTA WITH BROCCOLI RABE, GOAT CHEESE, AND ROSEMARY
Sicily

Serves 4

Greens such as broccoli di rabe are doted on throughout the lusty south, blanched and chopped, then tossed in olive oil and garlic, and served up with whatever pasta you fancy.

This dish reeks deliciously of garlic as you add half to warm in the hot oil and cook through, the rest raw just before serving. Goat cheese adds a lively touch, its tangy creaminess binding the pasta together, almost forming a sauce. If the pasta seems a little dry, drizzle each portion with a little extra olive oil at the table.

1 large bunch of greens such as broccoli di rabe, trimmed of their stalks

7 cloves garlic, crushed

3 tablespoons olive oil, plus a little extra if needed

1 pound flat pasta, cut into wide widths

6 to 7 ounces fresh tangy goat cheese, cut up or crumbled

Salt and black and cayenne pepper

3 to 4 ounces pungent grating cheese such as pecorino Sardo or asiago

2 teaspoons fresh rosemary, or to taste

1. Place greens in a saucepan with water to cover and bring to a boil. When greens are wilted and somewhat tender, remove from heat. Drain and rinse well with very cold water (I add a few ice cubes to it). Drain well, squeeze dry, and set aside.
2. Heat half the garlic in the olive oil in a large pan until the garlic begins to sizzle and turn golden. Add the greens and cook a few minutes in this mixture, then remove from the heat.
3. Meanwhile, cook the pasta in abundant rapidly boiling salted water.
4. Drain pasta, then toss with greens. Add goat cheese and toss well to mix and let the cheese melt slightly. Season with salt and pepper to taste.
5. Serve the pasta sprinkled with the grated cheese and fresh rosemary.

Le Mollica
TOASTED SEASONED BREAD CRUMBS
Sicily

Bread crumbs are a quintessential Sicilian topping for pasta, as *much if* not more so than cheese. Part of the reason is economical—bread crumbs are extremely frugal whereas cheese is costly. The crumbs also give a delightful crunch. They give texture to fish and pasta dishes in which adding cheese would confuse flavors.

When bread crumbs are added to Sicilian pasta, it is called *le mollica*. Crisp-fried crumbs seasoned with garlic and lots of fresh oregano also make a good substitute for cheese.

Be sure to use homemade bread crumbs. Commercially made ones are okay for frying but otherwise taste insipid, with a boring texture. To make your own bread crumbs, grate slightly stale sourdough bread. Grating gives a lighter, more pleasing texture than placing the bread in a food processor or blender.

About ²/₃ to 1 cup sourdough
   bread crumbs

3 tablespoons olive oil, or as
   needed

5 cloves garlic, chopped

3 to 4 tablespoons chopped fresh
   oregano

Brown the crumbs in olive oil until they turn golden brown. Remove from heat and continue to toss the crumbs a bit as they will continue to toast. Pour into a bowl and add garlic and oregano. Set aside while you cook pasta.

Penne con Fagiolini Verde, Noci, Formaggio di Caprina, e le Mollica
QUILL-SHAPED PASTA WITH GREEN BEANS, WALNUTS (OR HAZELNUTS), AND TOASTED GARLICKY BREAD CRUMBS

Sicily

Serves 4

Green beans and pasta tossed with toasted nuts, crumbs, and tangy cheese make an easy to prepare, simple meal or *primo piatto*. Goat cheese is used in Sicily, but crumbled Gorgonzola might be used elsewhere (often in my kitchen, and delicious *it is*).

½ cup bread crumbs

About 3 tablespoons olive oil

½ cup shelled walnuts or
hazelnuts

1 pound penne pasta

4 ounces green beans, trimmed
and cut into bite-sized pieces

4 to 5 ounces goat cheese such
as Sicilian caprina, California
chèvre, or French cheverie or
Montrachet

4 cloves garlic, chopped

Salt and pepper

2 tablespoons chopped fresh
basil or marjoram

1. Brown crumbs in about 2 tablespoons of the olive oil. Remove
   from heat and set aside.
2. To toast walnuts or hazelnuts: Place in an ungreased heavy frying
   pan and toss over a medium heat until fragrant and lightly
   browned. Or place on baking sheet in 400°F oven for about 10 to
   15 minutes, tossing and turning once or twice. Lightly toast walnuts or hazelnuts. If using hazelnuts, then place nuts on a towel
   and rub vigorously to remove their skins. Coarsely chop whichever
   nuts you use and set aside.
3. Cook penne in rapidly boiling salted water. When they are half-
   cooked, add the green beans and continue to cook until both are
   al dente.
4. Drain pasta and beans, then toss with reserved olive oil, nuts,
   goat cheese, garlic, and salt and pepper to taste. Serve sprinkled
   with toasted bread crumbs and basil or marjoram.

Pasta con i Carciofi
PASTA WITH ARTICHOKES, CARBONARA STYLE
Sicily

Serves 4

Combining raw egg with grated cheese, then tossing with hot pasta, is a carbonara-style treatment to a variety of vegetable pasta dishes in Sicily. The old man selling the artichokes described the dish to me, adding that if any last-minute guests arrive, you need only add a handful more pasta.

3 fresh artichoke hearts,
   blanched and diced
   (see page 138)

1 red onion, chopped

3 cloves garlic, coarsely chopped

About 3 tablespoons olive oil

1/2 cup chicken or vegetable
   broth

2 tablespoons chopped parsley

2 eggs, lightly beaten

3 to 4 tablespoons freshly grated
   Parmesan or pecorino Sardo

1 pound rigatoni

Salt and coarsely ground
   black pepper

1. Lightly sauté diced artichoke hearts, onion, and garlic in olive oil until artichoke is tender and onion is soft. Add broth and parsley, then cook down until it reduces into a small amount of sauce. Remove from heat and set aside.
2. Combine eggs and cheese. Set aside.
3. Cook rigatoni in rapidly boiling salted water until al dente, then drain. Toss the hot pasta with the egg and cheese mixture, mixing gently but well.
4. Add the artichoke mixture and its sauce, then season with salt and pepper. Serve immediately, with extra cheese if desired.

Variation: Add an ounce or two of prosciutto or diced browned pancetta.

PASTA with eggplant is the most Sicilian of foods. Fried little nuggets of the tiniest eggplants; whole eggplants fried so that they are creamy inside; slices browned and layered on the bottom of the pasta bowl or forming a sort of border or crust; diced eggplant browned and tossed with the pasta or simmered with the sauce . . . each city, town, village, home has its own version, depending on the tastes of the cook and the traditions of the region.

Pasta with eggplant is also called *pasta alla Norma,* in honor of Bellini's opera. At the time of the opera's success, Sicilian slang named anything that was very good, the best, "una vera Norma" after the opera written by its native son.

In Palermo you can buy whole eggplants at the *friggitore,* shops that sell fried foods. The vegetables are sliced at one end so that they fan out, then they're fried to a golden hue; buy one or two, then take them home for a near-instant *pasta con melanzane.*

Spaghetti alla Norma
SPAGHETTI WITH TOMATO SAUCE AND FRESH HERBS ON A BED
OF BROWNED EGGPLANT SLICES

Serves 4

The contrast between the textures, colors, and flavors of this dish is what appeals to me: browned earthy eggplant with its crisp edges and creamy middle, chewy supple strands of spaghetti, a cloak of tangy sauce, a scattering of pungent herbal leaves, a grating of cheese.

In addition to the browned eggplant slices surrounding the pasta like the petals of a daisy, I like to add an abundance of whole sprigs of the same herbs used to top the dish: marjoram, oregano, and so forth.

1 eggplant, sliced crosswise about ⅛ inch thick (if peel is tough, cut strips of it off the eggplant before slicing; otherwise leave unpeeled)

Salt

¼ to ½ cup olive oil, or as needed

1 onion, chopped

3 cloves garlic, chopped

4 cups tomato passata

A sprig or two of fresh marjoram or oregano, plus about 3 to 5 tablespoons chopped fresh marjoram, savory, or other mountain-scented herbs for sprinkling over the finished dish

Salt and black pepper

Pinch of sugar if needed

12 ounces spaghetti

Grated cheese as desired: pecorino, Parmesan, or asiago

1. Sprinkle eggplant slices generously with salt and let sit for 20 to 30 minutes. Rinse well and dry with absorbent paper or a clean cloth.
2. Sauté eggplant one layer at a time in a hot pan in as much olive oil as you need to brown the eggplant but not enough to turn the vegetable sodden. Take care as you turn each slice that the eggplant slices remain whole. As each slice is cooked, place on a baking sheet until all are lightly browned and cooked through. Set aside.
3. Sauté the onion and half the garlic in a tablespoon or two of olive oil until softened, then add tomato passata and sprig of herb such as marjoram or oregano. Cook over medium heat about 10 minutes. Season with salt, pepper, and a little sugar to balance any acidity. Remove herb sprig and discard, then add remaining garlic to sauce and keep warm.
4. Cook pasta in rapidly boiling salted water until al dente, then drain well.
5. Serve hot pasta on a platter surrounded by eggplant slices, then ladle the tomato sauce over the pasta. Sprinkle with fresh herbs and cheese, and garnish with sprigs of fresh herbs.

Ziti con Melanzane

PASTA TUBES WITH EGGPLANT SAUCE

Serves 4

The simplest pasta dish, inspired by a greedy meal in a Palermo market-place restaurant. The eggplant cubes are first fried, then added to a garlicky tomato sauce at the last minute, then tossed with ziti and topped with creamy-salty white cheese. Other pasta shapes would be good here, too, especially the chewy twists known as gemelli.

1 large or 2 medium to small
  eggplant, diced

Salt

¼ cup or more olive oil

3 to 5 cloves garlic, chopped

1½ cups diced tomatoes (canned
  okay), include juice

1 cup tomato passata
  (see page 264)

Pinch of sugar if needed

Salt and pepper

12 to 16 ounces ziti or other
  tubular pasta

3 tablespoons coarsely chopped
  fresh basil leaves, or more, to
  taste

4 to 6 ounces fresh pecorino,
  ricotta salata, or other
  pungent white cheese

1. Layer diced eggplant with generous sprinklings of salt in a colander and leave for 15 to 25 minutes to leech out its bitter juices. Rinse well and dry well on absorbent paper or a clean cloth.

2. Brown eggplant in oil over high heat (if the oil is hot enough, the vegetable absorbs less oil). Remove from pan with a slotted spoon and set aside on absorbent paper to drain.

3. Pour off oil in pan except for a tiny amount to cook the garlic in. Add the garlic and cook a few moments over medium heat until it is fragrant and only lightly golden.

4. Add tomatoes and tomato passata. Cook over medium heat for about 10 minutes or long enough for sauce to thicken and intensify in flavor. Season with a pinch of sugar if needed, and salt and pepper to taste.

5. Meanwhile, cook pasta in rapidly boiling salted water until al dente, then drain.
6. Add eggplant to tomato sauce, then toss with pasta. Serve right away, blanketed with basil and cheese.

Capellini con Pomodori Arrosti
THIN PASTA WITH ROASTED TOMATOES, GARLIC, AND BASIL

Serves 4

Roasted tomatoes taste of quintessential summer, of tomato essence distilled into a few bites. Fresher tasting than sun-dried tomatoes, they capture and intensify the flavor of the vine-ripened tomato. Roasting is also a good way to use disappointing supermarket tomatoes; the roasting intensifies the flavor and tends to get rid of mealiness and wateriness by concentrating the flesh.

About 8 roasted tomatoes (see page 167), skins removed and squeezed for their juices, the flesh diced, with the cooled and thickened juices from the pan

3 to 5 cloves garlic, finely chopped

3 to 4 tablespoons olive oil, or to taste

3 tablespoons chopped or thinly sliced fresh basil

Salt and pepper

10 to 11 ounces capellini or other very thin pasta

2 tablespoons coarsely grated pungent cheese such as asiago or pecorino, or to taste

1. Combine diced roasted tomatoes with garlic, olive oil, basil, salt, and pepper. Set aside while you cook the pasta.
2. Cook the pasta in rapidly boiling salted water for about 3 minutes or until al dente. Very thin pasta cooks very quickly.
3. Drain and toss with tomato mixture, then serve right away sprinkled with cheese.

Pasta with Meat Sauces
Pasta e Carne

MANY pasta sauces have bits of meat added: strong, flavorful meats such as pancetta, prosciutto, and sausage, which add great savor in small amounts.

In addition, the meat chapter has big, stewy, meaty dishes that can be used as pasta sauces, either as leftovers or in the traditional way of the sauce served with pasta as a first course, the meat served next as the main course. These big, long-stewed sauces are typical Sunday lunch and festival dishes: a simple tomatoey sauce in which enough rich meat simmers to last the coming week. You might find a whole chicken lying next to a stuffed veal or beef roast, a handful of pork or lamb sausages, everything adding its savory juices to the pot. The sauce will be ladled out onto the pasta, the meats saved for another course or another meal.

Pasta alla Contessa
PASTA RICH ENOUGH FOR A CONTESSA

Serves 4

In a crumbling villa by the sea it was the contessa among us who was macrobiotic and rather ascetic of table habits. We common folk were the ones who fell to the seduction of cream and other rich ingredients, though when the contessa wasn't fussing and muttering about dietary rules and regulations, she was known to polish off a nice big bowl of pasta with this sauce.

This sauce is an utterly delicious amalgam of tiny bits of liver, gizzard, broth and white wine, fresh tomatoes and onions, several slices dried mushrooms, all cooked down to a strong and savory mixture. A splash of cream finishes it off decadently.

While it is smooth, suave, and comfortingly rich, it is quite frugal to make if you do it a day or two after you have enjoyed a chicken dinner. Cook the chicken neck, heart, and gizzard to make the broth for the pasta sauce, then chop the gizzard and liver for sauce enrichment, and save a glass or two of white wine from the dinner to add to the sauce as well. You now have practically half the ingredients already. You could, in the name of practicality, save the neck, gizzards, and liver from your chicken and pop them into the freezer for the time you want to make this sauce.

The mushroom slices are optional, but I strongly recommend them. Since porcini are very expensive, I use one of the porcini's cousins, a mushroom gathered and dried in Argentina. It has a smoky, stronger flavor and is very good, though admittedly not porcini. You can find this mushroom at Napa Olive Oil Factory, St. Helena, California.

Serve this sauce with tender fresh pasta such as fettucine.

For the Broth:

- 1 chicken neck, heart, and gizzard
- 5 cloves whole garlic
- 1 carrot
- 1 onion
- 1 stalk celery
- 1 tablespoon parsley
- 2 cups chicken stock
- 2 cups water

For the Pasta and Sauce:

- 1 onion, chopped
- 2 tablespoons butter
- 2 tablespoons olive oil
- 1 chicken liver, chopped
- 2 slices lean, salted (not smoked) bacon, or prosciutto, or pancetta, chopped
- ½ cup dry white wine
- 5 to 6 ripe fresh tomatoes, diced
- 4 to 6 slices dried porcini-type mushrooms, such as the Argentine ones recommended in the introduction, broken into small pieces (about ⅓ ounce)
- 1 to 1½ cups whipping cream
- Salt and pepper

| 1 pound delicate ribbon type pasta such as fettucine, or tubular pasta such as penne or tubetti | Freshly grated Parmesan or pecorino cheese, to taste |

1. Make broth: Combine neck, heart, and gizzard with garlic cloves, carrot, onion, celery, parsley, chicken stock, and water. Bring to a boil, then reduce heat and simmer until liquid has a nice strong flavor. Cook down until it makes about 2 cups broth. Strain broth and remove solids, discarding everything except the gizzard (and heart if desired). Chop the gizzard and set aside.
2. Sauté onion in butter and olive oil until lightly softened. Add reserved gizzard, chopped liver, and bacon. When lightly browned, pour in wine and boil down until nearly completely evaporated.
3. Add tomatoes to the pan, stir, and let cook 5 minutes or so until saucy, then add mushrooms and reserved strained broth. Continue to cook until very reduced and full of flavor.
4. Add cream and cook through another 5 minutes or so until slightly thickened. Season with salt and pepper and keep warm.
5. Meanwhile, cook pasta in rapidly boiling salted water until al dente.
6. Drain pasta and toss with sauce, then serve immediately, each portion sprinkled generously with grated cheese.

Penne o Fusilli con Pomodori Arrosti, Salsiccia, Spinaci, e Formaggio Caprina

PENNE OR TWISTING PASTA WITH ROASTED TOMATOES, SPICY SAUSAGE, SPINACH, AND GOAT CHEESE

Sardinia

Serves 4 to 6

This marvelous dish gets its character from the bits of feisty, spicy sausage—lamb sausage, flavored with herbs and hot peppers, is especially delicious and very Sardinian. If unavailable, choose any interesting lamb or pork sausage, one with Italian flavors or even the delicious and fiery North African *merguez*.

10 roasted tomatoes, cooled, with their juices (page 167)

8 to 10 ounces spicy lamb sausage, spicy Italian sausage, or merguez, cut into bite-sized pieces

4 to 6 cloves garlic, chopped

2 to 3 tablespoons olive oil

12 ounces fresh spinach, cooked, squeezed, and cut or thinly sliced

5 ripe fresh tomatoes, preferably skinned and seeded, diced

1 pound twisting fusilli or other curly twists, or hollow tubes such as penne

6 ounces goat cheese, diced or crumbled

About 4 ounces mild milky cheese such as mozzarella

Salt and a shake of each pepper: white, black, and cayenne

1. Squeeze skins of roasted tomatoes to extract their flavor essence, then discard skins and combine the juices with the roasted tomatoes. Dice tomato flesh and set aside.

2. Brown diced sausage, then remove from pan and keep warm. Pour off any fat, but save any meaty juices and pour over the sausages.

3. In same pan, add garlic and olive oil and cook until garlic starts to turn golden. Add spinach and diced fresh tomatoes. Cook down until tomatoes are saucy. Return browned sausage to pan.

4. Meanwhile, cook pasta in rapidly boiling salted water until al dente. Drain and toss with spinach-sausage-fresh tomato mixture, the diced roasted tomatoes, goat cheese, and mozzarella, and toss over high heat for a few moments to warm through. Season with salt and the three peppers and serve immediately.

Rigatoni alla Moda dei Monzu

RIGATONI WITH MUSHROOMS, CHICKEN BREAST,
FRESH TARRAGON, AND CREAM

Serves 4 to 6

The traditional rich cooking of Sicily is a remnant of the past when French chefs ruled the kitchens of the prosperous and brought a taste of decadent indulgence to the tables of the rich and jaded. These chefs, called *Monzu* or *Monsu*, a corruption of the word *monsieur*, created dishes so smooth and refined, and often so elaborate, they are nearly baroque. A penchant for creamy concoctions is one of the culinary souvenirs of these times.

2 ounces (or as lavish an amount you can afford) porcini or other dried flavorful mushrooms, or a combination of mushrooms (I use an import from Argentina, a slightly smoky mushroom that is relatively inexpensive and very good)

3 cups boiling chicken stock

12 ounces boned and skinned chicken breasts, each cut into several 2-bite-sized pieces

Salt and pepper

1 bunch fresh tarragon, leaves pulled from the stems and chopped

Flour for dredging the chicken

3 to 4 tablespoons butter

3 cloves garlic, chopped

1/2 onion or 3 shallots, chopped

1 cup each sour cream and whipping cream (or use 2 cups nonfat sour cream)

Salt and pepper

1 pound ziti or rigatoni

1 cup grated Parmesan or pecorino cheese, or as desired

1. Combine porcini and boiling stock. Cover and leave to rehydrate for at least 30 minutes.

2. Remove mushrooms from soaking liquid and squeeze liquid back into the bowl. Set both aside.

3. Season chicken pieces with salt and pepper, then press about a third of the chopped tarragon onto the chicken. Dredge chicken with flour.

4. Heat half the butter and lightly sauté chicken pieces. Do not overcook; leave them slightly pink and translucent as they will continue to cook when added to the sauce. Set aside.

5. In remaining butter, sauté garlic and onion or shallots until softened, then add rehydrated mushrooms and stir in the fragrant mixture. Pour in about a cup of the soaking liquid, let cook down until it is only a few tablespoons, then repeat with another cup of the liquid. When that, too, is only a few tablespoons of concentrated flavorful liquid, add the remaining cup of liquid but leave the bits of grit and debris at the bottom of the soaking stock. When that, too, cooks down, stir in the cream and sour cream.

6. Add the chicken and about half the remaining tarragon to this sauce. Season with salt and pepper and keep sauce warm while you cook the pasta.

7. Cook pasta in rapidly boiling salted water until al dente, then drain.

8. Toss pasta with sauce and a few tablespoons of the cheese, then turn out onto a platter or individual bowls. Sprinkle with the remaining cheese and tarragon.

Canne al Vento

PASTA TUBES WITH A SAUCE OF SAUSAGE, LAMB, TOMATO, PEPPERS, PECORINO, AND A DAB OF CREAM

Sardinia

Serves 4

This recipe comes from Orgosolo, a typical Sardinian shepherds' village. Surrounded by vineyards and olive groves, it also produces wine and cheese, and is known for its folk art. But what it is really famous for is sheep-rustling, with centuries-old family feuds that intermittently break out with violence and viciousness.

It's no surprise to find bits of lamb in the village pasta specialty. Use lamb sausage, if you can find it, otherwise traditional Italian pork sausages are fine.

Canne is a name for pasta tubes, its roots in the word *cannelloni*. Use whichever pasta tube you favor, such as rigatoni or penne.

About 4 ounces flavorful Italian sausage, cut into bite-sized pieces

3 cloves garlic, chopped

4 ounces tender lamb, cut into thin strips

1 yellow pepper, cut into strips

1/2 cup dry white wine or stock of choice

2 cups tomato passata

Sprig of fresh rosemary or sage

1 pound pasta tubes such as small rigatoni

1/2 cup cream (optional)

Salt and coarsely ground black pepper

4 ounces pecorino, coarsely shredded or shaved

Garnish: About 2 tablespoons fresh herbs: sage, rosemary, marjoram, oregano, parsley, or any combination

1. Lightly brown sausage in pan, then pour off excess fat and add garlic, lamb, and pepper. Continue to sauté until lamb and pepper are both tender.
2. Pour in wine or stock and cook over high heat until liquid is nearly evaporated, leaving only a tablespoon or two. Add tomato passata and rosemary or sage. Continue to cook, letting the flavors intensify and the sauce thicken, about 15 minutes.
3. Cook the pasta in rapidly boiling salted water until al dente, then drain.
4. Add cream to sauce, season with salt and pepper, and heat through. Toss with pasta. Serve right away, sprinkled generously with pecorino and fresh herbs.

Gemelli con Carciofi, Prosciutto Cotto, e Pomodori

THICK CHEWY PASTA WITH ARTICHOKES, HAM, AND TOMATOES

Serves 4

I ate this at a vineyard on Sicily, but I've sampled similar dishes through-out Italy, islands and mainland. It's the sort of dish that typifies island food, full of sunny flavors yet uncomplicated to prepare.

This is also delicious using tender flat eggy noodles such as fettucine, or even the wider pappardelle. When basil is not available or I am not in the mood, I make this with chopped fresh rosemary instead.

1 onion, finely chopped

2 tablespoons butter or olive oil or combination

2 cloves garlic, chopped

2 artichokes, outer leaves and chokes removed, then blanched and diced; or 1 package (about 12 ounces) frozen artichoke hearts, defrosted

4 ounces very flavorful ham such as prosciutto, diced

½ cup dry white wine

2 cups diced tomatoes, including their juices (canned are okay)

Pinch of sugar, if needed

Salt and black pepper

12 to 16 ounces gemelli or other chewy pasta

3 to 4 tablespoons thinly sliced fresh basil

3 tablespoons freshly grated pungent cheese such as pecorino

1. Lightly sauté onion in butter and/or oil until softened, then add garlic, artichokes, and ham and continue to sauté a few minutes.
2. Add wine, bring to a boil, and cook over medium-high heat until nearly evaporated. Add tomatoes and cook until sauce thickens a bit and becomes flavorful. Season with a pinch of sugar if needed, and salt and pepper.
3. Cook gemelli or other pasta in rapidly boiling salted water until al dente. Drain.
4. Toss drained pasta with sauce, then turn out onto platter and strew with basil and grated cheese.

PASTA WITH FISH AND SEAFOOD

THE islanders combine pasta with whatever is hauled up in the fishing nets that day. Sautéed, simmered, crisply fried, or steamed, a wide array of fish and seafood is tossed with the bland, just-tender pasta, dressed with tomato sauce, spicy olive oil, seasoned butter, or rich cream. Crunchy nuts or crumbs, fragrant herbs, and occasionally pungent cheeses might be added for texture as well as flavor.

Pasta con Bottargu
PASTA WITH PRESSED TUNA OR MULLET CAVIAR

Serves 4

A specialty of nearly all the islands, especially Sicily and Sardinia, bottargu is typical island fare: tuna or red mullet eggs, salted and pressed into a sort of salamilike mass. It tastes strongly and delightfully fishy, and is eaten thinly sliced as an appetizer: with boiled potatoes, atop little slices of buttered bread, or mixed with olive oil and garlic and tossed with hot al dente pasta.

4 ounces bottargu

3 to 4 cloves garlic, chopped

1/2 to 3/4 cup olive oil

Freshly ground black pepper

12 to 16 ounces spaghetti or other pasta

2 to 3 tablespoons chopped parsley, preferably flat-leaf Italian

1. Slice the bottargu very thinly, then add the chopped garlic. Start adding the oil a little at a time, letting it combine well before adding more. Season this sauce with pepper and set aside while you boil the pasta.

2. Cook pasta in rapidly boiling salted water until al dente, then drain. Toss with sauce and sprinkle with parsley. Serve immediately.

Conchiglie con Broccoli e Alici

SHELLS WITH BROCCOLI AND ANCHOVIES

Sardinia

Serves 4

At the Sardinian villa of our Spanish friends, the talk was never far from food—how delicious everything was in Sardinia, how much like (or different from) our respective homes of Spain and California it all was. We'd spend hours lying in the sun and shade, idly, laconically, happily, picking up the conversations every so often with descriptions of dishes, places to eat, where to find this and that local delicacy.

Inevitably these conversations ended with us preparing big unhurried meals of what sounded particularly enticing at that moment. Gnocchetti was often the first course, since in addition to being a local specialty, it was our hostess's favorite.

1 pound conchiglie (or the shell pasta known as gnocchetti, or chewy cavatelli, little twists of gemelli, or any hollow pasta such as penne or ziti)

1 large bunch or 2 medium-sized bunches broccoli, broken into florets, the stem peeled and diced

3 to 4 tablespoons butter or olive oil, or mixture of the two

4 to 5 anchovies, chopped

4 to 5 cloves garlic, chopped

Black pepper or red pepper flakes

1. Cook pasta in rapidly boiling salted water until half cooked, then add broccoli florets and continue cooking until both pasta and broccoli are al dente. Drain (reserve water to make soup if desired).

2. Meanwhile, heat butter or oil with anchovies slowly until they "melt." Add garlic and warm a moment or two in the mixture.

3. Toss drained broccoli and pasta with the butter-anchovy-garlic mixture. Season with black pepper or red pepper flakes and serve immediately.

Spaghetti da Marina
SPAGHETTI WITH SEAFOOD, FROM THE WATERFRONT
Elba

Serves 4

All along the waterfronts, throughout nearly every resort and fishing village, you find trattorie and ristorante, all offering the catch of the day—fried, grilled, perhaps simmering in a soup, and always, some sort of seafood and pasta.

In Elba's Marciana Marina we feasted on this simple pasta: pristinely fresh seafood tossed with al dente spaghetti.

5 to 8 cloves garlic, chopped

3 to 4 tablespoons chopped parsley, preferably flat-leaf Italian

1 onion, chopped

3 to 5 tablespoons olive oil, or as desired

5 ripe tomatoes, diced

8 to 12 clams and/or mussels, soaked in cold water for at least 30 minutes to rid them of sand and grit

1½ cups dry white wine

4 to 6 squid, cleaned, the round bodies sliced thinly, the tentacles cut into short lengths

12 to 16 ounces spaghetti

Salt and pepper

1. Warm garlic, parsley, and onion in olive oil, then stir in tomatoes. In this mixture, sauté clams and/or mussels a few moments.

2. Add wine and cook, covered, over medium-high heat until the shells pop open. (Discard any that do not open.) Add squid and cook only a moment or two in this mixture.
3. Pour off liquid, keeping the seafood warm, and boil down the liquid until it forms a sauce. Taste for seasoning.
4. Meanwhile, cook pasta in rapidly boiling salted water until al dente.
5. Toss pasta with seafood and sauce and serve immediately.

Variation: In the little Ischian town of Lacco Ameno, in a small family restaurant on a terrace above the harbor, I ate Spaghetti con Vongole e Pomodori Secchi (Spaghetti with Clams and Sun-Dried Tomatoes). Prepare the above recipe using clams and omitting the squid. When clams are cooked through and have popped open, serve right away, scattered with several tablespoons of chopped marinated sun-dried tomatoes.

Pasta con Riccio di Mare e Carciofi
PASTA WITH SEA URCHINS AND ARTICHOKES
Erice, Sicily

Serves 4

The little town of Erice is calm, a tidy corner of an otherwise hectic island. Unlike the flamboyance and chaos of Palermo, Erice is understated, calm, private, with narrow cobbled roads winding around tranquil, shuttered houses overlooking the sea.

The scent and flavor of the sea gives its character to the food. Pastas and risotti often come with seafood sauces in Erice. Here I've added artichokes to the traditional dish of sea urchins and pasta. I purchased sea urchins from a little man sitting on the street, an upturned packing crate in front of him displaying an elegant mound of the spiky creatures, all very fresh.

You must take care to protect your hands against the porcupinelike needles of the urchins, so wear gloves. Once open you can eat them as is, dipping into their creamy orange-hued flesh with chunks of bread.

15 to 20 fresh sea urchins

3 to 4 tablespoons olive oil

3 to 5 cloves garlic, chopped

2 artichokes, trimmed of their thistles and prepared into hearts, then diced

3 to 4 tablespoons fish broth, clam juice, or water

2 tablespoons chopped parsley

Salt if needed and black pepper to taste

Juice of ½ to 1 lemon, to taste

12 ounces pasta of choice

1. Open urchins, protecting your hands with a towel or gloves. Using a small sharp scissors or knife, cut in half like a grapefruit.

2. Pour any juices into a strainer set on a bowl and rinse each shell, throwing away the brown insides. Scoop out the orange or yellow-colored roe, cut it up, and add it to the reserved juices that have dripped into the bowl.

3. Warm the olive oil and garlic over low heat, then add the artichokes and broth or water. Cook down until it forms a sauce. Add the roe and cook a few minutes. Season with parsley, salt and pepper, and lemon. Keep warm.

4. Cook pasta in rapidly boiling salted water until al dente, then drain and toss with sauce. Taste for seasoning and serve immediately.

Spaghetti con Barbalucci
SPAGHETTI WITH SNAILS

Serves 4

Barbalucci is the Sicilian name for snails; in other parts of Italy they are called *lumache*. Snails are doted on, sautéed in garlic, simmered in tomatoes, baked in butter, and often spooned over al dente pasta.

There are a number of different types of edible snails throughout the Italian islands. The most commonly eaten ones are *babbaluceddi* or *babbaluci du fistina,* which are very small and found on summertime grassy fields;

crastuni, a large field-crawling snail with brown strips; and *atuppateddu,* a large brown snail that lives underground and works its way to the surface after rainfall.

After rains, children with buckets come out to gather the snails from fields, gardens, and bushes, either bringing them home to Mama or selling them to local restaurants.

6 cloves garlic, chopped

3 tablespoons olive oil

2 cups tomatoes, chopped (canned are fine), include juice

½ teaspoon oregano or marjoram, or to taste

Hot pepper flakes

3 dozen live (see note) or prepared snails, each about the size of a cherry

12 ounces pasta such as spaghettini

1 tablespoon chopped parsley

1. Warm half of the garlic in the olive oil until golden, then add tomatoes and cook over medium-high heat for about 10 minutes.
2. Season with oregano or marjoram and hot pepper flakes to taste, and add the snails. Cook 15 minutes or until snails are very tender.
3. Meanwhile, cook pasta in rapidly boiling salted water until al dente. Drain and serve tossed with the sauce and remaining garlic, sprinkled with parsley.

Note: To prepare snails, place live snails in a container with lots of holes; a colander is fine if less aesthetic than the traditional basket.

Sprinkle the snails with bread crumbs or raw cornmeal, about 1 tablespoon per 2 pounds of snails, then cover the container with cheesecloth and seal it tightly over the top. Leave the snails with their frugal fare for 24 hours to give them a chance to purify themselves.

Rinse snails well with room temperature water, then place in a pot with room temperature water to cover. Keep covered with the cloth; eventually, depending on the temperature of the room, the little snails will crawl out of their shells. It may take a minute, or as long as several hours. Do not give up. Try not to disturb them as this may drive the little creatures back into their shells.

Place the pot on the stove, leaving the cloth still secured on top. Turn on very low heat to cook them gently and, I like to think, humanely. When the water is just past body temperature, about 110°F, the little snails will be past caring. Remove the cloth, raise the heat, and boil for 2 to 3 minutes.

Drain and rinse well. Remove the segment that is their digestive tract, leaving the little white-colored sac. They are now ready to sauté, simmer, or prepare whichever way you choose.

Pasta con Granchio or Aragosta
PASTA WITH CRAB OR LOBSTER, EATEN FROM A SHELL

Serves 4

We ate this on a lemon tree-shaded terrace on a too-warm day, our hot skin cooled by occasional breezes. Served in a whole crab shell, with the pasta spilling out onto the plate, it looked like a treasure from the sea.

Arrange the cooked pasta and crab or lobster in a crab shell or a large lobster tail with a few of the claws for garnish; if neither is available, any large shell will give similar visual appeal.

1 whole large crab or lobster, plus 3 extra shells, about 1½ pounds, or 12 to 16 ounces meat, picked over

6 cloves garlic, chopped

3 tablespoons olive oil

1 cup dry white wine

2 ounces tomato paste

1 cup diced tomatoes, either ripe fresh or canned (include juice)

Red pepper flakes

Salt if needed

12 ounces tagliarini or spaghettini

2 tablespoons chopped parsley or fresh basil

1. Remove meat from the crab or lobster. Clean the shells. Pick over the meat for any pieces of shell, then set aside.
2. Lightly sauté half the garlic in the olive oil, then add the wine and

boil until it is reduced to about half. Add tomato paste and tomatoes, season with red pepper flakes and salt if needed, then continue to cook until flavorful and saucelike, another 5 to 10 minutes.

3. Cook pasta in rapidly boiling salted water until al dente, then drain.

4. Add lobster or crab to the tomato sauce and heat through, then toss with the drained hot pasta.

5. Serve the pasta in and spilling out of the shells, and sprinkle with parsley or basil.

Fettucine con i Gamberi e Limone
Fresh Pasta with Lemon, Chives, Sautéed Shrimp, and/or Scallops

Serves 4

We were dining in a frighteningly chic area of the Sardinia coast, sitting just off the piazza, surrounded by willowy trees strung with twinkling fairy lights. Stylishness overwhelmed me; I was blinded by designer labels. I expected to be asked to leave any moment and busied about checking my clothing for stains, missing buttons, and little rips, anything that would get me ejected from such a well-manicured place.

As our waiter approached, I sat self-consciously, fearing great embarrassment and awaiting the dreaded moment. But the waiter walked past our table, over to the trees, and gently placed a bowl on the ground. Suddenly he was descended on by a motley collection of scruffy, voracious cats, who busied themselves with the food. And our devastatingly handsome, ever-so-chic waiter bent down to stroke the biggest, scruffiest cat: gently, with great tenderness.

A few minutes later he walked toward us again, this time bearing our dinner: a light, lemony pasta rich with shrimp and scallops.

8 ounces peeled and cleaned shrimp and/or scallops

Salt and red or black pepper

6 tablespoons butter, or more, as desired

1 pound fresh pasta such as fettucine

1 large bunch chives, finely chopped

Juice of 2 lemons

Grated rind of 1 lemon, or more to taste

1. Sprinkle shrimp or scallops with salt and red or black pepper, then lightly sauté in half the butter. When just turning opaque, remove from heat and set aside.
2. Meanwhile, cook pasta in rapidly boiling salted water until just tender; it will only take a few minutes.
3. Drain pasta well, then toss with remaining butter, chives, lemon juice, and grated lemon rind. Add shrimp, salt, and pepper, and serve right away.

Fregula
Tiny Pasta Crumbs
Sardinia

Makes about 2 cups, enough for 4 people

Made by rubbing semolina with moist fingers, fregula is a mixture of large and small crumbs, which are then separated into two piles. The small crumbs are served in soup while the large crumbs are served as pasta, with tomato sauce, vegetables, and/or fish.

2 pinches saffron threads or a pinch of turmeric

1/4 teaspoon salt

1/2 cup boiling water

2 cups fine semolina flour, more or less as needed

1. Mix saffron, salt, and boiling water. Let sit 10 minutes.
2. Spread about a quarter of the semolina flour in a flat, shallow bowl. Sprinkle a tablespoon or two of the warm saffron water over the semolina. Rub to form crumbs, then add about 1/2 cup more semolina and repeat with the water. Keep working the mixture until all of the water and semolina have been added and you have a big pile of uneven crumbs. If the crumbs are too dry, add a little more water; if too wet, a little more semolina.
3. Spread the fregula on a clean towel to dry and firm up for about 30 minutes.
4. Using your hands, brush the crumbs into a pile of big crumbs and a pile of small crumbs. Store in refrigerator, covered, for up to 5 days.

Gnocchi alla Caprese
GNOCCHI WITH TOMATOES, FRESH MOZZARELLA, AND BASIL
Capri

Serves 4

These chewy potato dumplings are tossed in tomato sauce with diced fresh mozzarella, then strewn with a handful of sweet basil leaves. I ate this dish one fine spring afternoon as the sun was growing warm and summerlike on the sybaritic island of Capri.

This is a classic dish throughout the Amalfi coast and the Pharagean Islands of Capri, Ischia, and Procida. Any kind of pasta can be used in place of the gnocchi: strings of spaghetti, tubes of rigatoni, twists of gemelli, ribbons of fettucine; each shape and texture offers its distinctive character to the simple sauce, cheese, and herb mixture.

4 cloves garlic, chopped or crushed

4 tablespoons olive oil

3 cups chopped or diced tomatoes (canned are fine; include the juice)

Pinch of sugar if needed

Salt and pepper

1 pound potato gnocchi

8 ounces fresh mozzarella, milky and tender, diced

A handful fresh basil leaves, coarsely torn (about 1/4 cup)

Grated fresh Parmesan or pecorino cheese

1. Puree garlic with 3 tablespoons olive oil and the tomatoes. Transfer to a pan and bring to a boil. Season with sugar if needed, and salt and pepper. Continue to cook until thickened, about 5 to 10 minutes.
2. Meanwhile, cook gnocchi in rapidly boiling salted water until just tender. Drain gently and toss with remaining tablespoon of olive oil.
3. Toss hot gnocchi with hot sauce and mozzarella cheese, then serve sprinkled with basil and cheese.

Malloreddus

SAFFRON GNOCCHI
Sardinia

Serves 4 to 6

Malloreddus are Sardinian pasta, sometimes called gnocchetti, shaped like huge, ribbed orzo. They are sold dried as well as prepared fresh, and they vary considerably, both in size and in flavorings: Some have no saffron but instead have spinach, tomato paste, or plain egg and flour.

Serve with a ragu typical of Sardinia, one that has the foresty flavors of field mushrooms, shreds of prosciutto, leafy greens, and bits of turkey and finely chopped lamb or beef. Or you could toss the malloreddus with a fresh tomato sauce in which you've cooked chunks of savory fennel-scented Italian sausage and tucked in the odd bay leaf or two. Alternatively, you could serve the ragu with al dente spaghetti or with tender fettucine.

2½ to 3 cups all-purpose flour	Large pinch of saffron
Pinch of salt	1 cup lukewarm water

1. Add salt and saffron to flour, then work in the lukewarm water until it forms a rather firm, sticky dough.
2. Knead until it is smooth and no longer so sticky, about 5 minutes. Then leave in a plastic bag for 30 to 60 minutes or up to overnight in the refrigerator.
3. Knead dough again, then break off into small walnut-sized lumps. Working one at a time, roll a lump between your hands to make a long ropelike strand, then lay down on floured board.
4. With a knife cut off lengths of ¾ inch or so, then roll each into a sort of half-closed shell shape. Use a fork to make striations along the side. Toss in flour and set aside while you continue with the rest of the dough.
5. Leave the floured pastas up to 2 hours until ready to cook. Cook

in rapidly boiling salted water until just tender, about 4 minutes; taste as you cook. Drain and serve with the following sauce and a generous dusting of Parmesan.

Culigiones
SARDINIAN RAVIOLI

Serves 4

Culigiones may be filled with a variety of mixtures, from mint-flavored fresh cheese, to vegetables mixed with tangy cheeses and yogurt. There is even a sweet pig's-blood filling eaten as dessert. I especially like the following eggplant filling. I serve this very traditional of dishes with the admittedly untraditional seasoning of cilantro added to the rosemary and parsley. It is particularly delicious.

1 eggplant, diced

4 tablespoons olive oil

1 cup ricotta cheese

1/4 cup freshly grated Parmesan, plus extra for serving

About 1/2 cup finely diced mozzarella or Jack cheese

1 egg, lightly beaten

1 tablespoon flat-leaf Italian parsley

3 to 4 tablespoons chopped cilantro

Salt and black and cayenne pepper

About 8 ounces fresh pasta squares (won-ton wrappers are excellent)

3 to 5 cloves garlic, chopped

2 cups tomato passata

Pinch sugar if needed

1 to 3 teaspoons chopped fresh rosemary

1. Prepare filling by lightly browning eggplant for 5 minutes or so in 2 tablespoons of the olive oil. Then cover the pan and continue to cook over medium-low heat until eggplant is very tender.

Occasionally turn, mashing with a fork as you do, and loosening the eggplant from the bottom of the pan. Let cool.

2. If the tender eggplant is not a rough sort of puree by now, mash it a bit more. Combine this chunky eggplant mixture with the ricotta, Parmesan, mozzarella or Jack cheese, egg, parsley, and 1 tablespoon of the cilantro. Season with salt and pepper.

3. Form ravioli by placing a tablespoon or so of filling in the center of each pasta square, wetting the edges, then topping with another square. Press the edges tightly and leave to dry on a floured plate.

4. Make sauce by sautéeing garlic in remaining oil until lightly colored and very fragrant. Add tomato passata and cook 5 to 10 minutes until flavorful. Adjust seasoning with salt, black and cayenne pepper, and a pinch of sugar if needed to balance acidity.

5. Cook ravioli in rapidly boiling salted water until tender, about 3 to 5 minutes. Drain carefully so the stuffed ravioli don't fall apart.

6. Serve pasta topped with sauce and sprinkled with rosemary and remaining cilantro. Offer grated Parmesan, pecorino Sardo, or asiago.

Cannelloni di Carciofi, Salsicche, e Funghi

CANNELLONI FILLED WITH RICOTTA CHEESE, CHOPPED ARTICHOKES
SAUSAGE, AND MUSHROOMS

Serves 4

Artichokes, sausage, and mushrooms add savory flavor to the creamy ricotta filling. This makes a lush *primo piatto*, say for a Sunday lunch or supper.

3 to 5 dried mushrooms such as shiitake; or 3 to 5 slices of a more fragrant mushroom such as porcini

1 cup boiling water

2 Italian pork sausages, diced, skin removed

About 12 artichoke hearts, marinated, either from a jar or a deli, coarsely chopped

2 cloves garlic, chopped

8 ounces ricotta cheese

6 tablespoons freshly grated Parmesan or pecorino cheese

1 egg, lightly beaten

Several large pinches oregano, thyme, or marjoram

Salt and a dash of cayenne pepper

8 egg-roll wrappers or fresh homemade thin noodles about 8 inches square

1³/₄ cups diced ripe, flavorful tomatoes; or 14-ounce can diced tomatoes (include juice)

4 ounces mozzarella or other mild white melting cheese, thinly sliced or shredded

3 tablespoons olive oil

About ¹/₄ cup fresh basil leaves, torn just before using

1. Combine dried mushrooms with boiling water and let sit to rehydrate. When cool, remove mushrooms and chop. Pour off the soaking liquid through a strainer, discarding the bottom gritty part. Reserve the strained liquid.
2. Brown sausage and add chopped artichokes, mashing with a fork until it is a chunky chopped mixture. Remove from heat and add reserved mushrooms, garlic, ricotta cheese, half the grated Parmesan, 1 egg, oregano or other herbs, salt, and cayenne. Mix well until it forms a slightly chunky paste.

3. Place about 2 to 3 tablespoons of this mixture on one edge of each pasta square, then roll each into a cylinder. Layer in the bottom of a 9 x 12-inch baking dish.

4. Pour the diced tomatoes over the top, then add the reserved mushroom soaking liquid. Sprinkle with mozzarella or other mild white cheese and remaining grated Parmesan or pecorino, then drizzle with the oil.

5. Bake, uncovered, in a 400°F oven for 15 to 20 minutes or long enough to cook the pasta, absorb the liquid, and melt the cheese.

6. Let sit a few moments, then serve, sprinkled with torn basil leaves.

RISOTTO

RISOTTO is a uniquely Italian dish of creamy yet firm grains of rice cloaked in a savory sauce. It is very different from the rice dishes of Asia or the pilaf dishes of the Near and Middle East. While Asian rice is steamed until just tender, risotto is stirred and stirred while the grains absorb the sauce. The rice, too, is a special variety, Arborio. Not only does Arborio absorb the liquid in the optimum way, it has a distinctive perfume and flavor.

To prepare risotto, begin by sautéeing aromatic vegetables such as onion, garlic, shallots, carrots, celery, and so on, then adding the rice. You do not want to brown the rice, merely gild it in the fragrant buttery vegetables.

Add the liquid of choice slowly, taking care that the liquid is absorbed before you add more. Broth of any kind—chicken, duck, meat, seafood, or vegetable—can be added to the risotto, as can red or white wine. Sometimes a risotto is finished with cream or a knob of butter to smooth it seductively.

Toward the end of cooking, a cup or so of vegetables, herbs, meat, and/or seafood can be added, as can such flavorings as sun-dried tomatoes or olives.

For most risotto I like to pass a chunk of Parmesan and a grater for each diner to grate a little of this fragrant cheese onto his or her own plate.

- ⑥ Use homemade stock: It has more flavor and less salt. If you must use a canned broth, double the amount of water and first simmer 30 minutes or so with a few bits of vegetables, a bone or two of chicken, etc.

- ⑥ Use only Arborio rice. Other rices will have too much or too little starch and not absorb the liquid properly. The result: sticky or mushy risotto.

⑥ Acids like tomatoes inhibit the ability of the rice to absorb liquid, so try to add tomatoes at the end of cooking, or adjust your amounts of liquid accordingly.

⑥ Have all ingredients ready to use. If the rice sits and cooks while you chop the other ingredients, the risotto will likely be ruined.

⑥ Serve risotto in warmed bowls. As it cools it mercilessly solidifies and goes unpleasantly gluey.

⑥ Do not make ahead. Reheated risotto is not the light, tender, and creamy dish it is when freshly made. It is stodgy and solid, good only for dishes such as Arancini (the Sicilian stuffed rice balls), Tortas, and other savory rice fritters.

USES FOR LEFTOVER RISOTTO

⑥ Torta: Bind leftovers with lightly beaten egg and grated Parmesan cheese, about 1 egg and 2 tablespoons cheese per cup of risotto. Spoon into a buttered baking pan, top with crumbs, and dot with butter, then bake in a 400°F oven until crumbs are golden brown and torta is heated through. Serve either hot or cool. Particularly good as *torta verde*, with a risotto made from spinach and/or herbs.

⑥ Form leftover risotto tightly into balls, coat with egg and crumbs and fry until golden. Serve in a bowl of hot homemade broth with cooked julienned vegetables of choice.

⑥ Make Arancini: See recipe on page 215.

⑥ Add risotto to a frittata.

⑥ Add risotto to a minestrone-style vegetable and bean soup, to thicken it.

⑥ Add a few tablespoons leftover risotto to a seafood soup to thicken it. Puree for a smooth, bisquelike consistency.

Risotto al Funghi e Anatra
WILD MUSHROOM RISOTTO MADE WITH DUCK STOCK

Serves 4

Duck stock makes a foresty risotto, along with the earthy field mush-rooms. I quick-start a decent duck stock by combining half canned low-salt chicken broth and half water with the next-day bones from a roast duck and a chopped onion and garlic clove or two, requisite broth season-ings. For further practicality, I keep duck bones in the freezer to tote out whenever I feel like making wild mushroom risotto.

2 cups canned low-salt chicken broth, more if needed

1 quart water

1 leftover carcass of a roasted duck, including defatted pan juices

1 onion, chopped

3 to 5 cloves garlic, whole or cut up

12 to 16 ounces assorted fresh "wild" mushrooms: porcini, shiitake, oyster, uovi, or flavorful domestic mushrooms, cut into bite-sized pieces

5 to 6 tablespoons butter or combination butter and olive oil

5 to 8 shallots or 1 onion, chopped

1 cup Italian Arborio rice

1 8-ounce cup dry white wine

Several dried mushrooms, broken into bite-sized pieces (optional)

3 tablespoons grated Parmesan, plus extra for grating or shaving at table

Salt and freshly ground black pepper

1. Make duck stock (this can be done a day or two ahead): Combine chicken broth with water, duck carcass and any juices, onion, and garlic. Bring to a boil, then reduce heat and simmer for 2 hours or until flavorful. Strain and defat. Discard duck bones and bits of vegetables.

2. Lightly sauté fresh mushrooms in half the butter (or butter and oil combination), then remove from pan and set aside. Heat

strained stock and keep it on a rolling simmer while you prepare the rice.

3. Lightly sauté shallots or onion in remaining butter (or butter and oil) until softened, then stir in rice and cook a few moments in the fragrant mixture. Slowly stir in a few ounces of the white wine, stir and let it evaporate, then repeat until all wine is used.

4. Add dried mushrooms and a ladle of broth, stirring until liquid is evaporated. Continue stirring in the remaining broth in small amounts every 5 minutes or so.

5. The rice should be almost tender—check the package directions for exact timing, as rices vary somewhat. Add the sautéed mushrooms plus any accumulated juices to the soupy rice, and stir in the 3 tablespoons of grated Parmesan.

6. Heat through, season with salt and black pepper, and serve with extra Parmesan.

Variation: Serve risotto as a bed for steamed or grilled asparagus.

Risotto al Verde
RISOTTO WITH SPINACH, LEEKS, BASIL, AND GARLIC BUTTER

Serves 4

A soupy risotto, green with spinach, young leeks, or green garlic and basil, finished with a glistening of garlic butter, it tastes of summer suppers eaten under a warm Italian sky.

Leftovers make a marvelous *torta verde*, bound with egg, topped with crumbs, and baked into a savory cake.

8 cloves garlic, chopped

3 to 4 tablespoons butter

1 tablespoon olive oil (optional)

1 cup Arborio rice

1 cup dry white wine

3 to 4 cups hot vegetable or chicken broth

1 leek, including tender greens, very thinly sliced and broken into rings; or 2 young (baby) garlics, thinly sliced

Salt and black pepper

1 to 2 cups washed and blanched spinach, cut up into bite-sized lengths (frozen, defrosted, is fine)

3 tablespoons freshly grated Parmesan, plus more for sprinkling

1/4 cup thinly sliced fresh basil leaves

1. Lightly sauté 3 cloves garlic in 2 tablespoons butter (or one table-spoon butter and 1 tablespoon olive oil, if using) until fragrant but not golden. Stir in rice, cook a moment or two, then stir in half the wine.

2. Stir and stir, cooking over medium heat until liquid is absorbed, then add rest of wine and stir, cooking, until this, too, is absorbed. Add 1/2 cup broth, continue stirring, then repeat as broth is absorbed.

3. When rice is nearly tender, add leek and finish cooking, about 25 minutes in total. Season with salt and black pepper, then add spinach and let warm through with rice.

4. Meanwhile, warm remaining garlic in remaining butter until just fragrant. Set aside.

5. Add Parmesan to risotto, stir well, then serve in hot bowls with a spoonful of the garlic butter drizzled over the top. Sprinkle with basil and serve immediately, with extra Parmesan.

Sbarrigia
CHICKEN RISOTTO FROM SICILY
Sicily

Serves 4

Sbarrigia is a Sicilian term that refers to any dish containing chicken, such as this traditional risotto, simmered in wine and studded with chicken breast, tomatoes, and green olives. Its scent of garlic is heady.

I was once wooed by a gentleman who used this risotto as a lure. He was right about the risotto: I could not resist, but my heart was won by someone who clearly enjoyed being on the other side of that risotto pot—the side that gets to brandish the fork.

1/2 onion, chopped

4 to 6 cloves garlic, chopped

3 tablespoons olive oil

1 1/2 cups Arborio rice

1 cup diced tomatoes (canned are fine), include juice

1/2 cup dry white wine (optional)

4 cups chicken broth, or more if needed

15 to 20 green olives (preferably Sicilian olives), pitted and halved

1 chicken breast, poached or roasted and cut into small pieces or shredded

1/2 teaspoon thyme

1/3 cup Parmesan cheese or as desired

Freshly ground black pepper

Fresh basil or parsley for sprinkling

1. Sauté onion and garlic in olive oil until softened, then add rice and warm through in the onion mixture.
2. Stir in the tomatoes and wine, cook down a few minutes, then begin adding broth, 1/2 to 2/3 cup at a time, stirring each time until the liquid is absorbed, then adding more.
3. When liquid is absorbed and rice is al dente, stir in olives, chicken, and thyme, then the Parmesan and black pepper.

4. Serve immediately in warmed plates, sprinkled with basil or parsley. Offer extra Parmesan at the table.

Variation: Con Melanzane
   CHICKEN RISOTTO WITH OLIVES AND EGGPLANT
Add 1 medium-sized diced and browned eggplant to the risotto at the end of cooking when you add the olives, chicken, and thyme.

Risotto di Fagioli, Salsicche, e Rughetta
SAUSAGE AND WHITE BEAN RISOTTO WITH CHOPPED ARUGULA
Ischia, Procida, Capri

Serves 4 to 6

This rustic risotto is filling and full of flavor, the sort of thing to spoon up on a cool night, sitting on a wooden bench and oilcloth-covered table surrounded by lemon trees, lilies, roses. Earlier in the day we had watched the elderly gardener pick the beans, tomatoes, and greens in the garden of the tiny restaurant, then sit in the sun and leisurely shell the beans.

1 onion, chopped

4 to 5 cloves garlic, chopped

1 Italian pork sausage, diced, skin removed

3 to 5 slices salami, chopped

1½ cups cooked white beans, drained, or 15-ounce can white cannellini beans, drained

1¾ cups diced tomatoes (14-ounce can is fine), include juice

1 cup Arborio rice

2 tablespoons butter

2 bay leaves

3 cups boiling chicken or vegetable broth

1½ to 2 cups coarsely chopped raw arugula

¼ cup grated Parmesan or pecorino, plus extra for sprinkling

About ¼ teaspoon (or to taste) dried thyme, oregano, or marjoram; or 1 teaspoon fresh herb, removed from its stems and chopped

1. Sauté onion, garlic, and sausage until sausage is lightly browned and onion softened. Add salami and beans and cook a few minutes longer, then add tomatoes and remove from heat. Set aside.

2. Lightly sauté rice in butter with bay leaves, then slowly add $\frac{1}{2}$ cup boiling broth, stirring and stirring as rice cooks and absorbs the liquid. When liquid is almost completely absorbed, add another $\frac{1}{2}$ cup, and continue repeating this until liquid is used up and rice is nearly cooked through, about 15 minutes (exact times will depend on your rice).

3. When rice is nearly cooked through, add the arugula and the reserved tomato-beans-sausage mixture and stir together. Heat through, then stir in grated Parmesan or pecorino, and serve each portion sprinkled with thyme, oregano, or marjoram and extra cheese.

Variation: Risotto di Broccoli e Fagioli Borlotti
RISOTTO WITH BROCCOLI AND BORLOTTI BEANS
Follow the above recipe, substituting borlotti beans for the white beans, and 1 bunch of diced, blanched broccoli for the arugula.

Risotto di Melone e Prosciutto
RISOTTO WITH SUN-SWEET CANTALOUPE AND PROSCIUTTO

Serves 4

Fruit risotti are widely prepared throughout Italy, and especially appreciated in sultry climates of the islands, when melons are so sweet and flavorful they can inspire poetry.

Some vendors set up stands, selling nothing but melons cut into wedges. I have eaten in a roadside restaurant that sold nothing but melons, which we chose ourselves from a cool swimming pool/tub set in the shade, filled with huge melons, bobbing up and down, chilling in the water.

The following risotto recipe was shared with me by a friend who lives in Liguria, Michael Greene, who sampled it as he sailed from island to island. I have tried preparing it vegetarian as well. I prefer it at room temperature, drizzled with a bit of olive oil and sprinkled with black pepper.

1 large ripe cantaloupe

3 tablespoons butter

3 shallots, chopped

1 1/4 cups Arborio rice

1/2 cup dry white wine

1/4 cup port wine

2 cups boiling chicken or vegetable broth, or as needed

2 slices prosciutto (about 2 ounces), thinly sliced or chopped

Black pepper

1/4 cup freshly grated Parmesan cheese, or a drizzle of olive oil

1. Cut melon in half and remove seeds. Spoon flesh out of shell and puree. Set aside.
2. Melt butter and lightly sauté shallots, then stir in rice and cook in the shallot butter a few moments.
3. Pour in white wine, bring to a boil and cook until liquid is absorbed. Add port wine and repeat process. Stir in 1/2 cup of the pureed melon, let it cook in, then add 1 cup of the broth and cook, stirring all the while. Repeat until all the broth is absorbed. Add the remaining melon last, along with the prosciutto, and cook together for the last few minutes until rice is al dente. Season with black pepper if needed.
4. Serve with Parmesan cheese or olive oil drizzled over the top.

Risotto con Salsa di Gamberi
RISOTTO WITH SHRIMP

Serves 4

Seafood, stirred into risotto, is eaten in a myriad of ways throughout the islands. In Ischia, I ate a risotto filled with a wide variety of seafood; in Palermo, a risotto studded with little clams.

This risotto was my summertime lunch one afternoon in Procida, a simple dish of rice cooked in wine and fish stock, tossed with shrimp sauce.

1 pound shrimp, in their shells

3 cups fish stock; or 1½ cups water mixed with 1½ cups white wine

¼ cup butter

1 onion, chopped

½ carrot, chopped

5 cloves garlic, chopped

1 teaspoon chopped parsley

Large pinch thyme

2 bay leaves

3 to 4 tablespoons brandy

1 tablespoon tomato paste

1 cup Arborio rice

½ cup dry white wine

1 tablespoon chopped fresh basil or flat-leaf Italian parsley

1. Shell shrimp. Set shrimp aside and place shells with fish stock or wine and water mixture. Bring to a boil and cook for 20 minutes to get a rich stock. Strain and set aside.

2. In half the butter, sauté half the onion along with the carrot, half the garlic, the parsley, thyme, and bay leaves. When onion is lightly browned, add brandy and let boil until nearly evaporated. Add a ladleful of the stock, bring to a boil, and reduce until half its volume. Then add tomato paste and reserved shrimp. Set aside while you make the rice.

3. Heat remaining butter in saucepan with remaining onion and garlic, lightly sauté until softened. Add rice and cook a few moments.

4. Ladle in ½ cup white wine, stir and cook until liquid evaporates. Ladle in the hot stock you have made from the shrimp shells, adding it ½ cup at a time, increasing to 1 cup as the rice cooks.

5. When rice is nearly cooked through, stir in the shrimp sauce, return to heat and finish cooking together.

6. Serve hot, sprinkled with chopped basil or parsley.

Couscous

Sardinia and Sicily lie in the Mediterranean, both 100 miles or so off the shore of North Africa, with which they share centuries of history and the foods that are a part of that past: couscous and couscouslike dishes (*sa fregula*).

In Sicily, couscous is usually steamed over a savory fish/seafood broth, then served with a spicy seafood stew; in Sardinia, vegetables tend to predominate, as in the following dishes.

Basic Cascasa, Cuscus, or Couscous Preparation, Italian Style

⑥ Adjust the amount of liquid by taste and common sense rather than following the directions on the package; they are not always accurate.

⑥ Before steaming, wet 1 cup couscous with ¼ to ½ cup water, enough to dampen all of the grains. Spread grains out on a baking sheet to swell for about 10 minutes. Crumble the grains in your hands to separate. If you have time, repeat the process for plumper, lighter grains.

⑥ You may steam the couscous over a fishy soup-stew, seasoned with ginger, hot pepper, and a little chopped cilantro and/or Italian parsley, ladling a bit of the fish stock over the couscous as it cooks. A traditional dish throughout the islands surrounding Sicily is a meat and vegetable couscous, with braised Mediterranean vegetables such as green beans, eggplant, zucchini, and lamb or beef braised in red wine and tomatoes.

You may cook the plumped couscous by pouring over it boiling stock of choice, covering the pot, and letting it sit for 10 minutes. Fluff up with a fork, season with salt and pepper, and toss with a little olive oil and other seasonings. Raisins, currants, pine nuts, chopped toasted almonds, cumin seeds, chopped parsley, a "batutta" of chopped sautéed onion, celery, carrot, and garlic, all may be added.

Serve cooked couscous spooned into a tomatoey seafood soup or a zesty braised lamb and vegetable dish or cook couscous in lamb broth and serve it with a garlicky sauce of tomatoes, sausage, and herbs, much as you would polenta.

Cascasa Carlofortina
SARDINIAN COUSCOUS FROM THE PORT OF CARLOFORTE

Also known as *sa fregula,* cascasa is prepared by steaming the couscous grains in a steamer above a pot of vegetable stew (which might contain carrots, potatoes, chick-peas, tomatoes, cabbage). The cascasa is then served tossed with chopped parsley, garlic, and olive oil, and accompanied by the vegetable stew over which it cooked.

Sa Fregula con Zucchini e Cecchi
COUSCOUS WITH SPICY ZUCCHINI AND CHICK-PEA SAUCE
Sardinia

Serves 4 to 6

Spicy zucchini and chick-pea sauce, ladled over cumin-scented raisin-studded couscous, is my variation on a traditional dish. It makes a zesty vegetarian main course and may be turned into a meaty main course by serving it alongside a selection of grilled meats.

1 cup dry couscous

1 cup cold water

1 onion, chopped

8 to 10 zucchini, cut into chunks

1 cup cooked, drained chick-peas

2 tablespoons olive oil

3 to 5 cloves garlic, chopped

3 cups diced tomatoes (canned are fine)

1 teaspoon chopped fresh rosemary

Hot pepper seasoning such as Tabasco, to taste

1 to 2 tablespoons chopped fresh basil or flat-leaf Italian parsley

2 to 3 cups boiling broth of choice: vegetable, chicken, or beef, or amount called for in couscous package directions

¼ cup raisins

¼ teaspoon cumin seeds

Salt and cayenne pepper

2 tablespoons butter

1. Combine couscous with water and work it through with your hands. Let sit 15 to 30 minutes and work it through with your hands once more.

2. Lightly sauté onion, zucchini, and chick-peas in olive oil until onions and zucchini are slightly tender. Add garlic and cook a moment. Stir in tomatoes and cook over medium-high heat until mixture is saucy and thickened, about 5 to 10 minutes. Add rosemary, Tabasco, and basil or parsley. Set aside.

3. Combine couscous with the boiling broth, raisins, and cumin. Cover and steep for 5 to 10 minutes. Season with salt and cayenne, then toss with butter.

4. Reheat sauce. Serve hot couscous with sauce ladled over it or alongside.

POLENTA

UNTIL recently, when polenta found itself very fashionable, this creamy, comforting cornmeal porridge has been eaten only in the home or in humble trattorie known for *cucina casalinga* (home cooking). In fact, the traditional way to eat polenta, especially in the mountains of Sardinia, is from a large wooden trough, a huge mound poured out onto the rough board, the eaters gathered around on a rustic bench, eating communally, each person spooning more sauce onto his or her individual portion as the meal progresses.

In Sardinia, polenta is traditionally served topped with meaty sauces and forest mushrooms, with tomatoes, herbs, game, and juicy browned sausages, or poured onto a board and cooled, then sliced and grilled. It has also long been a traditional dish in regions of Sicily.

Polenta may also be made with chestnut or buckwheat flour, a nutty brown hue, earthy and rustic, eaten on the neighboring French island of Corsica.

Basic Polenta

¹/₂ cup cornmeal

¹/₂ cup cold water

3 cups boiling salted water

1. Mix cornmeal with cold water and let stand 10 minutes or so.
2. Add ¹/₂ cup boiling water to the cornmeal, then slowly stir this cornmeal mixture into the remaining boiling water, stirring, stirring, stirring, until the cornmeal thickens and grows soft and

tender, not gritty. This will probably take about 30 to 40 minutes. Different cornmeals will take differing amounts of water and time; if the package lists directions and times, use that as a guideline.

3. Serve soft, soupy, and porridgelike (polentina), or tip the cooked hot polenta out onto an oiled platter and let cool. Carefully slice once it has cooled and firmed, then grill or brown, and serve as an accompaniment or breadlike base for other foods.

Suggestions for Serving Soft Polenta (Polentina):

⑥ Serve topped with melting sweet butter and a grating of Parmesan and black pepper to taste.

⑥ Stir a few tablespoons of moscarpone cheese into the hot cooked polenta, then stir in a grating of Fontina and/or a crumbling of Gorgonzola or goat cheese. Serve with a thin slice or two of prosciutto and a few crisp butter-browned sage leaves.

⑥ Serve topped with browned sausages (hot pepper or fennel-spiced) and a zesty tomato sauce.

⑥ Stir a few tablespoons cream or moscarpone into the just-cooked polenta, and top with a highly flavored homemade ragu as well as sautéed wild forest mushrooms. Blanket the whole thing with grated Parmesan or pecorino.

⑥ Rosemary polenta with mushrooms: Add several tablespoons chopped fresh rosemary to the polenta as it cooks. Serve dabbed with butter melting in, topped with sautéed mushrooms such as porcini or other field mushrooms and a grating of cheese.

⑥ Serve polenta with big meatballs, braised greens or broccoli, and a tomatoey sauce. Blanket with grated cheese.

Suggestions for Serving Firm Polenta:

Slice polenta and brush with olive oil. Grill, preferably over an open fire, leaving grill marks on its surface. Then serve:

- Topped with sautéed wild mushrooms, shredded Fontina cheese, and a drizzling of hot stock, then broil until the cheese melts.

- Hot, sprinkled with crumbled Gorgonzola and accompanied by grilled endive.

- In slabs, topped with braised chicken, quail, turkey, pheasant, or duck, in a winey tomato sauce seasoned with a handful of pitted, diced olives.

- As an accompaniment for a variety of grilled foods: sausage, goat cheese wrapped in vine leaves, kabobs of pork, herbs, and pancetta, asparagus, fresh porcini or other field mushrooms.

- Add diced sun-dried tomatoes to the polenta just as it finishes cooking. Pour out and let cool, then slice and grill or fry as desired.

- Cut into rounds about ¾ inch thick. Top with a thin slice of garlicky salami, then grill until hot.

- Top with a thin slice of Fontina, a little chopped garlic, and a little chopped sage leaves; grill until cheese melts.

- Top grilled polenta with garlicky sautéed mixed peppers and tomatoes, sprinkled with fresh oregano or marjoram, garnished with small pitted black olives.

Polenta al Forno
CASSEROLE OF POLENTA LAYERED WITH TOMATO SAUCE, FRESH ROSEMARY, AND FONTINA

Serves 4

Polenta, cut into slabs and layered with cheeses and tomatoes, much like a polenta Parmigiana, makes a satisfying and homey dish.

1 large batch cooked polenta, poured out onto a board or pan and left to cool (see basic recipe on page 108)

3 tablespoons olive oil

2 cups tomato passata

1 cup diced fresh tomatoes (or use 3 cups diced tomatoes in passata mixture)

3 to 6 cloves garlic, chopped

About 8 ounces Fontina or mozzarella cheese, thinly sliced or coarsely shredded

1 to 2 tablespoons chopped fresh rosemary

Grated Parmesan cheese

1. Cut the polenta into slabs. Layer in a 12- to 15-inch-long or 9- to 12-inch round baking pan that has been coated with olive oil, alternating polenta, tomato passata, diced tomatoes, garlic, rosemary, and Fontina or mozzarella. Reserve 2 cloves garlic for next step.

2. Sprinkle top with rosemary, reserved garlic, olive oil, and Parmesan, then bake in a 375°F oven about 30 to 40 minutes until the top is lightly brown and sizzling and the cheese has melted.

I Pesci, Crostaceo, e Frutti di Mare

FISH AND SEAFOOD

The sea provides so much of the food that nourishes island dwellers: silvery fish, spindly crustaceans, tender-fleshed mollusks. Cafes along the seafront or tucked into the hillsides offer *pesce del giorno* (fish of the day), lettered onto little signs or blackboards, sometimes on elegant menus, sometimes hand-painted in vivid colors.

The fish, of course, are nearly trembling with freshness, sold moments after being pulled from the sea, and cooked not long after that. (Unfortunately, pollution and overfishing are taking their toll; the abundance and variety of fish are declining.)

Usually fish are prepared simply: brushed with herbs and butter or olive oil, then grilled, baked, or roasted whole until the skin crackles and the flesh is tender. (Whole fish are considered at their best when full of roe.) When cut into chunks or fillets, fish are grilled quickly, or boiled in wine and seasonings, then served in their broth. They may be simmered with aromatics for a soupy stew, then ladled over crisp garlic croutons, polenta, or pasta.

One of the most unusual seafood dishes I came upon, however, was on a boat ride around Pantelleria, a volcanic island where hot springs abound. The captain plunged a steamer net filled with octopus into the bubbling sea, allowing it to cook in the boiling, salty water.

Since seafood and fish are so often served for antipasti, or simmered into soups, rice, and pasta dishes, be sure to refer to those chapters as well.

Brodetto de Pesce alla Marinara

FISH STEW

Tremiti Islands

Serves 4 to 6

Brodetto is a soupy fish stew eaten throughout the coast regions and islands of Italy. Each region has its own seasonings and flavor: This one is from the Tremiti Islands. (Sadly, this dish is seen less and less as so much of the local fish is sent off to Rome rather than eaten locally.)

The Tremiti Islands fishermen whip up this version, flavored with lots of tomatoes, hot peppers, and olive oil, on their boats from the bits and pieces of the day's haul that might not be worth sending to market. Trimmings such as fish heads go into the pot, as well as any creatures that are too small to bring in a profit, all full of the flavor that only freshness can bring.

Chunks of rough crusty bread and a bottle of equally rough red wine make perfect accompaniments.

5 to 8 cloves garlic, chopped (less if desired)

2 tablespoons chopped parsley (plus extra for sprinkling, if desired)

$^1/_2$ to 1 fresh hot chile, such as jalapeño, serrano, or Thai, chopped

3 to 4 tablespoons olive oil

1 cup diced tomatoes (canned are fine)

1 cup dry white wine

3 pounds mixed fish and seafood: cod, snapper, bass, mussels, clams, crab, lobster, eel, squid

Salt and pepper

Lemon wedges

1. Sauté garlic, parsley, and chile in olive oil until softened, then add tomatoes and wine and bring to a boil.

2. Gradually add the fish and seafood, beginning with those that take longest to cook, adding them at intervals so that by the time the last addition has cooked through, the rest of the fish and seafood are done. Take care not to overcook.

3. Taste a little of the soupy liquid. If it is too thin and needs a bit of flavor, pour off and keep the fish warm. Boil down the liquid until it is a flavorful saucelike consistency, season with salt and pepper, then pour over the warm fish and seafood.

4. Serve with lemon wedges and an extra sprinkling of parsley if desired.

Variation: Kassola

Kassola is the Sardinian version of *brodetto,* a casserole filled with sea creatures, simmering in a highly flavored tomato broth. Usually the broth is served first, ladled over either garlic-rubbed country toast or garlic-seasoned *sa fregula,* couscouslike pasta (see page 106).

To prepare kassola, increase liquid in above recipe by adding fish stock or broth along with the white wine. In Sardinia water would be used, but I find that when I prepare it with water in my American kitchen it just needs a bit of oomph and more flavor depth. Fish stock makes all the difference.

Pesce con Pomodori e Herbe
COD WITH TOMATOES, OLIVE OIL, AND FRESH HERBS
Capri, Ischia, Procida

Serves 4

Fresh white-fleshed fish, seasoned with tomatoes, onions, garlic, olive oil, and lemon, then tightly sealed and baked in its own juices makes a splendid dish. Its lusty flavor evokes memories of dinner on a terrace on the Isle of Capri, under the stars on an evening scented with night-blooming jasmine. It was too dark to see details of the sea, but silvery reflections on the water and the cozy sloshing sounds let us know it was there, all around us.

Begin the meal with a light but zesty pasta such as buttery fettucine with shrimp, chives, lemon, and a little chile pepper; for dessert, a plate of ripe cherries (chilled not in the refrigerator but tossed with a handful of ice cubes, letting the ice melt as it chills the sweet fruit), along with either a piece of creamy, deliciously stinky cheese or a bowl of red wine granita.

1½ pounds fresh cod, in large fillets or steaks

Salt, pepper, and crushed dried oregano to taste

1 medium onion, thinly sliced

3 cloves garlic, finely chopped

4 ripe fresh or canned tomatoes, diced or thinly sliced, include juice

2 tablespoons olive oil, or as desired

Juice of 1 lemon

2 tablespoons chopped parsley

½ teaspoon chopped fresh thyme or marjoram leaves

1. Place cod in earthenware casserole and sprinkle with salt, pepper, and oregano.
2. Top with onion, garlic, and tomatoes, then drizzle with olive oil and lemon juice. Cover tightly (parchment paper gives excellent results) and bake in a 375°F oven for 15 to 20 minutes.
3. Serve immediately, topped with parsley and thyme or marjoram.

Pesce con Arancia e Limone
ROAST SEA BASS WITH ORANGES AND LEMONS
Ischia

Serves 4 to 6

This dish combines two of the most essential flavors of the region: the excellent raw ingredients of fish and citrus fruit.

Begin the meal with Formaggio al Salsa Verde (page 34), then Vermicelli al Pomodori (page 56). For dessert, serve something chocolate such as dark chocolate ice cream topped with crushed chocolate-espresso beans, and a dollop of lightly whipped brandy-scented cream.

2 oranges

1 lemon

1 whole sea bass, sea bream, red mullet, or similar fish, about 2½ to 3 pounds, cleaned

Salt and pepper

8 to 10 bay leaves, preferably fresh

5 to 8 garlic cloves, peeled and halved lengthwise

3 to 5 tablespoons olive oil

2 tablespoons chopped parsley, preferably flat-leaf Italian

1. Grate the zest from 1 orange and set aside. Peel, seed, and slice the two oranges and the lemon. Mix with grated orange zest and set aside.
2. Rub fish all over with salt and pepper, then stuff its cavity with bay leaves and garlic.
3. Arrange orange and lemon slices in a baking dish large enough to hold the fish, then arrange the fish on top. Drizzle olive oil over it.
4. Bake in 375°F oven, covered, until fish is nearly tender, about 20 to 25 minutes, then remove cover and roast until top is lightly browned and the fish is fork-tender, another 10 to 15 minutes. If bottom of pan gets too dry with the citrus fruit threatening to burn, add a bit of stock or white wine when you remove the covering.
5. Taste for salt and pepper, then serve immediately, each portion of fish with some of the citrus pan sauce spooned over it, all sprinkled with the parsley.

The Mattanza

EACH YEAR WHEN THE HOT WINDS BLOW FROM THE SAHARA ACROSS THE SEA TO SICILY, THE ATLANTIC TUNA RETURN TO THE WARM WATERS TO REPRODUCE AND THE *MATTANZA*, OR ANCIENT RITUAL TUNA-KILLING, IS REPEATED.

THE *MATTANZA* IS MORE THAN A KILLING ORGY, HOWEVER, AND MORE THAN THE NECESSITY OF KILLING FOR FOOD. IT IS AN ALMOST RELIGIOUS EXPERIENCE THAT ORIGINATED AROUND 10,000 YEARS AGO. THE ISLANDERS VIEWED THESE MAGNIFICENT FISH AS GODS WHO SACRIFICED THEMSELVES SO THAT HUMANS MIGHT LIVE ON THEIR FLESH. A COMPLEX TUNAFISH CULTURE DEVELOPED, ENCOMPASSING SUPERSTITIONS, TRADITIONS, AND RELIGIOUS RITUAL, MUCH OF WHICH SURVIVES TO THIS DAY IN THE *MATTANZA*.

THE *MATTANZA* IS ORGANIZED BY USING NETS THAT ARE CONSTRUCTED INTO CHAMBERS, ALL OF WHICH LEAD THE TUNA (WHICH CAN WEIGH UP TO 1,800 POUNDS) TO THE FINAL "DEATH CHAMBER," WHERE THEY ARE STABBED TO THE CHANTS AND SHOUTS OF *"SPARA A TUNNINA!"* ("HIT THE TUNA!").

BEFORE THE *TONNARA*, OR THE HUNT FOR THE BEASTS, BEGINS, THE MIGHTY FISH ARE BLESSED BY A PRIEST: PRAISED FOR THEIR STRENGTH, BEAUTY, AND ESPECIALLY THEIR COURAGE: THEY DIE WITHOUT A CRY!

THIS RESPECT IS TURNED INTO KITCHEN FRUGALITY. NO PART OF THE TUNA IS LEFT TO WASTE. THE FLESH AND BONES PROVIDE OIL, FERTILIZER, AND AGRICULTURAL FEED AS WELL AS FOOD FOR THE TABLE. FOR THIS USEFULNESS, THE TUNA IS NICKNAMED "SEA-PIG" SINCE, LIKE THE PORCINE LAND CREATURE, EVERY BIT IS PUT TO USE.

WHILE THERE WERE ONCE MORE THAN TWENTY ANNUAL *MATTANZE* IN THE SEA AROUND SICILY AND SURROUNDING ISLANDS, THE PAST SEVERAL DECADES HAVE SEEN A STEADY DECLINE IN THE NUMBERS OF TUNA CAUGHT. THERE ARE ONLY ABOUT TWO *MATTANZE* A YEAR NOW,

SINCE THE FISH CAN BE CAUGHT MORE EFFICIENTLY ELSEWHERE AND KILLED IN AN EASIER, LESS BLOODY WAY. IT IS COMMON-SENSE ECONOMICS. (INTERESTINGLY, THE WORD *MATTANZA* IS NOW WIDELY USED TO DENOTE A MAFIA MASSACRE, IN HONOR OF THE BLOODY FISHERMEN'S RITUAL.)

FAVIGNANA, A SMALL ISLAND (PART OF THE EGADI) TO THE WEST OF SICILY, IS THE SITE OF THE MOST IMPORTANT PRESENT-DAY *MATTANZA*, ONE THAT HAS REMAINED VIRTUALLY UNCHANGED OVER THE CENTURIES. FAVIGNANA ISLANDERS HAVE MANY TRADITIONAL WAYS OF PREPARING TUNA, THOUGH WITH SO MUCH OF THE CATCH SOLD TO OUTSIDERS, SUCH SPECIALTIES ARE BECOMING RARER. THE EGGS OF THE GREAT FISH ARE TOSSED INTO PASTA SAUCE, THEIR BONES GROUND INTO FLOUR; OFTEN THE LUNGS ARE SALTED, TO BE REHYDRATED LATER, MUCH LIKE SALT COD; AND THE INTESTINES ARE MADE INTO SAUSAGES. AT ONE PENSIONE MY HUSBAND WAS SERVED A WHITE CREAMY PATTY, COVERED WITH CRISP CRUMBS, AND THE KITCHEN CURIOUSLY REFUSED TO SERVE ME THE SAME THING. "IT'S TUNA SEX, FROM THE MAN," EXPLAINED THE MOTHERLY PROPRIETRESS, HER CHEEKS BURNING WITH EMBARRASSMENT OVER MY INSISTENCE FOR THE DISH THAT IS "TOO DANGEROUS FOR A WOMAN."

Tonno in Agrodolce
SWEET-SOUR-SAVORY BRAISED TUNA
Trapani, Sicily

Serves 4 to 6

Traditional seafront fare, this Trapani specialty has the distinctive Arab-influenced flavor of sweet and tangy, with lots of mint and parsley to add freshness and fragrance.

1½ pounds tuna steaks, about
   1 inch thick

Flour for dredging fish

4 tablespoons olive oil

2 large onions, very thinly sliced

⅓ cup red wine vinegar

1½ to 2 teaspoons sugar

¼ cup dry white wine

¼ cup finely chopped mint

1 tablespoons coarsely chopped
   parsley

Salt and pepper

1. Dredge tuna steaks in flour, then shake off any excess.
2. Sauté tuna in 3 tablespoons olive oil over medium heat for a minute or two on each side, preparing in several batches if you need to. Remove tuna from pan and keep warm.
3. To sautéing pan, add remaining oil and sauté onions until golden and softened, about 5 to 8 minutes, stirring occasionally. Add vinegar, sugar, wine, mint, and parsley. Bring to a boil, then reduce heat and simmer a few minutes. Season with salt and pepper, then return tuna to pan, spoon sauce over the fish, and simmer a few minutes together, letting the fish absorb the flavors of the sauce. If the sauce is too thin, remove fish and boil down the sauce before pouring it over the fish. If the sauce is too thick and there is no liquid, add ½ cup water, white wine, or broth to the pan and boil a minute or two, scraping up the bits, until it forms a flavorful sauce.

Spada alla Palermo
SWORDFISH BASTED WITH OLIVE OIL AND LEMON JUICE
ON BRUSHES OF OREGANO STALKS
Palermo, Sicily

A description rather than a recipe: Baste skewered swordfish chunks with lemon juice and olive oil using little brushes made from oregano stalks. The brush adds its fragrance to the fish, but more than that, there is something very poetic and picturesque about using such a rustic and traditional tool. If you've prepared swordfish like this in a Sicilian kitchen or country-side, you'll find it much more evocative than an efficient and proper basting brush could ever be.

For the basting mixture, combine 2 parts olive oil with 1 part lemon juice and season with chopped fresh oregano or marjoram, salt and pepper to taste. Use to baste chunks of skewered swordfish as the fish is grilling.

Spada alla Caprese
SWORDFISH MARINATED, THEN GRILLED, THEN MARINATED AGAIN
Capri

Serves 4

A traditional island dish from Capri, swordfish is first brushed with marinade, then grilled over an open fire, then sauced with the remaining marinade. It is as delicious at room temperature as it is hot.

If swordfish is not available, it's very good with fresh tuna (see variation). The fresh tuna version is a specialty of the island of Lipari, north of Sicily, with a much spicier marinade than the Caprese dish.

4 cloves garlic, finely chopped

$1/2$ cup olive oil

Juice of 1 lemon, plus extra, to taste; or 2 tablespoons balsamic vinegar

Salt, pepper, and lots of fresh or dried oregano to taste

2 tablespoons chopped parsley

$1^1/2$ pounds swordfish steaks, cut about $1/8$ to $1/4$ inch thick

Optional garnish: 2 to 3 tablespoons diced roasted red pepper

1. Combine garlic with olive oil, lemon juice or balsamic vinegar, salt, pepper, oregano, and parsley.
2. Brush swordfish with the marinade, then grill over hot coals until lightly browned on the outside and just cooked through, about 6 to 8 minutes.

3. Remove fish from grill and arrange on platter. Pour reserved marinade over the hot grilled fish. Garnish with red peppers if desired, and serve right away, hot, or let cool to room temperature.

Variation: Tonno al Sammoriglio
FRESH TUNA STEAKS MARINATED IN HOT PEPPER MARINADE,
THEN GRILLED AND MARINATED AGAIN
Lipari

The *sammoriglio* in the title refers to the marinade the grilled fish is dressed with. The olive oil and lemon mixture is a traditional sauce for fish throughout Sicily and the nearby islands.

Proceed as above, but add a hefty jolt of cayenne pepper or chopped jalapeño to the marinade and substitute tuna steaks for the swordfish. Marinate the fish in half the marinade, using whatever is left in the bowl to baste the fish as it cooks. Use the rest of the marinade to dress the fish when it comes hot off the grill.

Pesce con Patate e Carciofi
BAKED SEA BASS ON A BED OF POTATOES AND ARTICHOKES
Sardinia

Serves 6 to 8

In Cagliari we wandered into a little trattoria filled with both blue- and white-collar workers, all enjoying the endless parade of zesty dishes. We forked up plates of *seppia con piselli* (squid with peas), *spaghetti con sugo di gamberi* (spaghetti with shrimp sauce), and *spaghettini con nero di seppia* (spaghetti with squid ink), and the simplest dish: olive oil-sautéed seafoods that tasted of the sea, all cloaked in the strong perfume of fresh garlic.

As the fish cooks, its flavors are absorbed by the bed of potatoes and artichokes. Tomatoes moisten and season the fish, as do garlic, olive oil, and herbs. If you can, cook this in a ceramic casserole; the slightly porous consistency seems to work delicious magic with the juices of the fish and vegetables.

This dish reflects Sardinia's shared history with the other Mediterranean islands, especially the Balearics.

²/₃ to ³/₄ **pound baking potatoes**

Olive oil

3 artichoke hearts, blanched and sliced (frozen are okay, but second-best; canned are not acceptable—better to simply omit the artichokes and increase the potatoes or add another vegetable such as 3 sliced zucchini or 1 sliced eggplant)

Salt and pepper

1¹/₂ **to 2 pounds sea bass, halibut, swordfish, or tuna steaks**

2 to 3 large ripe tomatoes, halved

6 cloves garlic, chopped

2 teaspoon chopped parsley, preferably flat-leaf Italian

2 green onions, chopped

¹/₂ **to 1 teaspoon chopped fresh rosemary**

¹/₂ **to 1 teaspoon chopped fresh thyme, marjoram, or oregano**

Lemon juice to taste

1. Boil potatoes in water to cover for 10 to 15 minutes, just long enough to stabilize their starch. Drain and let cool until you can handle them, then peel and slice about ¹/₄ inch thick.
2. Coat bottom of a clay or ceramic casserole or other baking dish with olive oil, then layer in overlapping slices of potato and artichoke, sprinkling with salt and pepper as you go.
3. Top with fish steaks, then tuck the tomato halves into any empty spaces. Drizzle olive oil over the top, then sprinkle with garlic, parsley, green onion, and herbs. Splash with a bit of lemon juice, then season with more salt and pepper.
4. Bake in a 375–400°F oven for 25 to 35 minutes or until fish and vegetables are cooked through.

Variation: If using zucchini or eggplant in place of artichoke, lightly brown in a small amount of oil before layering with the potatoes and fish.

Aragosta con e Fave
LOBSTER WITH FRESH FAVA BEANS
Sardinia

Serves 4 as a first course or lunch dish

Few dishes typify the Sardinian culinary character as does the combination of fish with vegetables. It seems to embrace the essential nature of Sardinia itself: a combination of its surrounding sea and its earthy, untamed interior.

Rather than give directions on cooking your own live lobster, I suggest that you ask your fishmonger to do the honor and that you simply warm the freshly cooked beasts when you cook the favas. If lobster is unavailable, you may use large prawns such as tiger prawns, in their shells.

1½ to 2 pounds fresh fava beans, in their shells

2 large lobsters, or enough for 4 people, freshly cooked; or 1 pound tiger prawns, in their shells

3 cloves garlic, chopped

6 tablespoons butter

3 tablespoons olive oil

Juice of 1 to 2 lemons

Salt and pepper

2 tablespoons thinly sliced fresh basil leaves

1. Shell favas, then boil for about 2 minutes or until they are barely tender. Remove from heat and drain, then rinse with cold water. When they are cool enough to handle, peel by cutting each bean with a sharp knife or fingernail to loosen the skin, then squeezing the bean out. Discard the skins and set the beans aside.

2. If using freshly cooked lobster, cut into 4 serving portions. If using large prawns, cook by placing in cold water with a lemon

half, then bringing to a boil. Reduce heat and simmer 30 to 60 seconds, then remove from the heat. Cover and let cool to warm room temperature. (The gradual cooling helps the flesh stay tender.) Drain and discard the lemon half.

3. Warm the garlic in the butter and olive oil, then add the favas and toss through the mixture, then push to the side and gently warm the lobster or prawns in the same pan.

4. When heated through, squeeze the lemon juice in, season with salt and pepper, and serve right away, each portion garnished with a sprinkling of fresh basil.

Cape Sante alla Rosmarino
ROSEMARY-GRILLED SCALLOPS
Capri

Serves 3 to 4

The sweet flesh of the scallop, like that of the delicate white meat of a chicken, takes good-naturedly to a marinade of garlic, olive oil, lemon juice, and rosemary.

Enjoy as is, accompanied by wedges of yellow, green, and red peppers and dollops of garlicky mayonnaise, or serve atop wilted spinach leaves, splashed with sun-dried tomato vinaigrette as a warm salad *nuova cucina* offering.

1 pound sweet fresh scallops, roe removed

3 to 5 cloves garlic, finely chopped

3 to 4 tablespoons olive oil

Juice of 1 lemon

2 tablespoons finely chopped fresh rosemary

Salt and pepper

1. Combine scallops with garlic, olive oil, lemon juice, rosemary, salt, and pepper. Let marinate, covered, at least 30 minutes, but not longer than 2 hours, turning once or twice.

2. Thread onto metal skewers (traditionally, rosemary branches might be used, but metal ones keep you from losing any scallops to branches catching fire).

3. Grill over a charcoal flame until just cooked through, only a few minutes on each side. Baste occasionally with any remaining marinade.

Seppie coi Carciofi
SQUID WITH ARTICHOKES
Elba

Serves 6

French influence—both Corsica's proximity and Napoleon's exile—is reflected in Elba's cuisine. The secret to keeping squid tender is to cook it either quick, quick, quick, such as deep-frying, or to simmer it long and slowly.

This is said to have been Napoleon's favorite dish, but judging from all of the dishes on the island that are said to have been Napoleon's favorite, I'm surprised he could bring himself to leave.

1 to 1½ pounds squid, cleaned of bone and ink sac, the tentacles left whole and the bodies sliced in half

3 tablespoons olive oil

1 cup fish or chicken broth

1 cup dry white wine

5 cloves garlic, crushed

Salt and pepper

5 to 8 shallots, chopped

¼ cup chopped parsley, preferably flat-leaf Italian

4 medium artichokes, cleaned of their chokes and quartered (if older, larger, and somewhat tough, blanch first; if young and tender, do not bother); or 6 to 8 artichoke hearts

Lemon juice to taste

1. Combine squid with 2 tablespoons olive oil, broth, white wine, and garlic, adding a little water if squid are not covered by the broth and wine. Bring to a boil slowly, then reduce heat and simmer, covered, for 20 to 25 minutes. Season with salt and pepper.

2. In the remaining olive oil lightly sauté shallots, parsley, and artichoke hearts until lightly golden; add to simmering squid and cook together until both squid and artichokes are tender and flavorful.

3. Pour off sauce and cook down until it is reduced to a flavorful sauce. Season with lemon juice to taste, then pour over the squid and artichokes. Taste for salt and pepper, then serve.

Pesce e Cozze con Finocchio
ROASTED FISH AND MUSSELS WITH FENNEL
Throughout the Islands

Serves 6 to 8

This combination of fish and seafood is lush and visually appealing, the flavoring of fennel particular to the Italian islands rather than the mainland. Though the recipe calls for only fish and mussels, by all means add whatever sea creatures are available: a handful of pink prawns still in their shells, or briny clams the size of coins.

Serve with couscous that you've steamed in fish broth and seasoned with hot pepper, garlic, and a squeeze of lemon.

2 pounds mussels, beards removed and cleaned of seaweed

1 medium onion, chopped

3 to 4 cloves garlic, chopped

1 cup dry white wine

1 fresh fennel bulb plus some of the feathery leaves, thinly sliced

1 to 2 teaspoons fennel seeds, as desired

½ cup diced sweet garden-ripe tomatoes, or well-drained canned tomatoes

⅓ cup olive oil

1 tablespoon fennel-flavored liqueur such as Sambuca, Pastis, or ouzo

1 whole fish, about 4 pounds, such as sea bass, or large fillets, cleaned

2 tablespoons chopped parsley, preferably flat-leaf Italian

Salt and pepper

1. Soak mussels for 30 minutes or so in cold water; rinse and discard and repeat.
2. Combine onion, garlic, white wine, fennel bulb, fennel seeds, tomatoes, olive oil, and liqueur in saucepan. Bring to a boil and cook over high heat for 5 minutes, to reduce liquid and intensify the sauce, then spoon into large baking pan or casserole.
3. Arrange fish on top, spooning some of the vegetable-sauce mixture into its cavity, basting the fish with the rest.
4. Bake the fish at 375°F until it is about 10 minutes from being done (this will depend on its thickness). Then add the mussels, baste with some of the sauce, cover, and cook over high heat until mussels open and fish is firm to the touch.
5. Sprinkle with parsley and season with salt and pepper if needed. If sauce is too thin, pour off carefully and boil down until reduced and flavorful.

I Polli, Galline, Anatre, Quaglie, e Uno Coniglio

CHICKEN, TURKEY, DUCK, QUAIL, AND ONE RABBIT

Unlike the foods from the sea that are a unifying element of Italian island cuisines, poultry dishes vary a great deal. Traditionally, domestically raised poultry has often taken second place to the wild birds and rabbits that are hunted in the fields and mountains. These game are cooked simply over an open fire or stewed in savory sauces.

Chicken, turkey, and duck are enjoyed with nearly as much enthusiasm as wild fowl, but without the verve and variety typical of seafood and fish. Sunday lunch will often center around a pot of chicken soup, the golden hen removed from her bath afterward and roasted quickly until browned and succulent, then eaten as the main course. Festive occasions nearly always begin with such a soup, and often chicken is simmered in a savory spicy sauce, along with peppers, tomatoes, onions, and the like, then served in two courses: pasta with the sauce first, then the platter of chicken.

A whole chicken may be roasted in the communal oven, its middle filled with chunks of lemon, cloves of garlic, and sprigs of fresh herbs. At other times, chicken might be marinated and cooked on the grill, or skewered onto a rotisserie where it revolves its way to crisp-skinned, juicy-fleshed succulence. Chicken breasts and slices of turkey breast are treated elegantly throughout Italy, including the islands, prepared the same way tender veal might be.

Small birds such as quail are devoured throughout Italy, and slightly larger ones such as game hens, poussins, and guinea hens are favored as well. Duck is prepared in a variety of ways: with fruit, aromatics, olives, and wine. Turkey is eaten roasted whole for special occasions, or sliced into cutlets and cooked with savory sauces, olives, and herbs.

The tourist culture of various islands has contributed the addition of international ideas (remember, in Italy, "international" means a dish from outside your neighborhood or region) and visiting chefs have brought their influences as well.

Pollo al Limone
CHICKEN WITH LEMON, MINT, AND ALMONDS
Sicily

Serves 4

I ate this vivacious lemon-scented chicken sitting under a tree-shaded table one sunny afternoon in Messina, Sicily. Lemon permeated the flesh of the chicken (from an overnight stay in the marinade) and gave the sauce the piquancy of a French vinegar essence, while fresh mint added freshness and almonds provided crunchy counterpoint.

To enhance its fruitiness, serve with Insalata di Pere e Parmigiana (page 9), bitter greens studded with bits of pear, cheese, basil, and mint, with a few spoonfuls of the pan sauce spooned over it, along with crusty bread and cooling wine.

1 chicken, cut into serving pieces

10 garlic cloves, coarsely chopped

1 cup fresh mint leaves, torn or coarsely chopped

Juice of 3 lemons (save several of the skins to toss in the marinade as well)

About 3 tablespoons olive oil

Salt and pepper

3 to 4 ounces slivered almonds

$\frac{1}{2}$ cup dry white wine

$\frac{2}{3}$ cup chicken broth

1. Combine chicken with garlic, about $\frac{2}{3}$ cup mint, lemon juice, $1\frac{1}{2}$ tablespoons olive oil, salt, and pepper. Cover well and refrigerate at least overnight.

2. Remove chicken from the marinade and wipe the pieces dry. Reserve the marinade for the sauce, including the chopped mint leaves, if desired.

3. Lightly toast the almonds in an ungreased frying pan on top of the stove, or in a shallow baking pan in a 400°F oven, then remove from pan and set aside.

4. Cook the chicken by browning the dark meat and wings first in the olive oil for about 20 to 25 minutes, then adding the breasts and browning for another 10 minutes, turning several times during cooking. Remove chicken pieces from pan and keep warm.

5. Pour fat out of pan, then add wine and cook over high heat until reduced by about half, then add the chicken broth and reserved marinade and continue to cook over high heat until it reduces to a flavorful, concentrated but thin sauce, about ½ cup in volume.

6. Taste for seasoning, then pour sauce over chicken and serve right away, sprinkling the top with reserved toasted almonds and reserved chopped fresh mint.

Variation: Instead of sautéing the chicken and preparing a sauce with the marinade, prepare the citrus and mint marinated chicken on the grill and serve sprinkled with fresh mint, toasted almonds, and wedges of lemon.

Pollo con Salsa di Olive
SAUTÉED CHICKEN WITH SAUCE OF OLIVE PASTE, VINEGAR, AND MIXED OLIVES
Ischia

Serves 4

This chicken sauté is for those who, like me, adore olives since it not only contains a variety of olives themselves, but the sauce is thickened with black olive paste. The chicken, of course, is sautéed in olive oil.

This is how much I adore olives: When I recently married, my husband and I bought an olive tree and planted it in the field overlooking the sunny vineyard where we held the ceremony. It is thriving; we can hardly wait for the first crop.

1 small to medium chicken, 2½ to 3 pounds, cut into serving pieces

3 tablespoons olive oil or as needed

10 cloves garlic, or to taste, coarsely chopped

2 to 3 small sprigs fresh rosemary (about 1 tablespoon leaves)

2 to 3 sprigs fresh thyme or marjoram, the leaves pulled off

2 cups dry white wine

2 tablespoons white wine vinegar

2 to 3 tablespoons black olive paste

1 cup mixed olives: small chiled green ones, big black Greek ones, wrinkly black oil-cured ones, etc.

1. Brown the chicken pieces in the olive oil, beginning with the dark meat ones, adding the breasts toward the end, allowing only 5 to 8 minutes browning. Every so often sprinkle with a little of the garlic.

2. When chicken is about half cooked, pour off the excess oil, add half the rosemary and thyme or marjoram, a little more of the garlic, and the white wine. Boil for 5 to 10 minutes or until the wine reduces to a saucelike consistency. Add the vinegar and reduce the heat and simmer 10 to 15 minutes. You want the strong vinegar taste to have dissipated with only a piquancy remaining, and the chicken to be tender and juicy.

3. Add the remaining garlic and black olive paste, and stir until it forms a smooth thick sauce, then add the mixed olives and remaining herbs.

4. Warm through and keep warm until ready to serve, adding a little water if sauce gets too thick.

Pollo Arrabbiata con Pomodori Secchi

FIERY CHILE-SPIKED CHICKEN WITH SUN-DRIED TOMATOES

Tuscan Archipelago

Serves 4 to 6

"Arrabbiata" means enraged and refers to any sauce that is rich with chile-heat. It is said that these spicy dishes edged their way into Italy via soldiers who had been based in Libya during World War II. These days you'll find *arrabbiata* dishes throughout the country, even in Tuscany where chile peppers are used far more judiciously than in the sunny south, where they might be tossed into the pot with scarcely a care.

Adding sun-dried tomatoes give the dish a more contemporary flavor. A delicious variation is to add trimmed asparagus spears to the simmering sauce, allowing enough time for the vegetable to just cook through. One-third to 1/2 pound is sufficient.

Serve a light and zesty soup to begin with, such as chicken broth with pastina and a little beaten egg, lemon, and Parmesan. Serve a side plate of room-temperature greens in olive oil, crusty bread, and a creamy comforting dessert.

5 cloves garlic, chopped

1/2 teaspoon or more hot pepper flakes

3 tablespoons olive oil

1 chicken, 2 1/2 to 3 pounds, cut into serving pieces

Salt

2 cups diced tomatoes, either fresh and very ripe and flavorful or canned, (include juice)

2 tablespoons tomato paste if needed

1 teaspoon fresh chopped rosemary, or to taste

1 cup chicken broth

10 to 15 marinated sun-dried tomatoes, halved or quartered

1 to 2 tablespoons fresh herbs of choice: basil, parsley, rosemary, marjoram, oregano

1. Heat the garlic and hot pepper flakes for a moment or two in olive oil, then add chicken and brown lightly in this mixture. Do

not let the bits of garlic turn dark brown or the sauce will have a bitter edge. Season with salt.

2. Add tomatoes, tomato paste, rosemary, and chicken broth, then cover and simmer until chicken is tender, about 35 minutes.

3. Season to taste, adding more hot pepper flakes if desired. If sauce is thin, remove chicken to a platter and keep warm, then boil sauce down until thickened and flavorful. Add sun-dried tomatoes to sauce and warm through.

4. Serve chicken pieces blanketed with the sauce, the whole sprinkled with fresh herbs.

Scallopini di Tacchino con Carciofi
TURKEY FILLETS SAUTÉED WITH ARTICHOKE HEARTS AND LEMON
Elba, Tuscan Archipelago

Serves 4

Tender scallops of turkey breast, quickly browned, then tossed with a sauce of sautéed artichoke nuggets and a splash of pan juices, white wine, and lemon—this is a straightforward dish, simple but full of artichoke and turkey flavors. Artichokes perform a curious thing with the tastebuds: The foods that directly follow them are rendered sweeter by the chemical effect.

Begin the meal with either a minestrone, rich with vegetables and beans, or a sunny salad of vegetables and herbs. Alongside the turkey scallops and artichokes, serve a simple risotto, or simply a chunk of bread. Finish the meal with a chunk of a creamy, deliciously stinky cheese such as stracchino, a piece of sweet fruit to eat with a knife and fork, and a glass of Moscato or other sweet dessert wine.

4 medium-sized or 2 large
   artichokes

1 lemon half or 1 tablespoon
   of flour

4 turkey scallops, each about 4
   to 6 ounces, lightly pounded
   to about 1/4 inch thick

Salt and pepper

1/4 cup flour or as needed

2 tablespoons butter, olive oil,
   or a combination of both)

3 to 5 garlic cloves, coarsely
   chopped or thinly sliced

1 cup white wine

1/2 cup chicken broth

Juice of 1/2 to 1 lemon, as desired

1. Prepare artichokes by bending back the outer leaves until they snap off. The edible bit at the end should remain on the heart, which you will cook for the sauce. When all the tough leaves have been snapped off and only the tenderest ones remain, trim them with a knife. First strip the stem of its tough skin, trim the base, and cut off the sharp top of the tender inner leaves. You now have artichoke hearts. Cut each heart into quarters and trim the inner choke away, then place the quarters in a saucepan with water to cover. Mix in the flour or add the lemon half. Bring to a boil, reduce heat, and cook a few minutes until artichoke quarters are al dente. Remove from heat, drain, and cool. This step may be done up to 3 days ahead.

2. Slice artichoke quarters into large bite-sized nuggets and set aside.

3. Season turkey scallops with salt and pepper, then dust generously with flour.

4. Lightly sauté floured turkey scallops in half of the butter and/or olive oil. Cook only a minute or two so as not to overcook them. (You are going to transfer them to the oven to keep warm and they will continue to cook.) Place in an ovenproof pan and then into 325°F oven to keep warm while you make the sauce.

5. Lightly sauté the reserved artichoke nuggets and the garlic in the remaining butter/olive oil. When fragrant and warmed through, pour in white wine and raise heat to very high and let boil down

until reduced to about half. Add chicken broth and cook down until you have a strongly flavored, but still thin, sauce. Add lemon juice, then return turkey scallops to pan and heat with artichoke and sauce for just a moment to warm through and absorb the flavors. Serve immediately.

Petti di Pollo con Salsa Gialla al'Zafferano
BROWNED CHICKEN BREASTS WITH YELLOW SAFFRON SAUCE
SURROUNDED BY SPRING VEGETABLES

Serves 4 to 6

This is an exquisite dish of simple browned chicken breasts surrounded by young spring vegetables: peas, asparagus tips, an artichoke heart or two, a few shreds of red peppers, sauced with a zesty saffron sauce. If the variety of vegetables is not available, just a handful of peas is fine, too.

Each little browned breast is wrapped in a thin slice of prosciutto. The ham flavor permeates the chicken breasts, giving it additional dimension. You could use any similar meat: sliced turkey, ham, bresaola, or simple smoked ham.

The sauce is what makes the dish special: much like a hollandaise in appearance, but not as impossibly rich since butter is used as a flavoring for a flour-thickened sauce, rather than the butter itself used as a thickening, as in the traditional sauce. *Salsa di gialla* means "yellow sauce," from its ingredients: saffron, egg yolks, tangy lemon juice, and an enrichment of butter. This traditional Sicilian sauce is usually served with seafood and fish.

3 egg yolks

1 tablespoon olive oil

Juice of about 3 lemons, added
a little at a time, to taste

1 tablespoon flour

5 to 6 tablespoons butter

Pinch of saffron threads

1/2 to 2/3 cup water

Salt and black pepper, tiny dash
cayenne pepper

Tiny pinch freshly grated
nutmeg

6 small to medium-sized boneless
and skinless chicken breasts,
about 3 to 4 ounces each

Flour for dredging lightly

Butter or olive oil for browning

6 thin slices prosciutto

Selection of vegetables, all
blanched: 1 cup tender small
peas; handful asparagus tips;
2 artichoke hearts, cut into
quarters, 1/2 red pepper, cut
into strips

1. Using a whisk or wooden spoon, combine egg yolks, olive oil, and
about 1 tablespoon lemon juice.

2. Warm over low heat in a double boiler, then stir or whisk in flour,
2 tablespoons of the butter, and the saffron. Cook over very low
heat, stirring, until yolks begin to thicken, then slowly stir in
water, cooking as sauce warms and thickens.

3. Continue cooking and stirring until sauce has thickened and the
floury taste has cooked out, then remove from the heat and add
the remaining butter, stirring it in until it emulsifies into the
sauce. Season with remaining lemon juice to taste, salt, pepper,
cayenne, and nutmeg. (Sauce may be prepared up to two days
ahead and kept covered in the refrigerator. To do so, omit butter
at end, then when warming up, stir in butter as in step 2.)

4. Sprinkle the chicken breasts with salt and pepper, then dredge
lightly with flour.

5. Heat a small amount of oil or butter in pan and lightly brown
chicken breasts on each side for about 1 minute per side. You do
not want to completely cook them through as they will warm in
the oven.

6. Remove chicken from pan and wrap each breast in a slice of
prosciutto.

7. Spoon about ¼ cup of the sauce into the bottom of the pan, then arrange the prosciutto-wrapped chicken on top. Spoon a few tablespoons sauce over the top of each. The dish may be made up to a day ahead to this point and kept covered in the refrigerator.

8. When ready to serve, arrange vegetables around chicken and spoon a bit of the sauce over that as well. Bake in a hot oven, about 400°F, for 6 to 8 minutes or long enough to heat the vegetables through and warm the chicken breasts, finishing their cooking.

Variation: In place of chicken breasts, you could serve a nice fillet of a firm white fish such as cod, wrapped in the prosciutto, then surrounded by a selection of shellfish: a few pink shrimp, a delicate scallop or two, and a handful of lightly steamed asparagus tips.

Pollastrello alla Griglia
GRILLED ROSEMARY-LEMON POUSSINS
Throughout Italy

Serves 4

Throughout both the mainland and the islands this is a traditional way of marinating and grilling chicken and smaller birds—especially on the islands, since poultry there is usually prepared very simply.

Few dishes are as tempting as this one: The fresh rosemary and garlic scent the flesh of the bird while the lemon tenderizes it and the olive oil keeps it all succulent. Flattening the birds the following way allows you to cook them whole on the grill by letting the marinade permeate them more evenly and letting the birds lie flat while they cook.

This is also an excellent marinade for chicken breasts, bones removed but skin left on.

4 game hens or 2 poussins	1½ tablespoons lemon juice
2 to 3 garlic cloves, chopped	3 tablespoons olive oil
2 tablespoons fresh rosemary	Salt and pepper

1. Flatten the birds for marinating and grilling: Cut off backs and save them for soups. Lay birds on a clean work surface, skin side up, and push down hard. This should break the breastbone and flatten the bird. Skewer it flat using bamboo skewers in a crisscross manner.

2. Combine with remaining ingredients and let marinate in the refrigerator overnight, covered, turning once or twice. The birds may be left to marinate for up to two days.

3. Prepare fire under the grill; when hot, remove birds from marinade and dry with absorbent paper. Grill on both sides over high heat to sear the outside, then place on the slower area of the grill and cook about 15 to 20 minutes, turning every so often until chicken juices just run clear. Do not overcook.

Anatra con Olive e Datteri

DUCK WITH OLIVES AND DATES AND MALVASIA OR SHERRY WINE

Ischia

Serves 2 to 3;
double the amount of duck and increase the water
or stock to 1 cup to serve 4 to 6

The combination of rich duck, meaty and crisp-skinned, with tart and tangy green olives and sweet earthy dates is an exciting one.

I often use sherry in place of the Malvasia in the pan sauce since it is often easier to find—and less expensive.

The final thickening of the sauce with a nugget of butter and flour—a *beurre manie*—is distinctly French but thickens the sauce nicely and smoothly.

Since the dish is quite rich and savory, the portions I've given are modest; you might wish to increase them. Serve the duck with tiny boiled new potatoes that are so fresh they still taste of the earth, or sliced steamed sweet potatoes, and spinach that you've seasoned with a bit of garlic or green onions and a dab of crème fraîche if desired. For dessert, offer fresh fruit such as nectarines with the strong flavor of high summer, or a light icy granita.

1 medium to large duck, about 5 pounds, cut into serving pieces, each breast half cut into 2 pieces, (reserve excess fat for another use such as fat for confits)

Dried mixture of Italian herbs: any combination of marjoram, oregano, thyme, rosemary, and sage

Salt and pepper

10 to 20 cloves garlic, half coarsely chopped, half whole

5 to 8 small to medium-sized tomatoes, halved or left whole

5 to 8 shallots, peeled and coarsely chopped

15 to 20 dates, pitted and halved

2 cups Malvasia wine or sherry (choose a medium-dry or lightly sweet one)

1/2 cup water or low salt broth

10 to 15 pimiento-stuffed green olives

2 tablespoons flour

2 tablespoons soft butter

1. Rub duck pieces with herbs, salt, and pepper. Place duck legs and thighs in roasting pan and sprinkle with the chopped garlic, and scatter several whole cloves around the bottom of the pan. Surround the duck with tomato halves and place in 350°F oven to roast for about 35 to 40 minutes. Periodically pour off the fat but save the meaty-tomato-scented juices; do this by pouring them into a cup and letting the juices settle. You can then pour or spoon off the fat. Save the fat for another use (such as cassoulet or cooking deliciously evil potatoes) and save the juices for the sauce.

2. Remove pan from oven and add duck breast, along with remaining garlic and chopped shallots. Return to oven and bake for

another 30 minutes or so, continuing to pour off fat as needed, separating the juices from the fat. When finished cooking, if the skin of the duck breast is not golden-brown and enticingly crisp, raise the heat to 400–450°F for 5 to 10 minutes.

3. Meanwhile, combine dates, wine, and water or broth and bring to a boil. Cook about 10 minutes or until liquid has reduced in volume by about a third. Set aside.

4. When the duck has finished roasting, pour off the juices from the pan and skim all fat from them. Place these juices in a saucepan, along with the reserved juices from pouring off fat as the duck roasted, and half the date-wine-broth mixture (reserve the rest).

5. Boil this mixture of pan juices and date sauce until well-reduced and flavorful; this will depend on how rich the pan juices already are, and this will depend on your duck, how many tomatoes you have used, how flavorful they are, the size of your pan, and so on. Use your sense of taste as a guide.

6. Add the olives and remaining date-wine-broth to the pan with the duck and return to oven while you make the sauce.

7. When sauce is concentrated in flavor and volume, use your fork to mix the flour with the softened butter, then whisk or stir into the hot sauce.

8. Remove duck from oven and set out on serving platter with the juices from the bottom of the pan, mixed with olives and dates. Pour sauce over the duck, olives, and dates, then serve immediately.

Anatra con Melagrana al Marsala

DUCK WITH POMEGRANATE, ORANGE, AND MARSALA WINE
Sicily

Serves 4

Marinating the duck breasts in Marsala overnight gives a sweet herbal flavor to the meat. This traditional dish is often prepared with quail or other game birds in place of duck breasts.

4 duck breasts, skin removed (save for another use; it's far too delicious to throw away)

Marsala wine to cover

Several sprigs of rosemary or other herb such as marjoram

3 to 4 ounces pancetta or bacon, sliced, to wrap the breasts

½ cup chicken or duck broth

Salt and pepper

1 orange, peeled and segmented and cut into small pieces

Seeds of 1 pomegranate

1. Place duck breasts in bowl and pour Marsala over them to cover. Add sprigs of herbs, cover, and refrigerate overnight.
2. Remove duck breasts from marinade and reserve the wine left in the bowl. Discard the herb sprigs.
3. Wrap each duck breast in pancetta or bacon and arrange in a frying or baking pan.
4. Brown either by roasting in a 450°F oven or browning on top of the stove until pancetta or bacon is browned and somewhat crisp, about 15 minutes. The inside of the duck should remain rare.
5. Remove duck from pan and keep warm. Pour off fat from pan, then pour in broth and reserved Marsala, then boil down until it reduces to only a few ounces of flavorful sauce. Season with salt and pepper.
6. Serve the warm duck breasts thinly sliced across the grain, with a bit of the sauce spooned over, garnished with bits of orange and a sprinkling of pomegranate seeds.

Anatra con Mori

DUCK BREASTS WITH BLACKBERRIES

Serves 4

If blackberries are unavailable, blueberries, fresh cranberries, or sliced peaches are excellent as well. Balsamic vinegar adds a sweet-sour edge to the fruit, and cinnamon gives an earthy yet sweet scent.

4 duck breasts, boned but with skin still on	1/4 teaspoon cinnamon (or more, to taste)
Salt and pepper	1/2 cup blackberries
2 tablespoons olive or vegetable oil	Pinch of sugar if needed
3 to 4 tablespoons balsamic vinegar	

1. Sprinkle both sides of duck breasts with salt and pepper, then heat oil in a heavy pan over medium heat. Reduce heat and place duck breasts on their skin side to cook over low heat, until the fat is melted and the skin golden.
2. Add vinegar, cinnamon, and berries, then cover and cook another 8 to 10 minutes.
3. Taste for seasoning, adding salt and pepper, or a dash more vinegar, as needed. If berries are very tart, add a pinch of sugar.
4. Remove duck from sauce and slice against the grain. Keep warm.
5. Spoon off any excess fat from top of sauce, heat through, then serve sliced duck breasts with sauce poured around and over them.

Gallina Faraone al Cioccolato
GUINEA HEN WITH SWEET-SAVORY CHOCOLATE SAUCE AND HAZELNUTS
Sicily

Serves 4

This sweet-sour chocolate-sauced roast guinea hen comes from the interior of Sicily, around Caltagirone. The sweet-sour flavoring is typically Sicilian in its Arab heritage, while the chocolate is reminiscent of Spanish rule.

Rabbit and oxtail are frequently prepared in place of the guinea hen; chicken thighs or dark meat turkey would also be just fine, too. Even Cornish game hens or plain old chicken will be good in this sauce.

The sauce should be rather sweet; indeed, when you taste it you might not be pleased. But combined with the savory roasted bird, the crunchy bite of toasted hazelnuts, and the herbal fresh chervil or fennel leaves, it makes a lyrically balanced and toothsome dish.

1 large or 2 small guinea hens split into 4 serving pieces

Butter for basting

Salt and pepper

1/4 cup hazelnuts

1 onion, chopped

2 celery stalks, chopped

1 parsnip, chopped

2 tablespoons olive oil

2 bay leaves

1 tablespoon golden raisins

Pinch of ground cloves

1/4 teaspoon fennel seeds

1 tablespoon sugar, plus extra if needed

1/2 cup white wine vinegar, plus extra if needed

About 1 1/2 cups chicken broth

2 tablespoons finely chopped or grated unsweetened chocolate

Chervil or fennel leaves, chopped

1. Rub guinea hen (or other choice of bird) with butter; sprinkle with salt and pepper.
2. Place in 350°F oven to roast for about 1 hour or until tender. Do not let overcook and dry out. (I roast them breast side down so that the moisture settles in the breast.)

3. Meanwhile, roast the hazelnuts lightly in an ungreased frying pan on medium heat on top of stove until golden and lightly browned in spots. Remove nuts to a towel and rub to remove their skins; leave whole or lightly chop some of them, as desired. Set aside.

4. Make the sauce: Lightly sauté onion, celery, and parsnip in olive oil until browned and very tender, about 10 to 15 minutes. Add bay leaves, raisins, cloves, and fennel seeds, then continue cooking a few more minutes.

5. Add sugar and wine vinegar, cook down a minute or two, then add 1 cup broth and chocolate. Cover and cook until sauce is thickened, adding extra broth if needed to keep from burning.

6. Season to taste with sugar, vinegar, salt, and pepper.

7. When bird has roasted to tenderness, remove to platter and keep warm. Pour off fat, then deglaze the pan with ½ cup broth, cooking down to concentrate flavors.

8. Add chocolate sauce to this mixture, then serve roasted guinea hen on a bed of savory chocolate sauce, sprinkled with both toasted hazelnuts and chervil or fennel.

Variation: Instead of guinea hens, use 1 rabbit, cut into serving pieces; or 8 to 12 chicken thighs; 1 to 2 turkey thighs; 4 individual poussins or Cornish game hens; or 1 chicken, cut into serving pieces.

Quaglie alla Zucchini
MARINATED AND WINE-STEWED QUAIL WITH ZUCCHINI
Elba

Serves 4

The simple country flavors of this dish are warming and comforting. The French influence reflects Elba's proximity to French Corsica.

Little birds are hunted and eaten so enthusiastically in Italy, both mainland and islands, that many places are completely bereft of birdsong. Instead of tiny quails, you could use game hens or poussins; chicken quarters are very good as well.

Serve in shallow bowls, the simmered birds with unfashionably well-cooked tender zucchini and the broth-sauce to spoon up. Slabs of grilled polenta make a good accompaniment; so does crusty bread.

4 game hens if allowing 1 hen per person, or 2 game hens if allowing ¹/₂ per person; or 8 quails; or 4 chicken quarters

About 3 tablespoons each coarsely chopped fresh herbs: rosemary, marjoram, sage

1¹/₂ cups dry white wine

6 to 8 ounces bacon or pancetta, diced

1¹/₂ cups chicken stock

Black pepper

4 medium-small, young and tender zucchini, cut into chunks

Garnish: About 2 teaspoons fresh marjoram leaves

1. Combine game hens or quails with herbs and white wine, taking care that each has lots of herbs inside. Include the necks, hearts, and livers. Marinate, covered, in the refrigerator at least overnight.
2. Remove from marinade and wipe each bird dry, leaving the herb stuffing inside. Strain marinade and reserve.
3. Lightly brown bacon bits; remove with slotted spoon and lightly brown the birds in the bacon fat.
4. Remove birds from pan, pour off the fat, then return birds to pan.

Add reserved marinade, chicken stock, and black pepper to taste.

5. Bring to a boil, then reduce heat and simmer, covered, until birds are tender, about 25 minutes. Halfway through add the zucchini.

6. When birds are cooked through and zucchini is very tender, taste the broth. If strongly flavored leave it as it is; if it needs to intensify a bit, pour off the liquid and boil down to reduce in volume just enough to have a nice strong flavor.

7. Serve each portion in soup bowls, the poultry and zucchini chunks awash in flavorful broth, the whole bowlful sprinkled with marjoram.

Coniglio all'Ishitana
RABBIT STEWED IN THE MANNER OF ISCHIA

Serves 4

This rabbit stew from the island of Ischia makes a typical countryside meal: The pasta is served as a first course, the rabbit carved up as the second. While you could serve the rabbit together with the sauce and pasta, it seems so crude: much more civilized to eat it in courses, Ischia style, the rabbit perhaps accompanied by a handful of little frisee leaves or arugula.

1 large rabbit, cut into serving pieces

Salt and pepper

Flour for dredging

Olive oil for browning

1 onion, diced

2 stalks celery, diced

2 carrots, diced

5 cloves garlic, chopped

2 to 3 bay leaves

2 cups diced tomatoes

2 tablespoons thinly sliced fresh basil; or 1 teaspoon fresh sage leaves; or 2 teaspoons chopped fresh rosemary

12 ounces pasta of choice (I recommend tender flat fresh fettucine)

1. Sprinkle rabbit with salt and pepper, then dredge rabbit pieces in flour and shake off the excess.
2. Lightly brown rabbit in a little olive oil until golden brown, then set aside. Remove any browned or burnt bits from the pan, then sauté the onion, celery, carrots, and garlic in pan, adding more olive oil if needed. When softened, add bay leaf and tomatoes, return rabbit to the pan, cover and simmer until tender, about 40 minutes.
3. Taste for seasoning, adding salt, pepper, and basil, sage, or rosemary to taste.
4. Cook pasta in rapidly boiling salted water until al dente, then drain and serve the sauce with the pasta as a first course, the tender rabbit as a second course.

Le Carne

MEAT

While fish and seafood is the primary Italian island food, meat is eaten either in small amounts as a flavoring, or in large amounts as a special occasion feast.

On Sardinia meat is an especially important food and reflects the traditions of the shepherds of the Barbagias, the heart of the island. The food of this area, *la cucina Barbagina,* is based on large cuts of meat—usually lamb, goat, or piglet—slowly roasted over an open fire or skewered onto spits. Restaurants specialize in this rustic cookery, offering a selection of antipasti and pastas to begin with, then plates of this simple savory meat.

Game is doted on—wild boar salami is one of Sardinia's specialties. If meat is not roasted over an open fire, it is probably stewed slowly with wine, herbs, and aromatic vegetables. Another Sardinian specialty consists of a large roasting pit in which meat is buried with hot stones, then slowly roasted underground.

While the dishes of the Mediterranean's largest island, Sicily, tend to be vegetable- and fish-based, small amounts of meat are eaten in everyday dishes such as pastas and soups. Sicilian sausages are renowned for their zesty flavor, and are grilled over a fire, simmered in soups or stews, or used as a topping for a platter of polenta.

Large meaty specialties are reserved for Sundays and holidays, and they are robust creations indeed. On any Sunday, walk into nearly any Sicilian kitchen and you might find a dish like this: a roasting pan filled with meats and fowl, a savory rolled roast of beef and perhaps another of lamb or pork, a handful of meatballs and sausages, or a chicken or two. These bake slowly in a piquant mixture of tomatoes, onions, garlic, and wine, and by the time the meat is tender you have a rich flavorful sauce for pasta, as well. Leftovers from this feast will be made into dishes and pastas for the week that follows.

The other islands generally do not have their own distinctive style of meat preparation and tend to follow the regional cooking styles of the mainland. Meat dishes on Elba reflect French traditions; while on Capri, Ischia, and Procida the lusty garlic-tomato scent of Napoli pervades.

Despite the array of different meats and cooking styles, one unifying fact comes to light. Unlike Americans, the Italians, especially peasants, are not squeamish about animal parts. All sorts of innards and offal are devoured with great relish. In one little book I picked up I found no less than three recipes that began with "take 1 liter of pig's blood" and five recipes for lamb's feet. Horse is also quite popular, whether grilled in steaks, simmered *alla pizzaiola* with tomatoes and garlic, or stewed with wine.

It's important to have an open mind when it comes to eating unusual cuts of meat. After all, if one kills the animal, how can one justify wasting the parts we are not used to? My husband, for instance, became quite fond of pig's testicles, fed to him by the farmer with whom he was helping with his accounts. And I think that grilled pig's ears deserve a second chance. The horse, however, got the thumbs down from both of us and you will not find any recipes for it here.

Agnello con Patate
LAMB AND POTATOES IN SAFFRON-SCENTED EGG-LEMON SAUCE
Sardinia

Serves 4 to 6

Throughout Sardinia you'll find dishes such as this one, rustic and robust preparations of meat and vegetables, simple and straightforward, yet with the haunting flavor of saffron, the piquancy of lemon, the richness of a little egg thickening. Though untraditional, I serve the dish garnished with a generous amount of black olives. They add a rambunctious accent to the tangy sauce, hearty meat, and flavorful potatoes.

As with all peasant dishes, amounts are to taste: More potatoes and less meat are quite fine. In artichoke season, prepare the dish with artichokes instead of potatoes (see variation), or use both vegetables combined.

2 pounds lamb boneless shoulder (if using meat with bones, allow extra weight)

2 to 3 tablespoons olive oil, or as needed

Salt and pepper

5 to 6 cloves garlic, coarsely chopped

4 medium-sized potatoes of choice, either baking or a more waxy variety, unpeeled

1 1/2 cups dry white wine

1/8 teaspoon saffron threads

1/4 cup warm water

1 egg, lightly beaten

1 tablespoon lemon juice

1. Lightly brown lamb in a heavy pan in 2 to 3 teaspoons of the olive oil. When lightly browned, place in a shallow casserole or baking dish, preferably making a single layer but with some overlap. Sprinkle with salt and pepper and add about two-thirds of the garlic, reserving the remaining third to add to the cooking potatoes.

2. Cut potatoes lengthwise into quarters, then brown in same pan meat was cooked in, adding the rest of the oil and seasoning the potatoes with salt and pepper. Toss the reserved garlic in with the potatoes as they sauté. When potatoes are lightly gilded but not cooked, remove from pan with a slotted spoon and add to the meat, arranging in the spaces between the lamb pieces.

3. Pour off the fat from the pan and add the wine. Bring to a boil and cook a minute or two to dissolve all of the browned bits from the meat and potatoes, then pour this over the meat and potatoes in the casserole.

4. Bake in a 350°F oven for 45 minutes, or until both meat and potatoes are very tender and browned.

5. Dissolve saffron threads in 1/4 cup warm water, then pour over the

meat and potatoes. Return to oven for another 15 minutes, long enough for the flavor to permeate the dish.

6. Combine beaten egg and lemon juice.
7. Remove meat and potatoes from oven and pour off juices to degrease (I find that carefully spooning the fat off gives a good result). Slowly add hot meat juices to the egg and lemon mixture, then pour over the hot meat and potatoes. It will make a creamy sauce; if it slightly curdles, it will still taste fine. Serve immediately.

Variation: Agnello con Carciofi
LAMB WITH ARTICHOKES

In place of the potatoes, add quartered artichoke hearts, preferably fresh ones. A combination of artichokes and potatoes is particularly nice.

Agnello alla Griglia con Ammyghiu
GRILLED LAMB OR KID WITH SICILIAN AMMYGHIU SAUCE
Sicily

Serves 6 to 8

In a country farm, cafe, or local tavern, Sunday lunch is the chance to get away from the pressures of the work week, to bask in the shade of an almond tree, to enjoy the delicious simplicity of life.

At its best, even in a country cafe, Sunday lunch is an outdoor feast: gaily colored tablecloth spread over a long table set in the garden, baskets of flowers. Bowls of olives, green onions, ripe tomatoes, and fresh sheep cheese are scattered over the tabletop, and there is crusty bread to nibble on while the meats roast.

Kid or lamb roasts on the spit, smelling irresistible. Sausages, seasoned with rosemary and other mountain herbs, brown on the grill, sputtering noisily as their juices drip onto the fire, and potatoes roast in a pan with tomatoes and onions, absorbing the smoky flavors of the fire as they cook.

The sauce that accompanies it all is the Sicilian specialty called ammyghiu, a refreshing uncooked sauce of fresh ripe tomatoes, oregano, and olive oil, to accompany the hearty roasted food.

2 to 3 pounds lamb or kid, cut
    into serving-size pieces
    or chops

Olive oil, lemon juice, salt,
    pepper, and dried or fresh
    oregano to taste

4 to 8 Italian fennel sausages,
    $1/2$ to 1 pound in total

Ammyghiu sauce (page 227)

1 to 2 teaspoons fresh marjoram
    leaves or flat-leaf Italian
    parsley, chopped

1. Combine lamb or kid with olive oil, lemon juice, salt, pepper, and oregano. Leave to marinate for at least 2 hours at room temperature or refrigerate overnight or up to 2 days, covered. Turn several times to coat well.
2. Remove from marinade and wipe the meatdry. Reserve the marinade for basting.
3. Grill meat and sausages to desired doneness, basting occasionally. Serve accompanied by the garlic-tomato sauce Ammyghiu and the fresh herbs.

Maiale Arrosto
PORK ROASTED WITH FENNEL SEEDS, ONION AND GARLIC, PANCETTA, AND TOMATOES
Ischia

Serves 4

This traditional dish of pork, roasted in a casserole with lots of savory ingredients, is delicious and simple to prepare. Though I ate it in Ischia, local variations are eaten throughout Italy and its islands.

It should be extremely savory, the bits of pork fat roasting to a crisp and delicious jacket covering tender meat. Ironically, these days pork is so lean it needs a little marinating, then a bit of olive oil and pancetta added to the cooking mixture to keep it succulent.

This is an excellent dish to make the day before; remove all fat that congeals as it cools, then gently reheat and serve.

2 to 3 pounds lean pork roast such as leg, cut into several large chunks

Juice of 2 lemons, or more

1 to 2 teaspoons fennel seeds

5 cloves garlic, chopped, and 2 heads garlic, broken up into cloves

2 tablespoons olive oil, or as needed

3 onions, cut into wedges

4 to 5 bay leaves

Salt and pepper

3 ounces pancetta or bacon, diced or coarsely cut up

1 to 1½ cups canned tomatoes, coarsely diced and lightly drained (reserve liquid for another use)

1. Combine pork with lemon juice, fennel seeds, chopped garlic and whole garlic cloves, olive oil, onions, and bay leaves. Season with salt and pepper, place in shallow ceramic casserole, and leave to marinate for at least an hour.

2. Add pancetta or bacon and place in 350°F oven. Roast for about 2 hours, or until meat is very tender and browned, turning occasionally. Add tomatoes, reduce heat, and return to oven for another 30 minutes or so.

Arrosto di Vitello o Porchetta
VEAL OR PORK COATED WITH SAGE PASTE, THEN ROASTED WITH BACON AND BAY LEAVES
Sardinia

Serves 4

This rustic roast of veal or pork has the mountain flavors of Sardinia, though in Sardinia the flavoring would be myrtle rather than the more readily available bay leaves. And the meat, if you are very lucky, might be one of the wild boars that roam the fierce mountain interior. Once, at sunset, as we sat on our terrace we saw a whole group of wild boars rustle through our backyard. There were huge adult pigs and tiny babies, and we were transfixed by their wild beauty and strength.

Begin the meal with a selection of antipasti: white beans and shrimp or octopus in olive oil and lemon; grilled porcini mushrooms; crostini of tomatoes, cheese, olive, and basil. Follow with a plate of simple pasta, then serve small portions of this rustic roasted meat, surrounded by a handful of frisee greens or—very Sardinian—wedges of fresh raw fennel, all accompanied by slices of rosemary bread. Follow with sweet fruit dripping with freshness. Digest it all with glasses of fiery strong grappa.

1/2 cup fresh sage leaves

1/4 cup parsley

5 cloves garlic, chopped

1/2 cup olive oil

Salt and pepper

2 pounds lean pork or veal stewing meat, cut into bite-sized pieces

4 ounces diced pancetta or bacon

3 to 4 bay leaves

1/2 cup white wine

1. Combine sage, parsley, garlic, and olive oil and whirl in blender or processor until smooth.
2. Sprinkle salt and pepper over meat, then combine with sage paste and leave to marinate for at least 2 hours.
3. Place meat in roasting pan along with pancetta or bacon, bay leaves, and white wine, then roast in a 350°F oven until meat is very tender and browned, about 2 hours. If the roast seems to be getting dry, reduce heat; if pan itself is too dry, add another 1/2 cup or so wine. If meat does not brown by the time it is tender, raise heat for the last 10 minutes or so of cooking time.

Variation: Porchetta di Tacchino
Substitute dark meat turkey chunks for the veal or pork in the above recipe. Reduce roasting time, checking the turkey after 1 hour, so that meat does not dry out.

Salsicche e Fagioli
SAUSAGES WITH TANGY PAN JUICES AND GARLIC-BASIL CANNELLINI BEANS
Elba

Serves 4

Meaty, spicy sausages resting next to a puddle of creamy, garlic-and-basil-scented white beans make this simple though extraordinary summer supper. It's the sort of dinner you might want to eat from a metal plate with an oversized spoon; in Elba we ate a similar dish in a wooden trough like contraption.

Choose any zesty fresh sausage: Italian for authenticity, or a selection of contemporary American ones such as sun-dried tomato and basil sausage, New Mexico sausage, or poultry sausage such as smoked duck or chicken, for a more complex dish.

4 to 8 spicy Italian or contemporary American sausages

2 tablespoons balsamic vinegar

3 to 4 cups cooked cannellini beans, either canned or freshly cooked

Salt and pepper

3 tablespoons butter

3 to 5 cloves garlic, chopped

About ¹/₂ cup chopped sweet basil leaves or pesto

Grated pecorino Romano, Parmesan, asiago, or dry Jack cheese

1. Brown sausages in a sauté pan until almost cooked through (time will depend on the type of sausage you choose). Pour off fat and sprinkle in balsamic vinegar. Stir to dissolve the brown savory bits in the bottom of the pan, then remove from heat.
2. Meanwhile, heat beans in a saucepan until bubbles form around the edge, then stir and slightly mash as they cook until the liquid evaporates and beans are both chunky and creamy.
3. Add remaining ingredients, then serve immediately, sprinkled with cheese and accompanied by the hot sausages and pan juices.

Gli Arrosti Misti

A BIG PAN OF MEAT AND POULTRY ROASTED TOGETHER
WITH RED WINE PAN SAUCE
Tuscan Archipelago

Serves 4 to 6 with leftovers

A platter of mixed meats, all roasted to a richly browned color and nearly unbearably good fragrance, makes a wonderful centerpiece for a large informal gathering.

I was served a similar dish one Sunday lunch in a vineyard in autumn; it was time for the *vendemmia,* the grape picking or "crush," and the air was just beginning to chill with the approach of winter. A long wooden table was set in the orchard alongside the vines, and after a day of picking that began at sunrise, we were ready for a hearty meal by afternoon.

Signora brought out tureens filled with an old-fashioned, very homey minestrone of tender creamy beans and chick-peas, chunks of long-cooked vegetable, and bits of pasta. Some workers splashed a bit of red wine into their soup. Then came great pans filled with assorted meats and chicken, their juices mingling together with red wine to make a light but strongly flavored sauce. There was a huge salad, and plates of lightly cooked greens, with crusty bread and endless bottles of red wine. Afterward we nibbled on rounds of rich cheese and sweet autumn pears.

Roasting a variety of meats and poultry together is a traditional way to feed a crowd. It gives delicious variety; each person can choose the cuts he or she would like, and the combination of meaty juices makes a complex sauce.

The important thing to remember with such a rich dish is to pour off as much fat as possible so that you are left with juices of straight, strong flavor, perfect for boiling down with a bit of wine and/or juice to make a thin, intense sauce that enhances the meats rather than disguising them.

1 tablespoon sugar

3 tablespoons strong Dijon-type mustard

10 cloves garlic, chopped, and 7 heads garlic, broken into cloves but left unpeeled

3 tablespoons chopped rosemary

Salt and black pepper

1 chuck roast, 3 pounds

1 roast of lamb, beef, veal,
or pork loin, 3 pounds

1½ lemons, quartered

8 fresh rosemary sprigs, each
about 4 inches long

2 cups broth of choice

1 whole chicken, 2½ to 3 pounds

1 to 2 cups dry red wine

Chopped parsley

1. Blend together the sugar, mustard, chopped garlic, chopped rose-mary, salt, and pepper. Rub the roasts and chicken with this mix-ture, then place the roasts in a roasting pan and scatter with 5 heads of the unpeeled garlic cloves. Set chicken aside and stuff with another head of garlic cloves, 4 lemon quarters, and 4 sprigs of rosemary. Set aside, reserving garlic cloves for the chicken and for additional seasoning.

2. Add 2 lemon quarters and 4 rosemary sprigs to the pan with the roasts, then pour broth around the meats. Roast in a 350°F oven for about 2 hours, or until meats are nearing tenderness. Remove from oven and spoon off excess fat.

3. Place chicken in pan with the meats.

4. Return pan to oven and roast for 1 hour or until chicken legs wig-gle with ease. Add more broth if needed to keep about ½ inch depth in the bottom of the pan.

5. Remove meats, chicken, and garlic cloves from pan and place on a hot platter in a very low oven while you make the sauce. Discard the bits of rosemary and lemon.

6. Spoon fat off from the pan juices, then add wine and cook over high heat, stirring and scraping any brown bits from the bottom of the pan. Add the juices from the platter of meats—the chicken will produce lovely lemony juices. Cook down until intensified; there won't be much but it will be delicious. Set aside.

7. Carve meats and chicken, arrange on platter with the cooked garlic cloves, then pour sauce over it all. Sprinkle with parsley.

Le Verdure e Contorni

VEGETABLES AND VEGETABLE SIDE DISHES

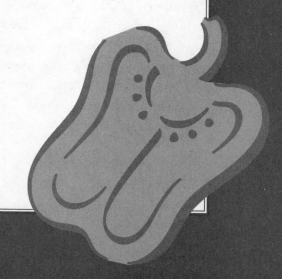

Verdure literally mean greens, and *contorni* refers to the wealth of small vegetable dishes that accompany the main course. A vegetable dish might be served as a *contorno* or it might be served as an antipasto, depending on the menu.

Little garden plots are often scattered throughout the Italian country-side, often in small strips of land that would have otherwise grown weeds or housed roadside litter. Carefully tended vegetables and herbs are seen alongside railroad tracks, behind industrial complexes, beside a country road. Weeds are also valued as many are edible and make their way onto tables and into stewpots.

Italian vegetables are often prepared very simply. Yet they seem to burst with flavor, no doubt because of the extraordinary care with which they are grown and the fact that they needn't travel huge distances to reach the eater. On the islands variety is often lacking; there may be only a few vegetables in season at any one time, but what is available is full of flavor.

Supermarket vegetables may not taste as good as the hand-tended vegetables that grace Italian tables, but for such flavor you must either grow your own garden, or support the dedicated work of small independent farmers by shopping at farmers' markets.

As vegetables are featured abundantly in soups, pasta, risotti, salads, and antipasti, be sure to peruse those chapters, too. Here, then, are the little plates of zesty vegetables that make eating in Italy a sensuous treat.

Pomodori Arrosti
ROASTED TOMATOES
Sardinia

Makes about 2 cups

Roasted tomatoes are somewhat halfway between the flavor and texture of fresh and sun-dried tomatoes: Their flavors have intensified but their flesh is moist and succulent rather than light and airy as fresh ones are, or chewy and dense as sun-dried are. Smaller tomatoes yield the best results.

While traditionally they are roasted and served as a vegetable, I find that the intensely tomato taste of roasted tomatoes tossed with a little garlic and olive oil makes a superb salsa for nearly anything: couscous, pasta, fish, thin green beans, even humble chunks of bread.

Roasted tomatoes also make an excellent base for soup: Combine with an equal amount of richly flavored broth of choice, then serve with tiny pasta and a handful of diced simmered vegetables, adding a drizzle of olive oil and hint of garlic and herbs at the end.

Enough ripe though firm smallish tomatoes to fill the bottom of the pan in a single layer

Several tablespoons olive oil

1. Fill the bottom of a heavy pan or casserole with the tomatoes and drizzle with the olive oil.
2. Broil under high heat until the tomatoes char and their skins begin to blacken and split.
3. Remove from broiler, then place in oven and roast slowly in a 375–400°F oven for 45 minutes or until the tomatoes have shrunk somewhat, collected quite a bit of liquid at the bottom of the pan (this will appear thin but will thicken as it cools) and smell terrific.
4. Let cool in pan, then remove skin from tomatoes and squeeze skin to get all of the flavor (alternatively, if making into a sauce, you can puree the skins along with the tomato flesh). Dice the tomatoes and combine with their juices and the juice squeezed from the skins.

Several Simple Dishes Using Roasted Tomatoes:

Gingered Couscous with Roasted Tomatoes and Green Beans
Prepare couscous with broth and season with a dash of ginger, then toss with diced roasted tomatoes and green beans, a nugget of butter melting into it all.

Green Bean and Roasted Tomato Broth
Cook a handful of tender green beans, cut into bite-sized pieces, in chicken or vegetable broth, then add a clove of chopped garlic, 4 to 5 diced roasted tomatoes, a pinch of fresh thyme or marjoram, and a drizzle of olive oil. Serve over a slice of dry country bread with mild cheese melted over it.

Cod with Roasted Tomatoes
Arrange plump slices of a mild white fish such as cod in an earthenware baking dish, then top each one with the diced flesh of 1 or 2 roasted tomatoes. Sprinkle with chopped garlic, parsley, fresh oregano, olive oil, salt, and pepper. Cover and bake at 375°F until fish is just tender, about 15 minutes. Serve along with its juices and a squeeze of lemon.

Two pasta dishes made with roasted tomatoes: with lamb sausage, spinach, and goat cheese (page 73), or mixed ravioli and rosemary-garlic-scented zucchini with roasted tomato sauce.

Funghi Arrosti
BAKED MUSHROOMS WITH GARLIC BUTTER AND NUTS
Sicily

Serves 4

The larger the mushrooms, the more pronounced the foresty mushroom flavor. This simply prepared yet savory dish is Sicilian, traditionally made with pine nuts, but I make it with hazelnut halves or quarters or slivered almonds when I have no pine nuts in the pantry or simply desire variety. The mushrooms bathe in the garlicky butter mixture, growing tender and succulent while the nuts toast to crisp crunchiness on top. It makes a delightful contrast in textures as well as tastes.

1 pound mushrooms, with caps as large as you can find

5 cloves garlic, finely chopped, or to taste

2 tablespoons butter or to taste

1 tablespoon finely chopped parsley

Salt and pepper

3 to 4 tablespoons nuts

1. Remove stems from mushrooms and save for another use. Arrange mushrooms in a single layer in a shallow baking pan.
2. Sprinkle tops with garlic, butter, parsley, salt and pepper, and nuts.
3. Bake in a medium to hot oven, about 375–400°F, until mushrooms sizzle and grow tender and nuts toast to a golden hue (take care that the nut topping does not burn—if it shows signs of cooking faster than the mushrooms, move the baking dish to a cooler part of the oven or reduce the temperature).
4. Serve hot, either as a first course, with crusty bread, or as a vegetable accompaniment.

Le Verdure con Aglio
LEAFY GREENS WITH GARLIC, BALSAMIC VINEGAR, AND OLIVE OIL
Throughout Italy

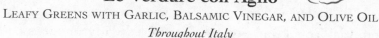

Serves 4

This treatment of greens is marvelous with any greens: beet tops, spinach, broccoli di rabe, older arugula, even tough cabbage leaves. I like it best with red chard. On the islands wild greens are often foraged for, then served in this classic way.

Try the garlic-sautéed greens as a bed for beets or toss with diced pan-browned pancetta as a bed for potato gnocchi or wine-stewed beef.

1 large bunch greens such as red chard or beet greens, cleaned, trimmed, and cut into bite-sized pieces

1 garlic clove, chopped

1 to 3 teaspoons olive oil

1 teaspoon balsmic vinegar

Salt and pepper

Combine greens, garlic, olive oil, and vinegar in sauté pan over moderately low heat. Cover and heat, stirring from time to time, until chard is just cooked through. Season with salt and pepper and adjust oil and vinegar as desired.

Le Patate
Potatoes

PASTA may be eaten at least once a day, but throughout many of the islands, especially Sicily, so, too, are potatoes. Potatoes might appear as a countryside supper, fried in olive oil and served with eggs or roasted fish. They might be boiled and mashed, then used to encase rich saucy mixtures as a savory pie. You'll find potatoes simmered with tomatoes and peppers in the Tuscan Archipelago, roasted with meats in Sardinia, and sautéed sweet-and-sour style in Sicily.

Also in Sicily, you'll find potatoes pureed with seasonings and cheese, coated with crumbs, then quickly fried to a golden brown. They are mischievously called *cazzilli*, the vulgar street name of the male anatomy, in honor of their thick cigarlike shape.

Cazzilli
POTATO FRITTERS
Sicily

Serves 4 to 6

Oh, Cazzilli, so naughtily named, so luscious to eat.

These cigar-shaped potato croquettes are classic Sicilian street treats, eaten from stalls that specialize in fried dishes, but they might be served for any occasion, such as an appetizer for a big party.

Their crisp crumbled exterior hides a creamy cheese-enriched mashed potato filling, studded with bits of ham and flecked with bits of fresh parsley. Some say they are addictive and I am inclined to agree.

1½ pounds baking potatoes, unpeeled

3 tablespoons softened unsalted butter

3 egg yolks

1½ ounces boiled ham, chopped

2 tablespoons chopped parsley

1½ ounces provolone, caciocavallo, or similar cheese such as Fontina, cubed

⅓ cup grated Romano or Parmesan cheese

Salt

2 to 4 tablespoons all-purpose flour

3 egg whites, beaten until fluffy

2 to 3 cups bread crumbs, either fresh or dried

Oil for deep-frying

1. Boil the potatoes until tender, about 40 minutes depending on their size. Drain and let cool slightly, then peel and mash while still hot. A ricer or sieve gives best results.
2. Stir butter and egg yolks into the hot potatoes along with ham, parsley, cubed cheese, and grated cheese. Season with salt to taste.
3. Shape mixture into 12 cylinder shapes, then coat each with flour.
4. Dip each cylinder first in beaten egg white, then in bread crumbs.
5. Heat oil until a piece of bread dropped into it sizzles instantly and turns golden brown. Fry the fritters, taking care not to crowd the

pan, until they are golden and crisp. Drain on absorbent paper and serve right away, hot and enticing.

Ciabotta
CASSEROLE OF POTATOES, CELERY, ZUCCHINI, EGGPLANT, AND TOMATOES
Portoferraio, Elba

Serves 4 to 6

This ratatouillelike vegetable casserole clearly reflects its French influences, and like the French dish, it makes an excellent side dish or main vegetable course, as good cold as it is hot. The first time I tasted it was at the Jewish celebration of Passover, when each guest brought a vegetable dish to the feast; our Elban guest brought this.

If served hot, offer a sprinkling of Parmesan; cold, it makes a grand lunch accompanied with spindly frisee leaves, olives, a plate of salami or cheeses, fresh fruit, and crusty bread.

1 red bell pepper

1 green bell pepper

3 to 4 tablespoons olive oil

1 pound baking potatoes, peeled and cut into bite-sized chunks

1 medium eggplant, diced

1 medium zucchini, cut into bite-sized chunks

2 medium onions, thinly sliced lengthwise

5 cloves garlic, coarsely chopped

4 stalks celery, cut into bite-sized chunks

1½ cups diced tomatoes

Salt and pepper

About ½ teaspoon sugar

2 tablespoons thinly sliced fresh basil leaves

1 tablespoon chopped parsley

1. Roast peppers until evenly charred, then let sit tightly covered to loosen skin. Peel when cool. (For full directions see page 211.) Slice peppers and set aside.

2. In a tablespoon or two of olive oil, lightly brown potato chunks and cook until half-tender. Place in a ceramic casserole and sprinkle with salt. Bake in 350°F oven while you prepare the rest of the vegetables.

3. In another tablespoon or so of oil, lightly brown the eggplant, then add this to the potatoes. Repeat with the zucchini, onions, garlic, and celery together. Add them to the eggplant and potatoes, along with the reserved roasted peppers, then add tomatoes, salt, pepper, and sugar.

4. Cover tightly, lower oven temperature to 325°F, and bake until vegetables are very tender and flavors have melded, about an hour. There will be a small amount of flavorful sauce.

5. Taste for seasoning, then sprinkle with basil and parsley. Serve either hot or cool.

Patate al Forno con Rosmarino
ROSEMARY-ROASTED POTATOES
Sardinia

Serves 4 to 6

One afternoon I picked an armful of rosemary on a hillside walk, along with a mass of wildflowers. Back at the house, our friend Franco whisked both the flowers and herbs into a plain water glass, then plunked it onto the table; their pure, natural beauty caused us to draw our breath in with delight.

In Franco's hand was a tuft of reserved rosemary: "For the potatoes!" he exclaimed happily, turning toward the kitchen and heading straight for the potato-filled oven.

The wildflowers and rosemary looked beautiful on the table, and those potatoes . . . those potatoes . . .

| 4 to 6 large baking potatoes | 4 to 6 tablespoons olive oil |
| Salt and freshly ground black pepper | 3 tablespoons chopped fresh rosemary, or more, to taste |

1. Peel potatoes or not, as desired. Cut into chunks. Boil until almost tender and drain.
2. Sprinkle generously with salt and pepper, then toss with olive oil. Arrange in a roasting pan so that they don't touch each other.
3. Roast in 350°F oven for about 45 minutes or until potatoes are golden brown. Toss with rosemary and return to oven for another few minutes, then remove from pan with slotted spoon, drain briefly on paper towels if they need it, and serve sizzling hot.

Patate con Basilica
BASIL-MASHED POTATOES

Serves 4

One midwinter, after the excitement of the holiday season and the annual onset of London's depressing season, gray wet weather with little to look forward to, I got a phone call from a friend in Spain. "Want to meet in Sardinia? Maria's boyfriend's family has a villa there and have offered it to us—can you be there by next week?"

The villa came complete with a cook, who, while not too pleased to have her solitude interrupted by a houseful of guests, fed us beautifully. I don't know where this dish originated; it's not particularly Sardinian, but I have eaten similar basil-scented potato dishes in Liguria.

Fragrant and green, it is very comforting for a late-night supper or topped with sausages, yet it is elegant enough to serve nestled next to pink roast lamb for a fashionable dinner party. It's good, too, as an accompaniment for *bollito misto,* and we also ate it as leftovers in the kitchen at midnight, dipping our spoons directly into the pot.

6 large baking potatoes, peeled and cut into quarters or bite-sized chunks

4 to 6 cloves garlic

3 tablespoons butter, or to taste

2 tablespoons cream, milk, or sour cream (light sour cream is just fine), or as needed

3 to 5 tablespoons pesto, or more; or about $\frac{1}{2}$ cup finely chopped fresh basil or to taste

Salt and pepper

1. Place potatoes in saucepan and cover with water. Add 3 to 4 cloves of garlic, coarsely chopped. Bring to a boil and cook until potatoes are tender, about 20 minutes. Drain (reserve garlic-scented potato broth for soup or another purpose).
2. Mash potatoes and season with remaining garlic, finely chopped, the butter, and a small amount of cream, milk, or sour cream.
3. Add pesto or chopped basil and mix well. Season with salt and pepper, and add more milk or cream to get desired consistency. Serve immediately.

Polpette di Melanzane con Ammyghiu
EGGPLANT CROQUETTES WITH UNCOOKED TOMATO SALSA
Sicily

Serves 6

Crunchily brown and crisp on the outside, inside they are soft and creamy. How the Sicilians love to fry vegetables in their beloved olive oil! These croquettes are among the wide variety of such fried delicacies that you might find in any of the *friggitorie* or *panellari* (sandwich shops).

A practical note: Take care to adjust the quantity of crumbs to match the moistness of your vegetable.

The sauce, ammyghiu, is the traditional fresh Sicilian sauce of uncooked tomatoes and basil. It is eaten with nearly everything: grilled fish, roasted meats, poached eggs, or plain bread.

1 large eggplant or 2 small to medium-sized ones (about 2 cups once cooked and pureed)

2 eggs, lightly beaten

6 cloves garlic, chopped

6 ounces ricotta cheese

2 to 2½ cups dry bread crumbs

¾ cup freshly grated Parmesan or pecorino cheese

Salt, pepper, and nutmeg to taste

About 1 to 1½ cups flour for dusting

Olive oil for frying at a depth of 2 to 3 inches

¼ cup coarsely chopped parsley

½ cup diced drained tomatoes (canned are fine)

1. Cut eggplant into chunks and steam or boil until very tender. Alternatively, eggplant may be pierced in several places, slivers of garlic inserted, then the whole thing baked in a 350°F oven until the eggplant deflates and is very tender.

2. Whichever method you use, once eggplant is tender, peel if skin is tough, then puree. Place eggplant puree in a fine-meshed strainer and leave for at least 10 minutes to drain of excess moisture.

3. Remove from strainer and mix with 1 of the eggs, half of the garlic, the ricotta cheese, 1 cup dry bread crumbs, Parmesan or pecorino cheese, salt, pepper, and nutmeg. Chill to firm.

4. Take walnut-sized spoonfuls of the mixture and roll first in flour, then in beaten egg, then in remaining 1 to 1½ cups crumbs.

5. Heat oil in pan until a cube of bread sizzles and browns when dropped in. Fry the *polpettes* without crowding the pan until each is crisply browned. Remove from oil and drain on absorbent paper. The croquettes may be either deep-fried or shallow-fried, as long as there is enough oil to keep the heat and let the croquettes brown quickly.

6. Prepare sauce by mixing parsley, remaining garlic, and chopped tomatoes. Serve the crisp *polpette* with a spoonful of the sauce on the side.

Carciofi Fritti con Formaggio di Caprina

ARTICHOKE HEARTS STUFFED WITH GOAT CHEESE,
COVERED WITH CRUMBS AND FRIED

Sicily

Serves 4

The vendor at the *friggitore* lowered his large hairy arm and scooped a net filled with crisp golden drumsticklike creations out of the vat of boiling oil. They were in fact not drumsticks, but just-tender artichokes with their stems, crisply crumbed and filled with a nugget of tangy fresh goat cheese. These make a memorable first course or side dish. You must use fresh artichokes for this dish—frozen or canned taste completely insipid.

Be sure to use enough oil in the pan; for best results they should deep-fry at a hot temperature until golden brown and crisply coated. If your oil is shallower than about 2 to 3 inches, let the filled artichokes first cook on one side until their coating is crisp and firm enough to hold them together, then carefully turn.

8 small to medium-sized artichokes

Dash of lemon juice or vinegar

Salt and pepper

3 cloves garlic, finely chopped

4 to 5 ounces delicate goat cheese such as cheverie or Montrachet

1 egg, lightly beaten

About 1 cup bread crumbs

Enough oil for a depth of about 3 to 4 inches (I prefer a combination of vegetable and olive)

Garnish: About 1 tablespoon thinly sliced fresh mint leaves

1. Pull the sharp tough leaves off the raw artichokes, bending them backward to snap off. Trim the edges of the base and stem. Cut each heart in half, then hollow out the choke and fuzzy part.
2. Place the artichoke halves in a pan of water to which you have added a dash of lemon juice or vinegar.
3. When all artichokes have been prepared, bring water to a boil and cook for about 5 to 8 minutes or long enough for the artichokes to

be almost tender but still somewhat crunchy. Remove from heat, rinse with cold water, and set aside to dry.

4. Sprinkle each artichoke with salt, pepper, and garlic. Fill each hollow with a generous spoonful of goat cheese, then stick together two artichoke halves.

5. Coat each reassembled artichoke with egg, then roll in the bread crumbs, coating well. Place on a plate to dry and solidify the crumbs, about 30 to 45 minutes.

6. Heat oil until hot enough for a bread cube tossed in to sizzle and turn golden.

7. Carefully add each filled and crumb-coated artichoke heart to the hot oil and fry until golden brown. If you need to turn them, wait until they are browned on one side first, then carefully turn. At this stage croquettes are very delicate and can fall apart, letting the goat cheese leak out.

8. When artichokes are golden brown, remove from oil and dry on absorbent paper.

9. Serve warm or at room temperature, rather than hot, garnished with a sprinkling of fresh mint.

Zucca Rossa alla Menta
SAUTÉED WINTER SQUASH WITH MINT
Sicily

Serves 4

Sautéed winter squash is sauced with vinegar and seasoned with fresh mint, making a tangy, almost pickled vegetable dish. Dressing cooked vegetables with vinegar is favored throughout parts of Italy and many of the islands.

1 pound winter squash, peeled and sliced ¼ inch thick

3 to 5 tablespoons olive oil or as desired

3 to 5 cloves garlic, chopped

Salt and black and cayenne pepper

½ to 1 teaspoon paprika, or more to taste

3 tablespoons thinly sliced fresh mint leaves

3 tablespoons red wine vinegar, or more to taste

1. Sauté sliced squash in the olive oil, a single layer at a time, letting it cook quickly to a golden brown color, sprinkling it with garlic, salt, black and cayenne pepper, and paprika as you cook it. When each batch is done, layer squash in a shallow casserole or flat bowl, sprinkling with the mint as you layer it.

2. When squash are all cooked, pour the vinegar into the sauté pan and bring to a boil, cooking down a few minutes, then pour over the cooked squash.

3. Serve at once, or let cool and enjoy at room temperature.

Variation: Pure di Zucca Rossa alla Menta

TANGY PUREED WINTER SQUASH WITH MINT

Bake or steam the squash instead of frying them; cooking should take about 35 minutes in a 425°F oven. When tender, scrape the flesh from the peel and mash with a fork.

Sauté garlic in olive oil until fragrant, then add the vinegar, mint, and spices, and add a tablespoon or two of sugar, to taste, as well. Mix with squash and heat together. Serve warm.

Zucca al Pomodoro
TOMATO-CASSEROLED WINTER SQUASH
Capri, Ischia, Procida

Serves 4 to 6

This hefty winter squash casserole layers the almost-sweet vegetable with pungent cheese and savory tomato sauce. It bakes into an almost mushy, polentalike consistency, and is even better leftover the next day.

1½ pounds winter squash, peeled and either diced or sliced ¼ inch thick

2 cups tomato sauce or puree

7 to 8 cloves garlic, chopped

3 to 4 tablespoons olive oil

3 ounces pecorino Romano or Parmesan cheese, shredded coarsely or diced

2 teaspoons fresh oregano, or more to taste

Salt and black pepper

½ cup vegetable or chicken stock or water, or as needed

1. Layer the squash with tomato sauce, garlic, olive oil, cheese, oregano, and salt and pepper, ending with a last layer of cheese.
2. Pour the stock over the top, then cover tightly and place in 375–400°F oven.
3. Bake about 30 minutes covered, then remove cover and continue baking until squash is tender, casserole is no longer soupy, and top is golden browned.
4. Serve hot or let cool and enjoy at room temperature.

Pizze, Focaccie, Panini, e Frittate

PIZZA, FOCACCIA, SANDWICHES, AND SNACKS

For snacks, little meals, antipasti, and street nibbles, you'll often find foods made with bread or bread dough, encased in pastry, or bound with eggs and cheese.

Pizza is the quintessential Italian snack: a round of tender dough stretched thin and smeared with sauce, topped with a scattering of savory morsels and a sprinkling of cheese, then baked in a wood-fueled oven. It emerges both chewy and tender, crisp around the edges and almost delicate toward its moist center. This humble dish at times is embellished to lavish proportions, with the addition of seafood, wild mushrooms, pungent olives, and garden vegetables. The dough itself varies from crisp and chewy to thick and breadlike, to the potato-enriched pizza dough of Sardinia.

Another typically enjoyed snack food is focaccia, the flat bread that is like pizza but topped with herbs or onions, coarse salt, a thin swipe of tomato paste, or with raisins kneaded into the dough. Italian sandwiches are often made on focaccia.

Italian sandwiches, known as *panini* or *tramezzini,* may be stuffed into any sort of roll or between thin bread slices. These little wonders are filled with nearly anything imaginable: vegetables such as spinach or mushrooms, cheese mixtures, cured or cooked meats, or fish, herbs, egg. Cafe-bars sell freshly made *panini* and *tramezzini,* and you'll find people snacking on them from late morning onward.

Crostini and bruschette are two bread dishes that are eaten round the clock, around the country, in an endless variety of guises. You'll find them in homes, cafes, and restaurants. As a first course in an elegant restaurant they might be topped with a salad of ripe tomatoes or grilled porcini; you might be served a plate of crostini as part of a lavish antipasto.

One dish synonymous with snacks, midnight suppers, antipasti, even as a filling for a *panino*, is the frittata. This flat cakelike omelet can be filled with nearly anything, from leftover pasta or dollops of tangy goat cheese and herbs, braised potatoes and peppers, to wild mushrooms. Frittate may be eaten hot or cool, and for nearly any occasion.

And, because there is nearly always a bit of stale bread left over from the last meal or two, the Italians have an unabashedly rich use for it. Layered with cheese and savory flavorings, it is drenched with cream and beaten egg, then baked. Called a strata, for the layers used in its assembly, it tastes much like a hearty, bready soufflé, and is irresistible.

Basic Pizza Dough

Makes enough to serve 4

For a crisp-crusted pizza, use a pizza stone according to directions, and spray a little water into the oven once or twice using an atomizer. Similarly delicious results can be obtained by filling a ceramic baking dish with hot water and placing it on the bottom of the oven before popping the pizza in.

2 packets dried yeast

1 cup warm water, 105°F

1 teaspoon sugar

1 teaspoon salt

2 tablespoons olive oil

3 cups all-purpose flour, more if needed

1. Dissolve yeast in warm water, then add sugar and let stand until foamy, 5 to 10 minutes.
2. Combine yeast mixture with salt, 1 tablespoon of the olive oil, and 3 cups of flour. Mix in food processor or by hand, starting with 2 cups and working the third one in. Mix until dough can form a ball. If mixture is too wet, add more flour; if too dry, a little more water. Mix until dough is smooth and firm.

3. Turn out onto a well-floured board and knead until dough is elastic, about 6 to 8 minutes.

4. Oil a large bowl with the remaining olive oil, then place the dough in the bowl and turn to coat the surface. Cover with a clean cloth and let stand in a warm place until doubled in size, 1 to 1½ hours.

5. Punch dough down, cover, and let rest and rise again 30 minutes before forming into pizza or focaccia.

Pizza on the Grill

Baking pizza on an outdoor grill gives it a lovely smoky scent as well as a crisp, chewy crust. Use a covered grill and place the baking pan—or tinfoil—with the pizza on it, on the cooking grid. Cover and bake in the hot smoky covered grill, occasionally checking the progress of the dough and toppings. It should take about 15 to 20 minutes.

Pizza con le Cozze
Pizza with Fresh Mussels in Their Shells

Serves 4

The mussels pop open as they bake, and their juices soak into the bread and saucy topping. While you could shell the mussels before topping the pizza so that it would be easier to eat, I recommend leaving them whole since the open-shell pizza topping is so beautiful to look at, and the shells add their ineffable sea-scent.

1 recipe Basic Pizza Dough
    (page 183)

1 cup tomato sauce or puree

3 cloves garlic, chopped

1/2 teaspoon dried oregano or
    1 teaspoon fresh, or more
    to taste

Several generous shakes of red
    pepper flakes

3 to 4 tablespoons olive oil

2 pounds mussels, soaked in cold
    water for at least 30 minutes
    to rid them of their grit, then
    rinsed and drained

2 tablespoons chopped parsley

1. Preheat oven. If using a pizza stone or water-filled baking dish,
    place in oven now.
2. Press dough out in oiled pizza pan or baking sheet, then cover
    with tomato sauce or puree.
3. Sprinkle with two-thirds of the garlic, oregano, red pepper, and
    olive oil. Top with mussels, then sprinkle rest of garlic, oregano,
    red pepper, and olive oil over the mussels.
3. Bake in 450°F oven until mussels pop open and bread is golden
    brown and puffy in places and cooked through, about 15 minutes.
    Sprinkle with parsley. Serve immediately, accompanied by a bowl
    for the discarded shells.

Pagnotta Sarda
SARDINIAN PIZZA WITH A POTATO CRUST

Makes 1 focaccia, to serve 4

Sardinian pizza is traditionally made with a potato dough crust: The potatoes give a soft round flavor and tenderness. The topping couldn't be sim-
pler: diced tomatoes, mixed cheeses, and lots of garlic. On Sardinia, fresh
local sheep cheese would be used, along with a milky mozzarella or

unsmoked scamorza, but you can vary the cheeses with whatever is available locally and it will be delicious: ricotta, mozzarella, unsmoked scamorza, pecorino fresca, even Monterey Jack.

If fresh tomatoes are not full of summer flavor, use well-drained canned ones; and if you can get multicolored tomatoes with their richly varied flavors as well as colors, they are delightful on this pizza.

10 ounces baking potatoes (about 2 small to medium), peeled and quartered

1½ cups flour

1 package dry yeast

1 teaspoon salt

½ to ⅔ cup lukewarm potato-cooking water, or as needed

¼ cup olive oil

10 cloves garlic, coarsely chopped

6 ounces goat or feta cheese, or fresh ricotta, crumbled

8 ounces mozzarella, Fontina, or similar white cheese such as Monterey Jack, coarsely shredded or thinly sliced

½ to 1 teaspoon crumbled dried oregano, or 1 to 1½ teaspoons crumbled fresh oregano

½ cup freshly grated pecorino Sardo, Romano, asiago, or Parmesan

6 to 8 very flavorful ripe or canned tomatoes, seeded and diced

1. Cover potatoes with cold water and bring to a boil. Cook until very tender, then pour off the water and let cool to lukewarm. Mash the potatoes.
2. Combine potatoes with flour, yeast, salt, and enough of the potato-cooking water to make a pliable dough.
3. With floured hands on a floured board, knead about 10 minutes or until elastic. Dough will be somewhat sticky.
4. Oil a large bowl and place dough in it. Cover with a clean cloth and leave overnight in the refrigerator. This step makes the dough roll out thinner and become tender rather than gummy.
5. Preheat oven to 475°F. If using a pizza stone or water-filled baking dish, place in oven now.

6. Punch down dough; it will be very tender and almost soft and slightly sticky. With oiled hands, stretch dough out until it forms a flat disc, then place on an oiled baking sheet.

7. Sprinkle with chopped garlic, goat cheese (or feta or ricotta), mozzarella (or Fontina of Jack), oregano, and a drizzle of olive oil. Sprinkle with pecorino or Parmesan and scatter with tomatoes.

8. Bake in a 475°F oven for 10 to 15 minutes or until top is golden brown and crusty. Serve right away.

Pizza con Spinaci, Polpette, e Formaggio di Caprina
PIZZA OF SPINACH, GOAT CHEESE, AND SPICY LAMB MEATBALLS
Sardinia

Serves 4

This rustic pizza is particularly good cooked over an open fire, to be eaten for a mountainside picnic. The goat cheese is fresh and tangy against the richness of the other ingredients. Lamb is a favored meat with the shepherds of Sardinia, who spend their days and nights watching over their sheep.

1 recipe Basic Pizza Dough (page 183)

3 to 4 tablespoons tomato paste

6 to 8 marinated sun-dried tomatoes, cut into thin strips or chopped

4 medium tomatoes, ripe, firm, and flavorful, thinly sliced

7 cloves garlic, chopped

3 ounces goat cheese or feta cheese, crumbled

1 cup cooked and squeezed-dry spinach, cut into bite-sized pieces

8 ounces mozzarella, shredded or thinly sliced

8 ounces ground lamb

$1/2$ teaspoon fennel seeds

$1/4$ teaspoon mixed Italian herbs

Hot red pepper flakes to taste

Salt

1 teaspoon crumbled oregano

Freshly grated pecorino Romano, pecorino Sardo, or Parmesan to taste

1. Preheat oven to 450°F. If using a pizza stone or water-filled baking dish, place in oven now.
2. Arrange Basic Pizza Dough on pan or baking sheet, using your hands to stretch it out as thinly as possible.
3. Spread dough with the tomato paste, then top with sun-dried tomatoes, sliced tomatoes, half the chopped garlic, dollops of goat cheese, and little piles of spinach. Sprinkle with mozzarella.
4. Combine ground lamb with remaining garlic, fennel, mixed herbs, hot pepper flakes, and salt to taste. Roll into meatballs 1 to 1½ inches in size, then arrange on top of pizza.
5. Sprinkle with oregano and pecorino or Parmesan and bake in 450°F oven for 10 to 15 minutes or until meatballs are cooked and lightly browned, the cheese topping melted and browned, and the crust baked through. Serve right away.

Pizza di Melanzane
EGGPLANT AND RICOTTA PIZZA
Elba

Serves 4

We stayed once in a villa, tucked away high in a hillside village. After a few days we heard a commotion in our back garden and poked our heads out to investigate. There behind the house we saw our neighbors pottering about, removing a large lid of some sort from a hole in the hill. They left, but returned an hour or so later, this time with a large filled baking pan, which they carefully placed inside the large hole.

The hole, it turns out, was a communal oven, and when this pizza emerged, our neighbor came to our door asking for a "coltello! coltello!" (a knife). She promptly cut off a big chunk of this pizza, offering it to us with grace and hospitality.

Though the eggplant and ricotta are reminiscent of French pizzas, I've eaten similar ones in Sicily, and actually throughout Italy in one version or another. The bland flavor of ricotta is lovely, but it is also terrific prepared with goat cheese.

1 recipe Basic Pizza Dough (page 183)

1 medium-sized eggplant, cut into bite-sized pieces

Salt for sprinkling onto eggplant

3 to 4 tablespoons olive oil, for browning

3 cloves garlic, finely chopped

12 ounces ricotta cheese

2 ounces finely chopped prosciutto, or marinated sun-dried tomatoes

4 ounces shredded white cheese such as mozzarella or a sharper cheese such as mild asiago

2 tablespoons finely chopped basil, or pesto

2 to 3 tablespoons freshly grated Parmesan or similar cheese

1. Stretch out pizza dough and press into large baking sheet or baking pan.
2. Generously salt eggplant cubes, then set aside for at least 15 minutes for the bitter juices to leech out. This will help with the browning, and most of the salt will be rinsed out.
3. Rinse eggplant, then dry well on absorbent paper or towels. Sauté the eggplant in the olive oil until lightly browned and tender. Toss with garlic and remove from heat.
4. Preheat oven to 450°F. If using a pizza stone or water-filled baking dish, place in oven now.
5. Mix ricotta cheese with prosciutto or sun-dried tomatoes, and half of the shredded mozzarella or asiago.
6. Top the pizza dough with a layer of the cheese mixture, then a layer of the basil or pesto. Top this with the reserved browned eggplant, sprinkle the top with remaining shredded cheese, then with the Parmesan.
7. Bake until dough is cooked through and cheese has melted and is spotted with golden brown bits, about 20 minutes. Eat immediately.

Pizzette

LITTLE PIZZAS WITH SIMPLE TOPPINGS

I've enjoyed little pizzas topped with the simplest of savory ingredients throughout Italy, including the islands—as a snack with a glass of wine or beer in a cafe; as a chic first course in a hillside restaurant; cooked over an open fire in the middle of a field; as part of an antipasto by the seaside, readying myself for the big fish that was at that very moment readying itself on the grill for me.

1. Preheat oven to 450°F. If using a pizza stone or water-filled baking dish, place in oven now.
2. Divide 1 recipe of Basic Pizza Dough (see page 183) into 6 to 8 balls and roll each of these out until thin and delicate. For smaller pizzas, divide the dough into 10 or 12 balls.
3. Top with any of the toppings listed below, then bake for 10 to 15 minutes or until dough is golden brown and cheese melted.

Toppings:

Olive, Fennel, Garlic, and Goat Cheese Pizzetta

Scatter ¼ cup black Mediterranean-type olives, pitted and halved or quartered, 2 tablespoons fennel seeds, 3 cloves coarsely chopped garlic, and 3 to 4 ounces crumbled goat or sheep cheese over the top of the dough. Drizzle with 1 to 2 tablespoons olive oil and bake as directed above.

Garlicky Tomato, Onion, and Caper Pizzetta

This is one of my favorites, the topping that seduced me into becoming a fan of capers. Spread the top of the dough discs with a thin layer of tomato paste, then scatter several tablespoons diced very ripe tomatoes over them. Sprinkle with chopped garlic, thinly sliced red onion, and a generous scattering of capers. Bake as directed.

Peperoni e Carciofi (Roasted Pepper and Artichoke Heart) Pizzetta
Spread dough discs with a thin layer of tomato paste, then sprinkle with
several cloves chopped garlic; 2 roasted, peeled, and diced red or yellow
peppers; and ⅔ to 1 cup marinated artichoke hearts. Top with a sprinkling
of shredded mozzarella or Fontina, sprinkle with dried oregano, and drizzle with olive oil. Bake as directed above.

Pancetta and Pecorino Pizzetta
Top dough with a mixture of 5 cloves chopped garlic and 4 ounces grated
pecorino or aged asiago cheese, 4 ounces diced pancetta or salami, and 2
tablespoons chopped fresh marjoram. Bake as directed.

Pizzette co'Cecinielle
LITTLE PIZZAS WITH FRESH SARDINES
Sicily

Serves 4

Fresh sardines or other small fish are pressed into the dough and baked,
their juices mingling with the tomatoes, garlic, oregano, and olive oil and
the chewy crisp-edged bread.

1 recipe Basic Pizza Dough
   (page 183)

About 1 cup tomato sauce
   or puree

About 1 pound fresh sardines or
   other small fish (anchovies
   or smelts), cleaned and boned

5 to 10 cloves garlic, chopped

½ to 1 teaspoon dried oregano

3 tablespoons olive oil

Coarse salt to taste

1. Divide dough into 4 or 8 portions, depending on the size pizza
    desired.

2. Preheat oven to 450°F. If using a pizza stone or water-filled baking dish, place in oven now.

3. Stretch and roll out each piece of dough until it forms a flat disc. Place on olive-oiled baking sheet.

4. Spread each disc with tomato sauce or puree, then top with several sardines, pressing them into the dough. Sprinkle with garlic, oregano, olive oil and coarse salt. Repeat until all of the dough is used up.

3. Bake in 450°F oven for 10 to 15 minutes or until the pizzas and fish are cooked through. Serve hot or let cool to room temperature.

Calzone
STUFFED PIZZA

Serves 4

This makes a traditional, lusty, non-trendy and utterly delicious calzone, the sort eaten throughout the region of Naples and the islands that lie off her coast.

I spread a small layer of sauce on top of the dough before baking, and serve the rest alongside the ready-to-eat calzone, as I find that with no sauce the dish can be a bit stodgy.

1 recipe Basic Pizza Dough (page 183)

1 cup ricotta cheese

About ¼ cup sun-dried tomatoes and/or roasted red/yellow peppers, diced

10 black oil-cured olives, pitted and halved

6 to 8 ounces mozzarella

4 to 6 ounces salami or prosciutto, diced, or lightly browned diced Italian sausage

1 recipe Garlicky Tomato Sauce (page 227)

Dried oregano to taste

Parmesan as desired

1. Preheat oven to 425°F. If using a pizza stone or water-filled baking dish, place in oven now.
2. Divide dough into 4 parts and, working one at a time, press out into flat discs.
3. Top each disc with a quarter of the ricotta, then a quarter of the sun-dried tomatoes and/or peppers, olives, mozzarella, and salami. Fold dough over and lightly wet edges and press together to seal. Place on a baking sheet.
4. When all calzone are filled, spread tops with a few tablespoons of the Garlicky Tomato Sauce, sprinkle with oregano and Parmesan, then bake at 400°F for 35 minutes or until lightly browned on the edges and cooked through.
5. When ready to serve, heat remaining tomato sauce and serve alongside the hot calzone.

FOCACCIA

FOCACCIA is pizza without the elaborate toppings, a flat bread often seasoned on top with herbs, salt, olives, green onions, chopped nuts, and/or a light swipe of tomato paste. It may be sold in a bakery that sells other breads or pizza, or from a shop, *il focacceria*, that sells nothing but focaccia.

This chewy flat bread may be stuffed and served as a sandwich, too. When you order a stuffed focaccia, you first choose the filling, then the flat pizzalike bread is slashed open into halves, then stuffed, closed up, and popped into the oven to heat through, served hot and sizzling.

Focaccia fillings change with the fashion of the moment: One day tuna and sautéed peppers are all the rage, the next day rich stracchino cheese, or braised onions, mozzarella with prosciutto and tomatoes. Or it might be a combination of goat cheese and braised peas, as it was last summer in my favorite little back-street *osteria* (inn).

Basic Focaccia

1 recipe Basic Pizza Dough (page 183)

1. Preheat oven to 450°F.
2. Stretch out dough to fit onto large baking or cookie sheet. The size of the sheet will determine the thickness of your focaccia, so if you prefer a thicker, breadier focaccia, use a smaller pan; for a thinner, more pizzalike bread, use a larger pan.
3. Press the dough into a large oiled baking sheet or pan, then bake until top is golden brown and bread is cooked through, about 15 minutes.

Foccacia con Olive Verde

Tomato, Onion, and Green Olive Flat Bread

Serves 4

Tear this crisp, savory bread into uneven hunks and serve it tossed onto a platter as an accompaniment to antipasto, salads, or stews, or simply as a partner for glasses of red wine.

This is delicious cooked outdoors on an open fire.

1 recipe Basic Pizza Dough (page 183)

1/4 cup tomato paste, or as desired

1 onion, thinly sliced

About 15 green olives, preferably slightly bitter Italian ones, pitted and halved

2 to 3 tablespoons olive oil, or as needed

Oregano and/or other dried herb, to taste

Coarse salt

1. Stretch out the dough and press into an olive-oiled, large flat baking or cookie sheet.
2. Spread with tomato paste, then top with onion slices and olives, pressing them all in. Drizzle with olive oil, sprinkle with oregano and coarse salt, then bake in 425°F oven for 20 to 25 minutes or until well-risen and golden brown in spots.

Seasoned Focaccia

Follow the recipe for Basic Focaccia, and add any of the following toppings:

Onion-Rosemary Focaccia

Press out twice-risen dough onto olive-oiled baking sheet, then press lots of browned onions into it. Top with chopped fresh rosemary and bake until the edges are golden brown.

Rosemary and Raisin Focaccia

Knead $1/4$ to $1/2$ cup golden raisins and 2 teaspoons chopped fresh rosemary into the dough, then roll out and press into the oiled baking sheet. Brush top with egg white, then sprinkle lightly with sugar, about 2 teaspoons. Bake at 375°F for 15 to 20 minutes or until top is golden and bread is cooked through.

Green Onion Foccacia

Top dough with lots of chopped green onions, olive oil, and salt, then bake until dough is cooked through.

Pancetta and Oregano Foccacia

Spread top of dough with a very light layer of tomato paste, then press in 6 to 8 ounces diced pancetta or salami, and sprinkle with 2 to 3 tablespoons chopped fresh oregano. Drizzle with olive oil and bake as above.

Garlic and Hazelnut Focaccia

Strew the top of the pressed-out dough with a mixture of $1/2$ cup coarsely chopped hazelnuts, $1/4$ cup grated Parmesan cheese, 4 to 6 cloves chopped garlic, 1 teaspoon fresh thyme, and 2 to 3 tablespoons olive oil. Bake as above.

Four Fillings for Stuffed Foccacia

—Braised Bitter Greens and Olives: To make the braised greens, warm 2 cups blanched, coarsely chopped greens such as escarole, spinach, Treviso, or a mixture of greens in olive oil to which you've added 3 to 5 cloves garlic. Cook softly for 5 to 10 minutes or until fragrant and tender. Slash open a focaccia, spread the cut edge with about $2/3$ cup ricotta, top with the braised greens, about 15 pitted oil-cured black olives, and a layer of thinly sliced mozzarella or other white cheese. Top with other side of focaccia and bake until hot and melty.

—Browned eggplant slices, fresh mozzarella, vinaigrette-dressed tomatoes, with whole leaves of sweet basil.

—Marinated artichoke hearts and shrimp, with enough mozzarella to hold it together when melted.

—Leftover swordfish or tuna, with diced tomatoes, pitted green olives, strips of roasted green peppers, garlic, and olive oil.

Four Cold Fillings or Toppings for Focaccia

—Diced ripe tomatoes with chopped garlic and basil leaves, dressed with olive oil and vinegar, on focaccia spread with goat cheese.

—Radicchio, leafy lettuce, toasted pine nuts, and shavings of pecorino, dressed in olive oil and vinegar.

—Diced fennel, chopped black olives, olive oil, and balsamic vinegar.

—Diced roasted chicken bound with an olive oil mayonnaise, seasoned with garlic, basil (preferably purple-leafed), and oil-cured olives.

BRUSCHETTE E CROSTINI

BRUSCHETTA typifies Italian flavor and spirit: rough, flavorful peasant bread that has grown stale in the Mediterranean sun, toasted over a wood fire, rubbed with fragrant garlic and anointed with freshly pressed olive oil. Topped with whatever fresh and savory bits are lying around the kitchen or growing lush in the garden, it is a feast of simplicity.

While bruschetta might be quintessential peasant fare, it has become as chic as any food could be from vineyard to posh restaurant, from Italy to London to California, often garnished with a wide variety of familiar and unusual toppings.

But the original garlic-scented bread, glistening with oil, is memorable on its own for its strong flavor and scent. I remember the first time I tasted it as a teenager, having never heard of such a thing. For some reason that I no longer remember, I was visiting a monestary high in the hills. The young priest was extremely playful and insisted we drink the monks' homemade wine, then visit the bones of the saint. Soon we were helping the monks press olives into oil between two big stone discs, thick green oil streaming out of the crushing rocks.

Then the priest toasted slices of bread over an open fire, rubbed them with garlic and poured on a little of the fresh, pungent green oil, scented with the flavor of an olive grove, peppery enough to catch the throat ever so slightly.

Basic Bruschetta

Serves 4

As brilliant as bruschetta is on its own, nearly anything is delicious spooned over it: tangy salads, thin slices of salami or prosciutto, marinated or grilled vegetables, cheese or seafood mixtures. Some of my current favorites follow the basic recipe.

8 thick slices of country bread, about ¾ inch thick

About 1 clove garlic per person, cut into halves

Olive oil to taste, preferably a big-flavored extra-virgin oil

Salt and pepper

1. Lightly toast bread, preferably over a charcoal grill, but if none is available, use the oven or broiler.
2. Rub cut side of garlic clove over toast, on one side or both sides, as you prefer.
3. Drizzle toast with olive oil, and season with salt and pepper to taste.

Bruschetta con Pomodori

BRUSCHETTA WITH TOMATO SALAD

Sardinia

Serves 4

Juicy tomatoes, marinated with olive oil and vinegar, fresh herbs, hot peppers, and lots of salty black olives, are marvelous spooned over bruschetta, as the toasted bread deliciously soaks up the savory juices. Roasted red peppers, a scattering of capers, and chunks of tuna or bits of chopped anchovies all make enticing additions.

This is an excellent antipasto before a bowl of spicy seafood spaghetti and perhaps a simple grilled fish.

1 recipe Basic Bruschetta
(page 198)

$^{1}/_{2}$ cup Kalamata or other
Mediterranean black olives,
pitted and halved

5 ripe tomatoes, diced

$^{1}/_{2}$ stalk celery, chopped

$^{1}/_{2}$ cup olive oil

2 to 3 tablespoons red wine
vinegar

$^{1}/_{2}$ cup coarsely chopped basil

$^{1}/_{2}$ cup coarsely chopped parsley

Dash cayenne pepper or hot
pepper flakes

1. Prepare Basic Bruschetta.
2. Combine remaining ingredients and spoon over bread. Let sit and absorb juices for a few minutes, then enjoy with a knife and fork accompanied by a glass of rustic and robust red wine.

Bruschetta Bianca e Nera
BLACK AND WHITE BRUSCHETTA WITH OLIVE PASTE AND MOZZARELLA

Serves 4

Pungent herbal black olive paste is spread over crisp-toasted garlic bread, topped with slabs of fresh milky mozzarella. Eat at room temperature, or melt lightly. And while it is delicious as is, a few slices of sweet vine-ripened tomatoes are luscious on the side.

Black olive paste, also known as olivada, is made from pounded or pureed pitted black olives. The purple-black spread tastes distinctly of the olive used but intensified and more vivid.

You may purchase black olive paste (and sometimes green olive paste) in specialty shops, usually imported from Italy or sometimes Greece, or buy tapenade from France. The latter has more flavor enhancements added to the paste: anchovies, garlic, herbs.

You can make olive paste yourself. Pit and cut up whichever olives you choose: I recommend an oily rather than watery olive. Place in food processor and whirl, adding a thin stream of olive oil as the olives chop finely, just enough to form a smoothish paste.

⅓ cup black olive paste

½ teaspoon fennel seeds (optional)

1 to 2 tablespoons chopped fresh rosemary

4 large or 8 small to medium-sized slices Basic Bruschetta (page 198)

About 3 ounces fresh mozzarella cheese, sliced into several thick slabs

1. Combine olive paste, fennel seeds, and rosemary.
2. Prepare Basic Bruschetta.
3. Spread olive-herb paste over bruschetta, then top each with mozzarella.

Variation: To serve hot, place under the broiler and heat until cheese just begins to melt. Serve right away.

Variation: Bruschetta Nera con Porcini
OLIVE BRUSCHETTA WITH SAUTÉED MUSHROOMS

Prepare the above Bruschetta Bianca e Nera and spread with olive paste. Instead of mozzarella cheese, however, prepare a mixture of sautéed wild mushrooms (or fresh domestic mushrooms mixed with a few slices of dried rehydrated porcini). Spoon the sautéed mushrooms over olive-spread toasts and serve immediately.

Bruschetta alla Palermo
CLAM OR TUNA AND ROASTED PEPPER BRUSCHETTA FROM PALERMO
Sicily

Top Basic Bruschetta (page 198) with roasted red, yellow, and green bell peppers, and garnish with chunks of tuna or nuggets of cooked clams. Sprinkle with chopped flat-leaf Italian parsley.

Funghi con Pane Rosmarino
SAUTÉ OF FIELD MUSHROOMS WITH ROSEMARY BREAD

Serves 4

If you are lucky enough to have access to a selection of the less common mushrooms, this starter is delectable and very simple to prepare.

1 pound mixed mushrooms of choice, sliced or cut up into large pieces all about the same size

3 to 4 tablespoons butter

3 to 4 tablespoons olive oil

3 to 4 cloves garlic, chopped

Salt, black pepper, and fresh chopped rosemary to taste

4 to 8 slices crusty rosemary bread or rosemary focaccia

3 tablespoons chopped parsley, preferably flat-leaf Italian

1. Lightly sauté the mushrooms in the butter and olive oil in a pan large enough not to crowd the mushrooms. Fry for 2 minutes or so, then add the garlic and cook until mushrooms are tender and golden brown. Season with salt, pepper, and rosemary to taste.
2. Meanwhile, toast or grill the bread and brush with olive oil.
3. Spoon the mushrooms over the toasted bread, then sprinkle with parsley and serve immediately.

Pane Guittiau
CRISP TOASTED FLATBREAD TOPPED WITH SALT AND OIL
Sardinia

Serves 4 for lunch or
6 for a snack or as part of an antipasto

You'll find this typically Sardinian snack brought to your table with wine, antipasti, or roasted meats. It consists of the crisp, toasted or fire-grilled flatbread known as *pane carasau* or *carte di musica*, dressed with olive oil and sprinkled with more salt than we like to think is healthy (but remember, the weather can be so hot . . .). Often Pane Guittiau is scented with lots of rosemary. Sometimes the garlic is brought separately, marinating in a bowl of olive oil; the dish is then known as *bruschetta Sarda*.

In the United States Sardinian flatbread is seldom available, so I use Armenian flatbread, lavosh, either fresh or dried. While a bit thicker than the original, it is every bit as deliciously addictive.

2 Armenian flatbreads (lavosh), either crisp-dried or fresh soft ones

3 to 4 tablespoons olive oil

5 to 8 cloves garlic, chopped coarsely

4 tablespoons chopped fresh rosemary

Salt for sprinkling

1. Run each sheet of lavosh under the tap, then leave to dry and soften; the fresh lavosh need only a 5-minute wait while the dried lavosh should sit 15 minutes or so.
2. Arrange each on an oiled baking sheet. For easier breaking once baked, roll a perforated wheel across the top to mark the size pieces you like. Spread with olive oil, garlic, and rosemary. Sprinkle with salt.
3. Bake in a 500°F oven for 10 to 15 minutes, then reduce heat to about 375–400°F until the rounds are golden brown and crisp. Remove from oven and serve, broken into pieces.

CROSTINI

LIKE bruschetta, crostini starts out as slices of stale bread, but unlike bruschetta, it follows a path of refined indulgence. These are cut into small pieces rather than the larger bruschetta, then either brushed with fragrant oil and baked to crunchy crispness or spread with rich pastes of liver, meat, truffles, cheese, fish, then grilled or fried until browned and sizzlingly crisp. They are fragrant and irresistible.

Tuscan crostini are especially famous: little crisp breads topped with savory chicken liver paste, served as antipasti with a platter of salami, prosciutto, and so on. Along the seafront, the crostini will be topped with a rich seafood paste and accompanied by a platter of little fresh sea creatures.

Crostini are a part of the everyday snacking patterns of much of Italy: A plateful late at night gets students through their studies; a crostini or two in the late morning gets housewives through their workday; and several savory crostini along with a glass or two of rustic red get cafe habitués through their afternoons. And nothing makes a more welcome antipasto than a plate of crisp crostini.

Crostini al Formaggio e Rosmarino
Garlicky Rosemary and Cheese-Topped Toasts

Serves 4

This is such a simple mixture, yet so delicious. Shredded cheese is mixed with fresh rosemary and garlic, then spread over crusty bread and broiled until browned and bubbly.

About 8 to 10 ounces mild white cheese such as Jack, Fontina, or mozzarella, shredded or diced finely

2 to 3 tablespoons chopped fresh rosemary leaves

2 to 3 cloves garlic, finely chopped

8 slices rustic country bread, sliced in halves, or baguette, each about 2 ounces (if using baguette, slice on a diagonal for a larger surface size)

Combine cheese, rosemary, and garlic. Spread onto tops of bread. Broil until cheese melts and lightly browns and edges of the bread turn crisp and browned. Serve immediately.

Variation: Flat tortillalike breads are delicious with the rosemary-cheese topping. In Italy use the pitalike *piadine;* in Britain, naan or chapatis; in the United States flour tortillas are perfect.

Stuzzicini e Tartine
Little Snacks on Bread

Little slices of well-buttered country bread or *ciabatta,* topped with savory ingredients, make up these little snacks. Unlike bruschetta or crostini, these are not cooked at all.

It is the contrast of the savory, strongly flavored morsels and the sweet butter as your teeth bite through to the tender bread, that is so exciting. Enjoy with an afternoon glass of wine or mineral water.

To prepare: Slice crusty Italian or French bread and generously butter with softened sweet unsalted butter. Top with any of the following:

- Green and black olive halves and bits of anchovy.
- A sprinkling of garlic, chopped black oil-cured olives, and prosciutto or bresaola.
- Chopped shallot and thinly sliced bottargu.
- Chopped garlic, black oil-cured olives, and basil.
- Black olive paste and mortadella.
- Thinly sliced little radishes.
- Chopped green onion and purslane.

PANINI AND TRAMEZZI
CAFE SANDWICHES

THE espresso machine hisses as it emits a steady stream of strong fragrant coffee. Sociable chaos reigns, conversations buzz around you, just made—it seems—for eavesdropping (now is the time those Italian lessons seem really worthwhile). Newspapers are being read, business conducted, lovers awaiting assignations: The cafe-bar hums with the vivacity of Italian street life.

Underneath the glass counter or waiting patiently on the counter, often covered with a light damp towel to keep in freshness (and, no doubt, keep off flies), are the Italian sandwiches known as *panini*, and probably also a pile of the more polite *tramezzini,* made on firm sliced bread, Italy's answer to teatime sandwiches.

Panini are usually crusty little rolls, though they may be made on pizza-like focaccia instead. They may be filled with a wide variety of ingredients: cooked spinach and sliced mozzarella; sautéed mushrooms; spicy salami; chunks of squid and tomatoes; tuna and peppers; wedges of frittate; and so on. The roll might be dressed with oil and vinegar or with a bit of mayonnaise, or it may taste only of the filling and the good bread. *Tramezzini* might be filled with higher-rent ingredients, though in a much thinner, more delicate layering: sliced chicken, porcini, homemade mayonnaise, radicchio, shrimp salad.

Since most anything that can sit atop bruschetta can lie between the covers of a *panino* or *tramezzino,* do read through the bruschetta recipes for additional ideas.

Panino di Pollo e Peperoni
CRUSTY ROLL WITH ROASTED CHICKEN BREAST,
PEPPERS, AND CAPER MAYONNAISE

Serves 4

This elegant little sandwich is not to be set out in the heat of the day or toted to the beach—with the mayonnaise, you are courting the disaster of food poisoning. Instead, prepare it for a special lunch, eaten on the terrace or simply near a window with a view. Serve with chilled juice such as peach or cherry, mixed with a little mineral water, or with a cooling white wine.

This is an excellent next-day sandwich after an evening meal cooked on the grill. Take care that you do not overcook the chicken, however, or this sandwich will be a disappointment.

3 to 4 boned chicken breasts, skin left on (this helps keep them succulent; the skin may be removed after cooking)

Salt and pepper

2 teaspoons chopped fresh rosemary

2 cloves garlic, chopped

2 tablespoons olive oil

1 tablespoon lemon juice

1/2 cup mayonnaise

2 to 3 tablespoons capers

1 tablespoon chopped parsley

4 crusty rolls, split (I especially like either whole-wheat sourdough or rosemary-scented rolls for this sandwich)

2 to 3 roasted red peppers, peeled and cut into strips (you may use the type from a jar, roasted and peeled but not pickled)

1. Combine chicken breasts with salt, pepper, rosemary, garlic, olive oil, and lemon juice. Let sit to marinate at least 30 minutes.

2. Remove chicken from marinade and dry with absorbent paper. Brown chicken breasts on their skin side, then turn over to brown other side, adding a little olive oil if necessary. You will only need to cook them about 3 minutes on each side. Remove from pan and slice; remove skin if you wish. You can make the sandwiches with either hot or cool chicken breasts.

3. Combine mayonnaise, capers, and parsley. Spread this mixture onto both sides of cut rolls, then top with chicken breast and peppers and close tightly. Enjoy right away.

Variation: Panino di Pollo col Carciofi
GRILLED CHICKEN SANDWICH WITH ARTICHOKES

To the above sandwich add sliced, cooked, and cooled artichoke hearts, steamed or grilled when you prepared the chicken.

Pani Cu'la Meusa, also called Guastelle

SICILIAN STREET SANDWICH OF BROWNED BEEF SPLEEN, FRESH RICOTTA, AND PUNGENT CACIOCAVALLO

Palermo, Sicily

Thin slices of beef spleen sizzle on the hot grill; they are then plopped between thick focaccia or a fresh roll, atop a layer of fresh ricotta cheese. The hot meat is then sprinkled with shredded caciocavallo cheese, with its slightly rank, provocative scent that seems so right with the other ingredients.

I confess that it was difficult for me to eat my first Pani Cu'la Meusa, mainly because in my younger days spleen was what I bought for my cat. Looking at it being browned for my sandwich gave me the impression that I should be putting it into a little bowl next to fish-shaped crunchies instead of enjoying it myself.

But pride has so much to do with the trouble we find ourselves in, at least in my life, and I couldn't admit to my companions that spleen was not to my taste (after all, I had already eaten the horsemeat stew, half a lamb's head, and bowlful of baby eels).

Stuffed into focaccia, dripping lusciously greasy juices, this makes a very nice sandwich, though I hasten to add that any thinly sliced beef, such as sandwich steaks sliced thinly and pounded, is a fine subsitute for the spleen, and provolone could be used in place of the ricotta and cacio-cavallo. In addition, I like to add pickled peppers to the sandwich, the ones that are just hot enough to brighten my smile.

Pani, by the way, is the Sicilian dialect for *panino.*

Panino di Prosciutto, Formaggio, e Pomodoro Arrosto
SANDWICH OF ROASTED TOMATO, PROSCIUTTO, AND MELTED CHEESE

Serves 4

The scent of coffee from the hissing espresso machine combined with the slightly acrid aroma of toasting sandwiches as I sat, nearly every morning one summer, in my local cafe.

This *panino* was what I—and everyone else—ordered. It's the sort of sandwich you don't mind having drip a bit down your chin. While I always meant it to be lunch, usually I couldn't wait, and it was breakfast instead.

Inevitably my little table was visited by the house kitten; I always shared, and once when I was surrounded by soulful dogs, I ordered them their own sandwich.

If you don't have a panful of roasted tomatoes on hand, use slices of fresh ripe tomatoes instead, crushing them lightly and pressing them into the bread.

4 crusty rolls, or 1 crusty loaf cut into 4 pieces

3 to 5 cloves garlic, halved or chopped

3 to 5 tablespoons olive oil

8 ounces Fontina, mozzarella, Jack, Manchego, or similar melting cheese, thinly sliced

6 to 8 roasted tomatoes, peeled and seeded, plus a little of their juices; or ripe raw tomatoes, thinly sliced

4 ounces prosciutto, thinly sliced

Handful of herbs: fresh basil, oregano, marjoram, parsley, etc.

1. Split rolls or bread and lightly toast. Rub with cut garlic halves or sprinkle with chopped garlic. Drizzle with olive oil, then top half the open bread surfaces with the sliced cheese.
2. On the other half of the garlic-and-olive-oil-anointed breads, spread the roasted tomatoes, then a layer of prosciutto and herbs. Place both sides together and press.

Savory Pastries and Fried Treats

THROUGHOUT Italy, both on the mainland and the islands, savory pies and pastries filled with meats, vegetables, fish, herbs, cheese, and the like are sold in shops, delis, and stalls. They are irresistible for nibbling as you walk and window-shop through the streets. They also make marvelous picnic fare, as well as convenient treats to tote home for an antipasto.

Torta Rustica
TURNOVER FILLED WITH SAVORY CURED MEATS, VEGETABLES, AND CHEESE
Sicily

Makes 1 large turnover or 4 to 6 individual pastries
to serve about 4

This exuberant pie is plumply filled with savory meats, garlicky spinach, marinated roasted peppers, and enough cheese to make it even richer. This essentially street snack also makes a lively antipasto and no doubt would be marvelous on a picnic, though each time I've tried to take it anywhere, we end up eating it in the car before we reach our destination. It smells enticing and tastes even better.

You can speed preparation by using canned roasted peppers.

Enjoy hot or at room temperature, with a crisp light green salad alongside, and a glass of wine or cool mineral water mixed with freshly squeezed fruit juice.

2 medium-sized red bell peppers

5 cloves garlic, chopped

1 tablespoon red or white wine vinegar

Salt and pepper

2 tablespoons olive oil

2 bunches spinach, about 2 pounds raw, blanched, chopped, and squeezed dry; or 1 package frozen chopped spinach, defrosted and squeezed dry

1 recipe short crust or pie crust dough for 2-crust pie

6 ounces pecorino Sardo, Romano, or aged asiago, thinly sliced

2 ounces boiled ham, thinly sliced

2 ounces garlicky dry salami, thinly sliced

1. Roast peppers over an open flame until their skin blackens and blisters. Place in a plastic bag or in a bowl; cover and seal tightly. Leave for at least 30 minutes or overnight, long enough for the peppers to cool and the skin to separate easily when scraped or rubbed.

2. When peppers are cool, scrape or rub them until all of the skin comes off. Remove seeds and stem, rinse in cool water, then layer with half the chopped garlic and all of the vinegar. Sprinkle with salt and set aside for at least 1 hour to marinate. (If using roasted peeled peppers from a jar, simply rinse and drain, then combine with the garlic and vinegar.) This may be done up to a week ahead of time. Drain before using.

3. Heat remaining garlic in the olive oil until just fragrant, then add the blanched chopped spinach and cook a few moments. Season with salt and pepper and let cool.

4. Preheat oven to 400°F. Roll out the pastry and place onto work surface. For one large pie or turnover, use the pastry whole, in one large disc. For smaller individual pastries, separate the dough into 4 to 6 pieces and roll each out until it forms a thin disc.

5. Placing the filling in the middle (you are going to fold the edges up to meet each other on top to minimize juices running out of the

pastry). Begin with a third of the cheese, then the spinach, a layer of ham, the second third of the cheese, then the drained marinated peppers, sliced salami, and finally the remaining cheese. Pull the edges of the crust together and pinch to seal. It does not matter if it doesn't meet completely on the top.

6. Carefully place the pastry or pastries onto a large baking sheet and bake in a 400°F oven until golden brown, about 20 to 35 minutes. Serve either hot, warm, or at room temperature.

Calzone alla Carnevale
BASIL-SCENTED CHEESE- AND PEPPER-FILLED PASTRIES
Elba

Serves 6

These crisp pastries are filled with the scent of basil, bound together with creamy ricotta cheese, and dotted with bits of roasted pepper and ripe tomato. I ate them in a nameless market in a forgettable town, one warm morning when we docked our boat and headed out for adventure. The pastries were very hot, the cheese dripping in sizzling little strings, mildly dangerous to our tender tongues.

1 recipe short crust or pie crust dough for a 2-crust pie, or puff pastry for 6 cream puffs

3 to 4 tablespoons pesto or chopped fresh basil leaves

10 to 12 ounces mozzarella, Fontina, asiago, Jack, or Manchego, diced

1 roasted and peeled red bell pepper, cut into strips or bite-sized pieces (or about 3 tablespoons roasted, peeled red peppers from a jar)

1 tomato, diced, or 2 tablespoons diced canned tomatoes

4 ounces ricotta cheese

1 clove garlic, chopped

1. Divide the dough into 6 equal pieces, then roll into round flat discs. Place on baking sheet.

2. Spread half of each pastry with pesto, or sprinkle with basil leaves, taking care to leave a border at the edge, as you will fold the pastry over and seal it.

3. Mix the remaining ingredients, then place a spoonful or so on top of the pesto-spread dough or basil leaves. You will very likely have leftover cheese mixture—it is delicious for topping crostini, spreading onto panini, or as stuffing for boned chicken breasts (see variation below).

4. Fold pastry over, wetting the edges with a little water. Press edges together to seal, then bake in 400°F oven for 15 to 20 minutes or until golden brown. Eat very hot, the cheese dripping in sizzling little strings.

Variation: Pollo Ripiene con Ricotta

CHICKEN BREASTS STUFFED WITH SAVORY RICOTTA

Use the leftover cheese mixture as stuffing for chicken breasts. Lay 4 to 6 (depending on the amount of leftover cheese mixture) skin-on chicken breasts skin-side down on a working surface. Slightly flatten breasts with a mallet or rolling pin, then top with a tablespoon of the cheese filling. Roll up into little parcels and secure with a bamboo skewer.

Lay the cheese-stuffed chicken breasts in a baking pan and pour in dry white wine to cover them about three-quarters of the way. Roast in a 375–400°F oven until golden and just cooked through, about 10 to 15 minutes. Do not overcook. The skin helps keep the meat moist on the outside while the cheese filling moistens it from within.

To serve, remove chicken parcels from baking dish and keep warm on a platter, then add 1/2 cup chicken stock to the wine and pan juices and boil down over high heat until it forms a well-reduced essence. Taste for seasoning and pour several spoonfuls over each chicken parcel. Sprinkle with chopped parsley or basil, and serve right away.

Gnocco Frito

PASTRIES FILLED WITH GORGONZOLA AND BASIL LEAVES

Capri, Ischia, Procida

Serves 4 to 6

The name translates as "large lump," in much the same way that pastalike dumplings are known as "little lumps," or gnocchi.

We were served these rich, browned turnovers one mild summer evening as we helped out in our friends' vineyard. We sat, chores done, drinking wine, gathered around an open fire when our friends brought out the makings of this snack. The already risen dough, a heavy pan, and a chunk of cheese were on the tray; we picked the basil ourselves, then assembled the pastries, with a little slab of cheese and leaf of basil in each disc of dough, sealing them up and tossing them into the pan to brown.

They emerged crisp on the outside yet soft and chewy inside, filled with the pungent scent of Gorgonzola and bits of sweet, fragrant basil. It is at its best with a really stinky blue cheese, so if your Gorgonzola is mild, use Danish or Oregon blue.

1 recipe Basic Pizza Dough (page 183)

4 ounces strong blue cheese such as Gorgonzola, Danish, or Oregon, sliced

25 to 30 fresh sweet basil leaves, whole or roughly cut up

1 to 2 cloves garlic, chopped

1 to 2 tablespoons olive oil for frying

1. Divide the dough into 12 pieces, then roll each out into a flat disc.
2. In the center of each disc, place a piece or two of blue cheese, a little fresh basil, and a sprinkling of garlic. Fold over and seal edges well.
3. Heat pan or skillet and add just enough olive oil to coat the pan. Cook the pastries, several at a time, until golden and lightly brown-flecked on each side. They will cook in about 5 minutes. Serve immediately.

Arancini
RICE CROQUETTES
Sicily

Serves about 8

Arancini are round crisp-fried golden croquettes filled with either a savory meat mixture such as a rich ragu mixed with peas, or with a cube of cheese that melts as the rice balls cook in the bubbling oil. They are named *arancini,* or "little oranges," for their shape and nearly golden color.

This is a specialty of Sicily, but also found in the area around Naples where they are filled with cheese and called *suppli al'telfono,* for the way the melted cheese forms strings that look like telephone wires.

Arancini are a good way of using leftover risotto.

2 cups cooked rice or leftover simple risotto

3 to 4 tablespoons grated Parmesan or similar cheese

2 eggs, lightly beaten

1 cup cold ragu or savory meat sauce mixed with $1/4$ cup tender cooked green peas; or 8 to 12 ounces mozzarella or similar cheese, cut into bite-sized pieces

1 cup dry bread crumbs, or as needed to coat the rice balls

Oil for frying to a depth of about 3 inches

1. Combine rice with grated cheese and one of the eggs. Mix well.
2. Form a round ball about the size of a lemon, then make a hole in it with your thumb. Fill the hole with either the meat and pea mixture or with a cube of cheese. It should now be the size of a small orange.
3. Roll rice balls in remaining beaten egg, then in crumbs. Set on a plate to dry as you finish crumbing each ball.
4. Heat oil until a tiny cube of bread turns golden when tossed in.

5. Fry stuffed, crumbed rice balls in hot oil, taking care not to crowd the pan, until balls are evenly colored golden brown. Remove from pan and dry on absorbent paper. Serve right away.

FRITTATE
FLAT OMELETS AND SAVORY VEGETABLE CAKES

FRITTATE are Italian omelets: flat and firm, unlike the custardy, quivering filled and rolled omelets of France. Frittate are more like the Spanish tortilla or the Persian eggah: beaten eggs tossed with savory vegetables, maybe bits of meat, seafood, cheese, and/or crumbs, then poured into a heavy pan and fried into a big savory cake.

Frittate may be filled with any vegetable: broccoli, spinach, zucchini, potato, eggplant, green beans. One of my favorites is sautéed red onion and lots of raw fresh basil, bound with egg and made into green frittate. Another is diced potatoes, peppers, and tomatoes with diced fresh pecorino or feta cheese.

When preparing frittate, lightly sauté the vegetables with aromatics and herbs, then cool a moment and combine with beaten egg. Let it sit for at least 10 minutes, then pour into the pan. The egg soaks up flavors from the vegetables as it sits. All of the following recipes call for large eggs, but smaller eggs may be used. Obviously, you can use one more or less, depending on the needs of the frittata.

These flat omelets are as delicious cold as they are hot; some—myself included—say they are better cold. Frittate are eaten as an appetizer, stuffed into a sandwich or *panino* as an afternoon nibble or picnic lunch. As if frittate are not luscious enough on their own, try spreading something savory over the top: creamy goat cheese, pesto, seasoned pureed artichoke, or sun-dried tomato tapenade.

Frittata di Fagiolini Fresci con Pesto
ROMANO BEAN AND PECORINO FRESCO FRITTATA WITH PESTO TOPPING

Serves 4

This frittata of Romano beans is studded with bites of pungent cheese and spread with a thin layer of pesto. Romano beans are flat Italian green beans, heartier than other green beans, with a more defined inner bean. If Romano beans are not available, any green bean may be used instead.

Serve at room temperature in little wedges along with a glass of wine and bowl of olives and raw vegetables for an antipasto, or serve large chunks warm for a supper dish along with a crisp salad of radicchio and lettuce, studded with toasted pine nuts.

1 cup Romano beans, preferably fresh (frozen are acceptable — barely)

2 to 3 cloves garlic, chopped

3 tablespoons olive oil

6 ounces fresh pecorino or feta cheese, cut into bite-sized nuggets

6 eggs, lightly beaten

About 3 tablespoons pesto (either frozen or homemade)

1. Blanch Romano beans until bright green and crunchy-tender. Drain well.
2. Heat garlic in olive oil until just fragrant, then add beans and toss through the fragrant oil. Add cheese to the eggs, then pour mixture in with the beans.
3. Cook over medium-low heat, occasionally lifting the edges and letting the liquid egg run under. When bottom of eggs are cooked and frittata is fairly set, place under hot broiler until top is lightly browned and firm.
4. Serve hot or cool, spread with the pesto.

Frittata di Asparagi e Caprina
ASPARAGUS AND GOAT CHEESE FRITTATA
Elba

Serves 4

This frittata, like the omelets of neighboring Corsica, is scented with the sweet mint that grows everywhere on the island. It was whipped up for me at the pensione where I stayed for supper one night, along with an antipasto salad of ripe tomatoes, tuna, and string-thin green beans.

When using mint from shops in the United States, however, I often combine it with its cousin basil, which can tame any harshness and brings out not only the mint's sweetness, but its savory flavor as well.

Any type of fresh goat cheese is delicious in this; if it is crumbly, add it to the egg mixture; if soft and creamy, spread it over the finished frittata. The frittata is, however, equally good without any cheese at all, eaten cold in little wedges as part of an antipasto or as a filling for a goat-cheese-spread crusty bread sandwich (see variation below).

1 bunch asparagus, about 1 pound, trimmed of tough ends and cut into ¾ to 1 inch lengths

2 cloves garlic, chopped

2 tablespoons butter or olive oil

3 eggs, lightly beaten

Salt and black pepper

1 teaspoon each chopped fresh mint, and basil; or 2 teaspoons chopped fresh mint

4 to 6 oz fresh tangy goat or sheep cheese

2 tablespoons olive oil

1. Cook asparagus in frying pan with garlic and butter for 2 minutes or so or until still crunchy. Cover and let cool.
2. Combine cooled asparagus with eggs; season with salt and pepper, mint and basil. If you are using crumbly goat cheese, add it now.
3. Heat olive oil in pan, then pour in asparagus and egg mixture. Cook until edges are lightly browned, lifting the edges to let the liquid egg run under. When nearly firm through the middle, place

under broiler until the top is golden brown in spots and puffy (puffs will subside when the frittata cools).

4. Serve hot or at room temperature. If you are using soft goat cheese, spread it over the frittata.

Frittata di Peperoni e Pecorino Fresco
ROASTED PEPPER AND FRESH PECORINO (OR FETA) FRITTATA

Serves 4

While most frittate are as delicious cold as warm, this one is best hot and freshly made, the cheese soft and the eggs tender. Serve for supper as a first course, perhaps garnished with tender cooked fava beans, steamed and warmed in a little garlicky olive oil.

1 medium-sized red bell pepper, roasted, peeled, and sliced (page 211)

1 medium-sized green bell pepper, roasted, peeled, and sliced (page 211)

3 cloves garlic, chopped

3 tablespoons olive oil

4 eggs, lightly beaten

4 to 6 ounces fresh pecorino or feta cheese, diced

Salt and pepper

Dried oregano to taste

1. Lightly sauté red and green pepper with garlic in 1 tablespoon of the olive oil, just enough to bring out the flavors. Remove from pan and stir in eggs and diced cheese, taking care not to break the cheese up too much. Season with salt and pepper.

2. Heat remaining olive oil in pan and pour in egg mixture. Cook over medium heat until bottom is golden brown, then place under broiler to cook the top. Sprinkle with oregano and serve immediately.

Piselli alla Sarda
PEA, TOMATO, AND BREAD FRITTATA
Sardinia

Serves 6

This frittata, while it is a sturdy bread and egg pancake, is known as Piselli alla Sarda, that is, Sardinian-style peas. It is at its best the next day when it has solidified into a firm and bready savory cake. It makes wonderful brown-bag or picnic fare, along with thin slices of prosciutto and sweet fresh fennel, or as an accompaniment for grilled sausages.

1 onion, chopped

3 cloves garlic, chopped

3 to 4 tablespoons olive oil

2 cups young peas (frozen are fine)

Salt and pepper

2 to 3 ripe tomatoes, chopped with any juices (canned are fine)

3 to 4 ounces (or 3 to 4 slices, each 3/4- inch thick) country bread, cut into 3/4 to 1-inch cubes

4 eggs, lightly beaten

Herbs of choice: a pinch of thyme, oregano, marjoram, fresh sweet basil

1. Lightly sauté onion and garlic in half the olive oil until softened, then toss in the peas. Let cook in the fragrant oil until peas are tender. Sprinkle with salt and pepper, then add tomatoes and cook through about 5 minutes until tomatoes are tender and mixture is not too saucy.

2. Add bread cubes and let cook with this mixture a few minutes.

3. Combine eggs with peas-tomato-bread mixture, season with herbs, and let sit 5 to 10 minutes to soften the bread.

4. Heat remaining oil in heavy skillet, then pour in egg mixture and cook over medium heat until bottom is lightly browned and frittata is not runny on top. (You do not need to lift the edges on this frittata as the mixture is quite thick.)

5. Place under broiler until top is cooked to a golden brown, then remove and serve either hot or cool.

Variation: Frittata Sarda con Carciofi
FRITTATA OF BREAD, TOMATO, AND ARTICHOKES
Instead of peas, use 10 to 15 small tender artichoke hearts, blanched and diced (frozen, defrosted, are fine).

CRISPELLE
CREPES

CRISPELLE are Italian crepes, thin pancakes found in a variety of guises: in thin strips floating in clear broths, rolled around cheeses or rich forcemeat mixtures, or stuffed with pureed vegetables and gratinéed.

Following are two distinctive and delicious crispelle recipes, one from Elba that reflects the French influence as well as the island's affection for chestnuts, the other a classically flavored tomato-sauced cheese-filled concoction from the Aeolian Islands.

Crispelle di Castagne
CHESTNUT AND ROSEMARY CREPES
Sardinia

Serves 4 to 6

These thin pancakes made from pureed chestnuts are scented with rosemary and taste vaguely sweet yet earthy and savory. Serve as an antipasto, along with glasses of cooling white wine, the little pancakes spread with a bit of soft garlic butter and/or sprinkled with Parmesan cheese.

In Sicily, interestingly, similar chestnut crepes are prepared with sugar rather than savory flavorings, and eaten as a sweet snack or dessert.

5 to 8 cloves garlic, chopped

About ¼ cup butter

2 tablespoons olive oil

2 cups pureed chestnuts (canned are fine). To prepare from scratch, peel by scoring along the flat side, then boiling for 10 minutes to loosen the skin. Let cool and peel. Puree peeled chestnuts in a food processor.

2 eggs, lightly beaten

4 tablespoons olive oil

1½ cups milk

¾ cup flour

¼ to ½ teaspoon salt

1 to 2 teaspoons chopped fresh rosemary

1. Make garlic butter: Heat garlic in butter and olive oil until fragrant and garlic bits are lightly golden, not browned. Pour into a bowl and set aside.

2. Combine pureed chestnuts, eggs, 3 tablespoons olive oil, and milk and mix well until smooth. A blender or food processor is excellent for this.

3. Stir in flour, salt, and rosemary; the consistency should be light, like lightly whipped cream, rather than thin and runny like a typical crepe batter.

4. Heat 1 tablespoon olive oil in a heavy frying pan, then when hot spoon a few tablespoons of the batter into the pan. Reduce heat to low-medium and use a spoon to spread the batter carefully out to form a thin pancake. Cook until pancake darkens and appears firm rather than runny.

5. Loosen pancake with a spatula, then place a plate over top of pancake and invert. Flip over into the hot pan and cook the other side.

6. Brush hot pancakes with garlic butter and keep warm until you are finished preparing the last pancake. Serve hot, in wedges, sprinkled with Parmesan if desired.

Variation: Chestnut-Rosemary Crepes Gratinéed with Cheese
Lay several chestnut crepes on a baking sheet, taking care that they don't overlap. Omit the garlic butter, and sprinkle each crepe with several heaping tablespoons grated Fontina or sharp white cheddar cheese. Broil until cheese is melted and crispy brown around the edges. Serve immediately.

Volette all'Eoliana
CREPES IN THE STYLE OF THE AEOLIAN ISLANDS

Serves 4 to 6 (8 filled crepes)

Tender crepes filled with creamy white cheese, then baked with tomatoes and served with a sprinkling of fresh basil, this specialty of the Aeolian Islands is vivacious and full of bright flavor, much like the lightest, most delicate lasagne you could desire.

The name *volette*, interestingly, means the sails of ships, referring to the shape of the edges of the crepes as they are folded over and baked until lightly crisped.

Crepes:

3 eggs, lightly beaten

1/2 cup milk

1/2 cup water

1/4 cup oil

1/4 to 1/2 cup flour, or as needed

Filling:

8 ounces ricotta cheese

4 ounces mozzarella or similar mild melting white cheese, diced

1 lightly beaten egg

1/3 cup freshly grated Parmesan or pecorino

Black pepper to taste

1 1/2 to 2 cups diced ripe tomatoes (or use 14-ounce can diced tomatoes, plus juices)

3 tablespoons olive oil

About 1/4 cup thinly sliced or chopped fresh basil

1. Make crepes: Whisk together eggs, milk, water, oil, and flour. The consistency should be that of heavy cream.
2. Let sit a few minutes to dissolve any lumps (a few are okay and will either dissolve or not be noticed).
3. Ladle batter into a hot, lightly oiled heavy flat pan, preferably one used only for crepes, then swirl batter around and pour out any excess. Cook on one side until lightly flecked golden brown, then turn and cook a few moments on the second side, letting it stay creamy colored. Remove from pan, stack on a plate, and set aside. The crepes may be made up to three days ahead and kept covered in the refrigerator, or stored in the freezer for up to two months.
4. For the filling, combine ricotta with mozzarella, egg, 2 tablespoons Parmesan, and black pepper.
5. Preheat oven to 375°F. Spread ¼ to ½ cup of diced tomatoes in the bottom of a large baking dish, or 2 tablespoons in the bottom of small individual ramekins.
6. Place a generous spoonful of the cheese filling onto one quarter of each crepe, then fold first in half, then in quarters to make a cheese-filled triangle-shaped parcel. Place in baking pan or ramekins, in a single, slightly overlapping layer.
7. When all crepes are filled and arranged in pan or ramekins, cover with the diced tomatoes and juices, drizzle with olive oil, then sprinkle with another 2 tablespoons Parmesan.
8. Bake in a 375°F oven for about 20 minutes or long enough for the stuffed crepes to sizzle enticingly and be flecked golden on top.
9. Serve sprinkled with the remaining Parmesan and the fragrant fresh basil.

Salse e Ragu

SAUCES AND RELISHES

Unlike French sauces, Italian sauces are usually an integral part of the dish, with all of the ingredients stewing together in the pot, their juices combining into a seductive and irresistible liquid.

At other times, especially in the islands, a sauce may be a sprightly mixture of zesty and strongly flavored ingredients, stirred together into a light sauce or relish, or ground into a fragrant paste. Sicily, especially, makes a tomato-basil salsalike sauce, *ammyghiu,* as well as a tomato, basil, and almond pesto from Trapani. *Ammoghiu,* from Pantelleria, is also an uncooked tomato sauce, but this one is filled with herbs and incorporates the ingredient Pantelleria is most famous for: capers.

Sometimes a sauce may be no more than pickled vegetables, chopped into a relishlike sauce for grilled or cold meat or fish. The simplest sauce you will find throughout the islands is olive oil and lemon juice whisked together. Sometimes it is seasoned with oregano, at other times thinned with a bit of seawater, but always it is the essential taste of the Italian islands, indeed of all the Mediterranean.

Then there are the deep dark sauces, ragu, full of flavor that develops from a wide array of savory bits and pieces and a long slow simmer in a heavy pot.

Ammyghiu
UNCOOKED SAUCE OF TOMATO, GARLIC, AND HERBS
Sicily

Makes about 2 cups

This typical sauce combines pureed garlic with ripe flavorful tomatoes, herbs, and olive oil. To be at its best, the tomatoes must be at their best. When summer's sweetest tomatoes are no more, I make Ammyghiu using roasted tomatoes.

Ammyghiu may be eaten with roasted chicken or fish, or simply spread on bread. For a refreshing summer lunch, quickly grill thin slices or steaks of halibut, then layer with Ammyghiu sauce and let sit and macerate until tepid. Eat with chunks of bread.

6 cloves garlic, very finely chopped

6 to 8 very ripe flavorful tomatoes, diced

3 to 4 tablespoons olive oil

Salt and pepper

Dash of red wine vinegar

1 to 2 tablespoons fresh chopped oregano, rosemary, or parsley; or 3 tablespoons chopped basil

Whirl garlic and tomatoes together with olive oil, in a blender or food processor, then season with salt and pepper. Add red wine vinegar to taste, then stir in the herbs. Serve right away.

Ammoghiu
UNCOOKED TOMATO SALSA
Pantelleria

Makes about 2 cups

The island of Pantelleria, just off the coast of Sicily, is famous for capers, used in abundance in this traditional sauce. Like Ammyghiu, its Sicilian counterpart, Ammoghiu is based on fresh tomatoes and garlic but is seasoned forcefully with tangy ingredients such as vinegar and capers.

This raw sauce is eaten with all sorts of grilled and roasted fish and meats; its zesty astringent quality is especially good with rich lobster or lamb.

3 tablespoons capers

2 tablespoons white wine vinegar

3 cloves garlic, chopped

3 to 4 tablespoons thinly sliced basil leaves

5 large ripe tomatoes, diced and drained (save juice for another use; canned tomatoes are fine for this, as are roasted tomatoes if ripe flavorful fresh ones are not available)

1/2 cup coarsely chopped parsley

1/2 cup olive oil

Black pepper to taste

Tiny pinch of sugar if needed

Caper juice if needed

1. Combine all ingredients except for the olive oil, black pepper, and sugar in a food processor or blender and whirl to puree. Slowly add olive oil as if you were making mayonnaise, letting the oil amalgamate into a rich sauce.

2. Season with black pepper. Add a tiny pinch sugar if tomatoes are too acidic. Add a bit of caper juice if salt is needed.

Pesto Trapanese

Sicily, Pantelleria

Makes about 2 cups

The addition of ground almonds and tomatoes to the Ligurian basil puree known as pesto is a traditional sauce from the Sicilian town of Trapani; on Pantelleria, it is known as *pesto Pantesco*.

Just before you reach Trapani there is a lookout point: huge sheer cliffs that drop dramatically and terrifyingly 2,500 feet to gentle green fields and, off in the distance, the sea. Resting in the sea are the Egadi Islands: Levanzo, Marettimo, and Favignana. This lookout point is a very nice spot for a picnic: crusty bread spread with this unusual pesto, perhaps a plate of prosciutto, and a basket of sweet fruit.

2 cups chopped basil leaves, tightly packed

3 to 5 cloves garlic, chopped

1/2 cup olive oil, or as needed

1/2 cup grated Parmesan or similar cheese

6 ripe tomatoes, diced (canned are fine)

1/2 cup finely chopped blanched or raw almonds

Whirl the basil, garlic, and olive oil in blender or food processor until smooth, then add cheese. Stir in tomatoes and almonds and serve as desired.

Variation: Nearly instant pesto Trapanese using store-bought pesto: Combine 1/2 cup pesto with 6 ripe chopped tomatoes (canned, drained, tomatoes are fine) and 3 to 4 tablespoons finely chopped blanched or raw almonds.

Salsa di Giardiniera
RELISH OF GIARDINIERA, FENNEL, AND RED PEPPERS
Elba

Serves 4

This simple sauce of chopped pickled vegetables bound with a bit of olive oil is absolutely marvelous spooned over thin slices of rich rare roast beef, perhaps resting on a bed of arugula. Similarly, it would be good spooned over carpaccio.

¼ to ½ cup bottled pickled
giardiniera vegetables

2 tablespoons olive oil

1 bulb fennel, cut into small
wedges or strips, sprinkled
with lemon to keep it from
discoloring

1 red bell pepper, either roasted
and peeled or raw, cut into
strips

Coarsely chop giardiniera vegetables, then drizzle with olive oil.
Arrange on a plate, surrounded with fennel and red pepper.

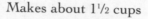

Salmoriglio
OLIVE OIL AND LEMON SAUCE
Sicily

Makes about 1½ cups

Olive oil is whisked into a nearly creamy consistency with hot water in
this very traditional Sicilian sauce for seafood, fish, vegetables, and
roasted meats. Once, in a boat, we came upon a thermal pool, and dipped
our bowl into the hot seawater to make this sauce.

1 cup olive oil

¼ cup hot but not boiling water

Juice of 2 lemons

1½ tablespoons chopped parsley

1 tablespoon chopped fresh
oregano or sweet marjoram

Salt

Beat the olive oil in a warm bowl, then gradually whisk in the hot
water, lemon juice, parsley, and oregano or marjoram. Add salt to taste.
Warm the sauce, whisking as you do, over gentle heat or in a double
boiler. Serve immediately, poured over grilled or roasted fish or meat.

Tapenado Rosso
RED SUN-DRIED TOMATO AND CAPER SPREAD
Tremiti Islands

Makes 1½ cups

Spread onto a sandwich or used as a condiment for boiled fish or meat, this spunky sauce is intensely flavored with sun-dried tomatoes and capers.

Use oil-marinated sun-dried tomatoes in this dish, taking care that you choose ones that are supple and juicy rather than leathery and chewy.

About ½ to ⅔ cup oil-marinated sun-dried tomatoes

2 to 3 tablespoons capers

1 to 2 cloves garlic, chopped

1 to 2 tablespoons coarsely chopped parsley

3 tablespoons olive oil

2 teaspoons red wine vinegar, or mixture of vinegar and caper juice

½ to 1 teaspoon Dijon or English strong mustard

Tiny pinch sugar

Garnish: Fresh sweet basil or thyme

In blender or food processor, combine all ingredients except herb garnish. Whirl until it forms a chunky-textured paste. Chill until ready to serve, then garnish.

Salsa Verde alla Capperi
GREEN PARSLEY AND CAPER SAUCE
Elba

Serves 4

Versions of salsa verde are eaten throughout much of Italy, especially the northern regions where pots of mixed simmered meats or fish are a specialty. This version is tangy from capers and mustard, and bright green from chopped parsley. Serve with steamed mussels or other simple seafood, or with rich boiled or simmered meats.

2 tablespoons chopped parsley	2 tablespoons lemon juice
2 to 3 teaspoons capers	½ to 1 teaspoon caper juice
3 tablespoons olive oil	½ to 1 teaspoon strong mustard such as Dijon or English

Combine all ingredients in a blender or food processor and whirl until smooth and green. Chill until ready to enjoy.

Salsa di Noci
WALNUT SAUCE FOR PASTA
Sardinia

Makes 1½ cups

This reflects the Ligurian influence of walnuts in the pestolike sauce, as well as the particularly Sardinian inclusion of buttermilk or yogurt.

½ cup walnuts	Black pepper
½ beef or vegetable bouillon cube	Parmesan cheese for sprinkling
¼ cup whipping cream	
¼ cup buttermilk (or an extra ¼ cup cream plus a tablespoon of yogurt)	

In processor or blender grind nuts into a fine meal. Crumble bouillon cube into the nut mixture, then add the cream and buttermilk. Whirl until it forms a smooth sauce. Serve tossed into pasta, with pepper and Parmesan to taste.

Ragu Tradizione
TRADITIONAL RAGU

Long-simmered, richly flavored and thick with an almost magical blending of ingredients, a traditional ragu bears little resemblance to the stuff in jars that goes by the same name.

This takes lots of ingredients and ends up with a dark rich sauce. Save it for a rainy day that begs for a kitchen project, and invite friends over to share in the eating. A practical note: You can make a saucepan of 4 portions, as this recipe calls for, or you can double or triple the recipe, then freeze in several-portion parcels. Defrost and heat another day, seasoning with any of the following variations: lemon rind, artichoke hearts and chunks of chicken, bits of chicken livers, bacon. Ragu layered with lasagne and bechamel is sublime.

A practical through untraditional note: I often stretch the beef in this rich sauce with textured soy protein, and sometimes ground turkey as well.

The sauce should be so well-reduced and strongly flavored that each portion of pasta needs only two spoonfuls or so of sauce.

2 tablespoons butter

2 tablespoons olive oil

4 ounces pancetta or unsmoked, salted bacon, diced

1 medium onion, chopped

1 stalk celery, chopped

3 cloves garlic, chopped (actually, garlic is optional; the sauce is also lovely without it)

1 carrot, chopped

12 ounces lean braising beef such as chuck or flank, preferably coarsely chopped

4 to 6 chicken livers, roughly chopped

$^1\!/_2$ ounce dried porcini or other flavorful mushrooms

$^2\!/_3$ cup dry red wine

$1^1\!/_2$ cups roughly chopped tomatoes (canned are fine)

2 tablespoons tomato paste

$^1\!/_2$ cup beef broth

3-inch piece lemon rind

1 teaspoon chopped parsley

Sprig fresh rosemary and/or marjoram

2 bay leaves

Salt and coarsely ground black pepper

$^1\!/_4$ cup milk or cream

1. Heat butter and olive oil with pancetta or bacon and brown gently, then add chopped onion, celery, garlic, and carrot, cooking gently until the onion has softened.
2. Add meat and cook over medium heat until it colors. Add chicken livers and dried mushrooms, cook a minute, then pour in the wine. Cook over medium heat until wine has almost evaporated.
3. Add tomatoes, tomato paste, broth, lemon rind, and herbs and simmer very slowly for at least 2 hours. This is not fast food.
4. Add salt and pepper. Taste for seasoning. If too thin, raise heat to reduce; if too thick and threatening to burn, add a little more broth.
5. Add milk or cream, then serve as desired.

Variation: Lemon-Scented White Wine Ragu
Omit chicken livers from above recipe and substitute white wine for red wine and a lemon half for the lemon rind.

Variation: Ragu alla Sardegna
LAMB RAGU FROM SARDINIA
Prepare the basic ragu using lamb instead of beef. Omit the lemon and cream/milk finishing and season with a generous handful of fresh chopped mint toward the end.

Variation: Ragu con Olive e Salsicche
RAGU WITH OLIVES AND SAUSAGES
Prepare ragu omitting lemon and cream. Add a savory sausage or two instead of meat or bacon. Just before serving add a handful of diced black oil-cured olives.

I Dolci

SWEETS AND DESSERTS

The islands, like the rest of Italy, enjoy a wide array of elaborate, almost baroque sweets. In Italy, you would buy these from specialty shops, or in Sicily, from convents famous for their sweets. Indeed, entire books have been written about the sweets of Italy and her islands.

When in Italy, sample the crisp little cookies, scented with the peel of lemon, or the dry biscotti, brittle as a bone and delicious when dipped into a glass of wine or a cup of coffee. Blush as you ask for the bishop's buttocks or the nun's breasts, both names of various cookies.

Try the almost translucent confection of grape must (see Special Ingredients), known in Sardinia as *sapa* or *saba*, in Sicily as *mustarda,* often used as filling for cookies, pastries, and sweet breads. If you are adventurous, try this unusual dessert from Sardinia: *culingionis di sanguinaccio,* sugar-sweet pig's blood ravioli.

In Sicily admire the little sugar figurines so festive and beautiful, specially prepared for the feast-days, and wonder over the sweet almond paste goodies that are a specialty of the medieval town of Erice, a town of cobbled streets that sits dignified on a hillside overlooking the Mediterranean.

For blissful cannoli, travel to Palermo and visit the good sisters at the Benedictine Convent. Their crisp, nearly greaseless pastry shells are filled at the last minute with a sweetened ricotta mixture. Such a delicacy has saved even the most recalcitrant of souls.

Italian frozen desserts such as *gelati, granite,* and *sorbetti* are exceptional throughout the islands. They are made from sweet fruits, flowers, even ricotta cheese, and Sicilian gelato is seriously delicious. Sometimes ice cream is made from sheep's milk and is richer, softer, more delicate than cow's-milk ice cream could ever be.

In Sicily, ice creams and ices are often constructed into elaborate concoctions such as the traditional summer watermelon ice shaped like a melon, complete with little seeds made of chocolate. Watermelon is also turned into a refreshing jellylike pudding.

Layered concoctions of liqueur-soaked cakes with custard and cream, preserved fruits, and bits of chocolate; crisp cannoli and creamy tiramisu; sweetened ricotta cheese and delicate cheesecakes, are displayed in dizzying array in pastry shops and cafes where they are purchased for special occasions or as the mood requires. I therefore offer only a few recipes and descriptions, preferring to concentrate on the desserts and fruit-based sweets one would prepare in the Italian home.

FRUIT DESSERTS

IN the home, fruit is the most common dessert, delicious little dishes of fruit, lightly sweetened and/or flavored with wine or liqueurs. In Italy fruit is often grown on small plots for flavor rather than for mass consumerism; it tastes sweeter, more intense than fruit elsewhere. Sometimes I think that the fruit of the islands in particular is all the more flavorful for its suffering in poor soil, strong salty winds, hot sultry air.

Nectarines taste like essence of nectarine, strong with summer perfume; pears are sweet and juicy with an echo of almond; berries burst with flavor; and watermelon is such a delight that entire stands or restaurants are set up in the streets to sell it. I doubt you will ever find a more delicious melon.

When the season is over you will not find the fruit in the market: That is the price you pay. (Here in the United States, for fruit with the brightest, most intense flavor, either grow your own or frequent your local farmers' market.)

In Sicily and on many of the neighboring islands, the Arabic custom of bringing refreshing vegetables to the table along with fresh fruit at the end of a meal is still practiced. Celery, fennel, cucumber, and red peppers are as sweet and juicy as fruit for dessert.

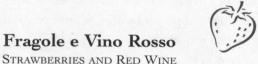

Fragole e Vino Rosso
STRAWBERRIES AND RED WINE

On a warm early summer evening, when strawberries are at their sweetest and most fragrant, place two bowls on the table, one filled with strawberries, the other with red wine.

The bowl of red wine is for dipping the strawberries, one by one as you eat. Shake off the excess and dip into sugar, too, if you like. The red wine amplifies the berry flavor in a delightful way.

Mori e Melone con Porto o Marsala
BLACKBERRIES AND MELON WITH PORT OR MARSALA

Serves 4

I like the fruit for this dessert chilled to cool refreshment, but not refrigerated for days on end to a chilly numbness. A Tuscan favorite eaten in the islands off its coast.

2 cups blackberries

3 tablespoons sugar

1/2 cup port, Marsala, blackberry brandy, or similar fortified wine or fruit brandy

2 ripe cantaloupes, cut into wedges

1. Combine blackberries with sugar and wine or brandy. Macerate for about an hour if possible; the best way to do this is to macerate the berries before dinner. When it comes time for dessert, the berries have absorbed the wine flavor.
2. Serve spoonfuls of berries and their sauce next to wedges of sweet flavorful melon. Serve immediately.

Variation: Fragole e Melone
STRAWBERRIES AND HONEYDEW MELON
Use strawberries in place of the blackberries and honeydew in place of the cantaloupe. In place of port, use kirsch, brandy, or *liqueur frais de bois.*

Pesche con Amaretti e Mandorle
FRESH PEACHES WITH AMARETTI AND ALMONDS

Serves 4

So simple and so very delicious, this is my favorite summer sweet: juicy peaches, crisp crumbs of amaretti, crunchy nuggets of toasted almond, all topped with dollops of crème fraîche.

¼ cup sliced or slivered almonds

8 ripe sweet peaches

Sugar to taste

A few drops almond extract

Dash lemon juice

10 small amaretti, crumbled (Amaretti are crisp almond meringue cookies; usually purchased rather than home-baked, they get their distinctive aroma from apricot pits.)

4 tablespoons lightly whipped cream, crème fraîche, or sour cream (light is fine), ice cream, or frozen yogurt

2 tablespoons strawberry preserves or about 8 fresh strawberries

1. Lightly toast almonds in an ungreased frying pan on top of the stove until lightly golden brown around the edges. Leave to cool.
2. Peel and slice peaches, then toss with sugar, almond extract, and lemon juice. Chill until ready to serve.
3. Arrange peaches in bowls and serve each portion sprinkled with the crumbled amaretti and garnished with a dollop of cream, a dab of the preserves or several fresh berries, and a scattering of the reserved toasted almonds.

Pesche al Forno con Mori Freschi
ROASTED PEACHES IN RED WINE WITH FRESH BLACKBERRIES

Serves 4

Baking emphasizes the fruity taste of peaches, intensifying both their flavor and perfume. Fresh blackberries, lightly moistened with a little wine and sugar, make a fresh contrast to the rich peaches. The peaches can be served either hot, warm, or cool.

8 peaches

¼ cup sugar or to taste

1 cup red wine or enough to come to a depth of about ½ to ¾ inch in baking pan

Dash of almond or vanilla extract

1 cup blackberries

1. Score the skin of the peaches lengthwise, dividing the peaches into what look like wedges. Plunge the peaches into hot water and blanch for a minute or two. Remove and let cool; the skin will peel right off.
2. Place peaches in a single layer in a baking dish and sprinkle well with about 3 tablespoons sugar. Pour red wine between the peaches, then bake in a 375°F oven for 45 minutes or until lightly caramelized and tender, adding more wine or water if needed to

keep a shallow layer of sauce. Remove from oven and season sauce with a dash of almond or vanilla extract.

3. Mix berries with remaining tablespoon sugar, or to taste. Serve each portion of the peaches with a little of the pan sauce and some of the berries spooned over.

Variation: Puree the fresh berries along with the pan juices; sieve if you like. Serve the sauce spooned over the roasted peaches.

Aranci alla Zingara
BLOOD ORANGES WITH MARSALA
Sicily

Serves 4

No one knows when or where blood oranges originated, though many say they are native to Sicily. Legend has it that a prince of Salerno, besieged by Saracens in 1002, used blood oranges as incentive to the Normans to conquer southern Italy.

A blood orange is distinctive from the more common orange not only for its striking scarlet shade, but also for its full, fragrant flavor. Often sharper, sometimes sweeter, blood-orange juice is thick, aromatic, and delightful. When choosing blood oranges, search for red splotches on the skin, a sign of lush red-hued flesh, and that aromatic flavor that distinguishes the blood orange from the ordinary one. If they are not available, however, use any flavorful juicy orange for this traditional dish.

4 to 6 sweet, fragrant, and very red blood oranges, peeled and sliced	Sugar to taste Several spoonfuls Marsala

Arrange sliced blood oranges on plates and sprinkle with sugar to taste. Drizzle with Marsala and chill until ready to eat.

Melagrana al Liquore

POMEGRANATE SEEDS MARINATED IN BRANDY

Tremiti

Serves 4

We arrived by boat and after we docked were taken to a restaurant that was little more than a sparsely decorated room up a narrow flight of stairs.

Yet the meal was as vibrant as the decor was nonexistent: a rough wooden table laden with antipasti, pasta with a fiery sauce, and a huge fish, stuffed with herbs and roasted until crisp-skinned and tender-fleshed.

When it was over we were brought a big bowl filled with pomegranate seeds—sweet, tangy, slightly bitter, all awash in a sauce of brandy and liqueur.

4 pomegranates

Juice of 1 lemon

6 tablespoons sugar

3 tablespoons brandy

3 tablespoons orange or raspberry liqueur

Peel the pomegranates and place the seeds in a bowl. Dress with lemon juice, sugar, brandy, and liqueur. Chill at least 2 hours.

Melone Tricolore

THREE COLORS AND FLAVORS OF MELON
Sicily

Serves 4

Melons that you find in Italy are so utterly delicious that you need do nothing more to them then wield a knife and develop skills at seed spitting. Throughout Italy, in high season, special roadside restaurants are set up, garishly painted with bright colors and cartoonlike paintings that have to do with watermelons and melon-eating. The focal point of these restaurants or melon stands is often a swimming pool-sized tank filled with great melons, bobbing up and down in the cooling water.

This recipe is slightly gilding the lily. Try it when you have eaten your fill of plain melon and long for something with a bit of panache. The combination of the three colors—red, orange, and green—is very nice indeed, and each of the melons has a slightly different flavor. If you have four kinds of melon, all the better.

I have added a dash of orange flower water, a scent sometimes added to sweets in Sicily. It makes the melon delightfully flower-scented, but it may not be to everyone's taste. You can omit it.

1 pound watermelon, peeled and cut into chunks (seeded if needed)

½ to 1 honeydew or Galia melon, peeled and seeded, then cut into chunks

1 cantaloupe, peeled, seeded, and cut into chunks

Several teaspoons sugar

Dash of lemon juice

Dash of orange flower water (optional)

Combine all ingredients, then chill.

Torta di Mori

BLACKBERRY TART

Elba

Serves 8

Down the dusty road we discovered a huge blackberry patch, and set about filling buckets with the fragile berries. A neighbor watched us set out, then when we returned, offered to make us this simple pie.

Enough short crust for 1-layer
pie crust

3 tablespoons sugar, or as needed

3 cups blackberries

Lightly whipped cream

1. Sprinkle pie crust dough with sugar and bake at 325°F until crust is lightly, crisply, golden and sugar has caramelized, about 20 minutes. Cool.
2. Just before serving, fill crust with blackberries and serve with lightly whipped cream.

Cassatta alla Pera

WINE-POACHED PEAR AND ALMOND CAKE, WITH WHIPPED CREAM

Sicily

Serves 8 to 10

This layered tort of wine-poached pears, ground almonds, and whipped cream is nearly baroque in its grand richness and it makes a splendid celebration cake. This is the sort of cake you could add nearly anything to:

fresh strawberries, bananas, nectarines, or poached peaches, bits of chocolate, or crushed crunchy toffee. And feel free to really soak the cake with liqueur, syrup, fruit, almonds . . . it is even more irresistible.

I make this with store-bought cake for quick assembly.

8 ripe but still firm pears, peeled and diced

3 cups dry white wine

½ cup sugar (or more)

Dash lemon juice

½ to 1 teaspoon almond extract, or to taste

½ cup ground almonds or almond paste

Sugar to taste

⅛ teaspoon cinnamon

1 pint whipping cream

Confectioners' sugar to taste

½ teaspoon vanilla extract

3 thin layers sponge cake, homemade or purchased

2 to 4 ounces brandy, rum, or other alcohol

⅓ cup flaked almonds, lightly toasted

1. Place pears, wine, and sugar in noncorrosive saucepan and bring to a boil. Reduce heat and simmer 10 to 15 minutes or until pears are tender. Remove pears from liquid with a slotted spoon and set aside.

2. Bring liquid to a boil and cook down until reduced in volume to about 1 cup. Taste for sweetness, then add a dash lemon juice and half of the almond extract. Set aside.

3. Combine ground almonds or almond paste with sugar and cinnamon and remaining almond extract. Set aside.

4. Whip cream until firmly whipped. Flavor with confectioners' sugar and vanilla to taste.

5. Place one layer of sponge cake on cake plate and drizzle top with a third of the pear syrup and a third of the brandy. Crumble the almond mixture over the top and layer half of the pears, then spread a third of the whipped cream. Top with the second layer.

6. Repeat with the drizzle of syrup and brandy, the remaining pears, and a third of the whipped cream. Top with last layer of cake, and drizzle that with the last of the syrup and brandy.

7. Frost the top with remaining whipped cream, then sprinkle the top with lightly toasted flaked almonds. Refrigerate until ready to serve.

Mandorlata
FRAGRANT ALMOND PASTE CAKE WITH TOASTED ALMOND TOPPING

This is adapted from my previous book *Sun-Drenched Cuisine*. It is reminiscent of the islands and tastes like delicate marzipan cake with a crisp glazed almond topping. Nibble with a cup of coffee in the morning or a glass of brandy later in the day.

If possible, let cake sit a day before serving, as it improves. Keeps well for about 5 days.

1½ cups raw unblanched almonds (measure before grinding)

½ cup flour

¼ teaspoon baking soda

¼ teaspoon baking powder

Pinch salt

4 tablespoons butter, preferably unsalted

½ cup sugar

1 egg

1 teaspoon almond extract, or to taste

½ cup sour cream (low-fat is okay)

¼ cup brandy

¼ teaspoon cinnamon or to taste

¾ cup sliced almonds

¼ cup confectioners' sugar

1½ tablespoons milk

1. Preheat oven to 350°F.
2. Grind raw almonds in a nut grinder, blender, or food processor until mealy in consistency. Set aside.
3. Mix flour with baking soda, baking powder, and salt. Set aside.
4. Cream butter with sugar, then beat in egg. When smooth, add ½ teaspoon almond extract, or more if desired, along with sour cream, brandy, cinnamon, and ground almonds.

5. Combine flour mixture with butter-sugar mixture, stirring only enough to make a thick batter. It should retain some lumps—they will bake away.

6. Pour into an 8 x 8-inch pan, either a nonstick pan or ordinary one sprayed with nonstick spray. Top with sliced almonds and bake at 350°F for 40 to 45 minutes, or until topping is golden. Because cake is quite thick and rich with ground almonds, it may remain too moist for a tester to come out clean.

7. Mix confectioners' sugar with milk and enough almond extract to give it a strong almond flavor. Pour evenly over the top of the cake and return cake to oven. Bake 5 to 10 minutes or until the topping sizzles and the almonds are beguilingly browned.

8. Remove from pan while still warm. The sugar syrup cools to a rather hard consistency and makes removal from the pan difficult. If cake cannot be removed from pan easily, serve it from the pan.

Biscotti di Vino
RED WINE BISCOTTI

Makes 40 cookies

These dry, hard little cookies are delicious dipped into a glass of red wine or coffee. Cookies made with red wine have been eaten since Roman times.

4½ cups flour

¾ cup sugar

2 teaspoons salt

1 tablespoon baking powder

1 cup vegetable oil

1 cup full-flavored dry red wine

1. Combine 4 cups flour, the sugar, salt, and baking powder and make a well in the center. Pour in the oil and wine, and mix from the edges, as if you were making pasta, until all of the flour mixture is incorporated with the liquid and it forms a soft dough.

2. Knead in remaining ½ cup flour, then divide the dough into 40 little balls.

3. Roll each ball into a 5- or 6-inch length, then form these into rings, pinching the edges together.

4. Place on nonstick baking sheets and bake at 350°F for 15 to 20 minutes. Reduce heat to 300°F and finish baking the cookies for another 15 to 20 minutes or until they are golden. Let cool on racks. Store in airtight containers.

GRANITE, SORBETTI, E GELATI
FROZEN DESSERTS

THE most delicious accompaniment to an Italian ice or gelato is a generous portion of the Italian national pastime: people-watching. Buy a cone of pistachio or strawberry ice, *ciocolatto* or zabaglione, and stroll the streets, wandering along the cobblestones. Take time to look in the shop windows, admire the passersby, ponder over the espresso drinkers sitting in the cafes, all the while licking at the ice cream as it melts in the hot afternoon or evening.

Whether it is the icy treat of granita, the fruity light ice, sorbetto, or creamy ice cream gelato, frozen desserts in Italy are intensely flavored and come in a wide and often wild array. A visit to a *gelateria* can be a dizzying experience.

I have included only a few of my favorites here, icy treats that are easy to prepare in the home kitchen and refreshing on a summer day.

Basic Granita Directions

The grown-up treat of granita, crushed crystals of strongly flavored ices, makes a refreshing and often provocative sweet. Not smooth and creamy like gelato, nor smooth and light like sorbetto, granita is almost crude, shockingly simple, utterly delicious.

I think about dark, strong, almost bitter espresso coffee frozen and forked up into a frisson of light fluffy ice, topped with a dollop of cream; this conjures up memories of sultry summer afternoons sitting in cafe-bars after the siesta as the town is just coming back to life. I recall, too, a young boy with a huge chunk of flavored ice and hand grater, ready to grate bits of ice into a cup individually, as each customer ordered it.

The thing to remember about granita is that texture is everything, or nearly so. The aim is to achieve uniformly small and separate, light and fluffy little ice crystals, like tiny grains (hence the name).

The best way to do this is not with an expensive machine but with an ordinary, heavy-duty fork, scraping at the ice rim around the edge of the liquid every so often as it forms. Repeat this, scraping and mixing it with the liquid, every 30 minutes or so (begining about an hour after you have placed it in the freezer) until the mixture forms a smooth consistency with lovely, light grains separate like newly fallen snow. It should then be eaten immediately, but if you stir and fork it every so often you can keep it for several hours.

Granita di Espresso
ESPRESSO GRANITA

Serves 4

Dark and deliciouslly bitter, Granita di Espresso is lovely served with a
dollop of lightly whipped cream or a tiny scoop of vanilla gelato.

4 cups freshly made strong
espresso-type French-roast
coffee

Sugar to taste

Combine and freeze according to directions above.

Granita di Limone
LEMON GRANITA

Serves 4 to 6

Possibly the most favored flavor of granita, along with Granita di
Espresso, lemon granita is exquisitely refreshing as its light and fruity
coolness spreads from your throat throughout your body, cooling you
from the unremitting summer heat.

Sometimes cafes spoon a scoop of this granita into cooling glasses of
iced tea or lemonade.

1 cup sugar

3 cups water

1 cup freshly squeezed lemon
juice

Combine sugar with water and bring to a boil. Cook until sugar is dissolved, then allow to cool. Add lemon juice and freeze as in Basic Granita
Directions (page 249).

Variation: Lime Granita
Instead of lemon juice, use freshly squeezed lime juice and about $1/2$ teaspoon grated lime zest.

Granita di Gelsomino

JASMINE GRANITA

Sicily

Serves 4 to 6

This is quintessentially Sicilian, the scent of flowers and cinnamon perfuming the icy granita.

2 cups freshly picked unsprayed
    jasmine flowers

3 cups water

3/4 cup sugar

Pinch of cinnamon

Juice of 1/2 lemon or to taste

Dash of orange flower water

1. Place jasmine flowers in bowl and cover with 2 1/2 cups water. Cover and let steep overnight (flowers are at their best when picked in the evening as that is when they open and give off their perfume).
2. Combine remaining water and sugar and bring to a boil just until sugar dissolves.
3. Strain jasmine flowers from the steeping liquid, then combine with the cooled sugar syrup. Season with cinnamon, lemon juice and orange flower water. Freeze according to Basic Granita Directions.

Granita di Mortelli

CRANBERRY GRANITA

Ischia

Serves 4 to 6

4 cups cranberry juice cocktail

2 ounces peach brandy
    (optional)

Squeeze of lime

Combine and freeze as above.

Cremolata di Mandorla
ALMOND GRANITA
Sicily

Serves 4 to 6

On the eastern coast of Sicily, granita is often called *cremolata*. This one is made from almond milk or almond syrup combined with water, then frozen. It is sweetly scented, and for those who love almonds as I do, irresistible.

4 cups water	**1 cup commercial almond syrup, or to taste**

Combine and freeze as in Basic Granita Directions (page 249).

Variation: In place of commercial almond syrup, boil ½ cup sugar with 3 cups water, then let cool. Add a generous dash of almond extract.

Sorbetto all'Aranciata
BLOOD-ORANGE SORBETTO
Sicily

Serves 4

The juice of the blood orange, so essentially Sicilian, adds its distinctive flavor and color to the sorbetto.

1 pint blood-orange juice (from 7 to 8 oranges)	**2 tablespoons Grand Marnier or Cointreau**
1 cup sugar	**1 tablespoon fresh lemon juice**

1. Combine all ingredients and stir until sugar is dissolved. Taste, and add more sugar if necessary, more lemon or orange juice if it is too sweet.
2. Freeze in an ice cream freezer or in an ice tray, removing and scraping every so often as it freezes.

GELATO

ITALIAN ice cream is full-flavored though surprisingly often much less creamy than its American counterpart.

Unlike commercial ice creams and gelati, with their emulsifiers and sophisticated machinery, homemade ice cream and gelato must be eaten as soon as it is frozen, or within a few hours. Otherwise, it becomes icy and hard, and its flavor seems to freeze into oblivion.

Gelato di Pesche alla Siciliano
PEACH GELATO

Palermo, Sicily

Serves 4

This fresh gelato is very appealing: creamy, fruity, and sweet, yet made with *crema rinforzata* (a very light cornstarch-based custard) instead of cream. Other fruit is equally delicious—strawberries, blackberries, mango, apricots, poached pears, banana, or your own combination.

It must be eaten as soon as it is frozen or it begins to turn rock-hard; however, all is not lost: In this hardened ice-bound state it makes a delicious addition to a frozen yogurt *frullato* or shake.

2¹/₂ cups milk

2 tablespoons cornstarch

³/₄ cup sugar

1 egg yolk

3 to 4 ripe summer peaches, peeled or unpeeled as desired, mashed with a fork

Dash of almond extract

Dash of vanilla extract

1. Heat 2 cups of the milk until boiling. Meanwhile, combine remaining milk with cornstarch, sugar, and egg yolk and mix well.

2. Remove scalded milk from heat and slowly stir into the milk-cornstarch-sugar-egg mixture, then return it all to the saucepan and cook over medium heat, stirring constantly until mixture just comes to a boil and is thickened. Remove from heat and let cool.

3. When cool, add peaches and almond and vanilla extracts, then pour into an ice cream maker (or a pan for freezing, removing every so often and scraping, as if making granita). Freeze until creamy and well-iced.

Variation: Serve the peach gelato topped with an almond praline. To make praline lightly toast 1 cup flaked almonds until golden, then sprinkle with 3 to 4 tablespoons sugar and lower the heat, continuing to toast as the sugar caramelizes; take care it doesn't burn. Transfer to a plate immediately and let it harden.

Gelato Cioccolato Doppio
DEEP DARK DOUBLE CHOCOLATE GELATO
Sicily

Serves 4

I like my chocolate gelato to taste of chocolate, chocolate, and more chocolate. This one does, but if it is still not enough, fold ½ cup chocolate sauce into the nearly frozen mixture for a chocolate swirl.

2½ cups milk

6 to 8 ounces semisweet chocolate, broken into bits

2 tablespoons cornstarch

½ cup sugar

1 egg yolk

Dash vanilla extract, to taste

1. Scald 1 cup milk, then remove from heat and add chocolate bits.
2. Combine remaining 1½ cups milk with cornstarch, sugar, and egg

yolk and mix well. Heat over medium heat, stirring contantly until custard is creamy and thickened and just begins to bubble. Remove from heat and let cool.

3. When both mixtures are cool, combine and add a dash of vanilla extract. Freeze in an ice cream freezer or in freezer tray, removing and scraping as for granita.

Variation: Gelato "Baci"
To the chocolate ice cream, add chunks of rich hazelenut-scented *baci* chocolates, along with toasted and coarsely chopped hazelnuts.

Affogado al Caffe
COFFEE MILKSHAKE

Serves 1 to 2

Strong coffee whirled with ice cream: the most delicious way to get caffeine pumping through your bloodstream on a hot day.

²⁄₃ cup strong cooled brewed espresso	Dash brandy or other spirit if desired
2 scoops gelato: 1 scoop chocolate, 1 vanilla or espresso bean	Garnish: Unsweetened or lightly sweetened whipped cream; grated chocolate

Mix espresso, gelato, and brandy in blender and whirl until smooth and creamy. Serve at once, topped with a dollop of cream and a shake of grated chocolate.

Special Ingredients

Few exotic ingredients are absolutely necessary to capture the essential flavors of the islands. It is the simple foods—fresh seafood, olive oil, local vegetables, and rustic cheeses—that flavor the cuisine. There are, however, some ingredients that are either favored or peculiar to the islands, and other Italian ingredients that call for some basic description and/or directions.

Borage: Also known as *burrania;* in Sicily especially, borage is enjoyed as a fresh and sprightly herb and also for the blue blossoms that appear in spring, which are scattered deliciously atop salads and almost anything else. Borage may occasionally be bought as blossoms or leaves from specialty greengrocers or farmers' markets, or you may grow it from seed.

Borlotti beans: Brown beans with a round, rich flavor, much like pinto beans or the American Southwestern Anasazi bean. Fresh cranberry beans are much like borlotti beans.

Borlotti beans are often available in cans, imported from Italy, where they are eaten in soups, risotto, and pasta, marinated as salads, or cooked with mushrooms or other aromatic vegetables.

If borlotti are unavailable, use cranberry, Anasazi, or pinto.

Bottargu: Tuna or cod roe, salted and pressed into sausagelike shapes, then left to dry. The result is much like a deliciously fishy salami, eaten thinly sliced atop a small slice of buttered bread or tomato salad as an antipasto. From Sardinia to Sicily, bottargu is eaten grated over pasta, risotto, or stewed white beans in olive oil; mixed with butter and spread over grilled beef or pork steaks; sprinkled over vinaigrette-dressed celery; tossed into beef, turkey, or swordfish scallopine. Truly it captures the flavor of the islands.

Capers (Capperi): These flower buds grow wild along the shores of much of the Mediterranean, especially central and southern Italy. Sicilan capers are renowned for their delicious briny scent, and those that come from the tiny island of Pantelleria are bigger, with bigger flavor, often preserved in salt rather than vinegar. Capers have a peculiar, saline scent, and much like olives can be a bit controversial—people either love them or hate them. And like olives, capers can grow on you.

Add a tiny spoonful or two of capers to any quick sauté of fish or poultry, or scatter into vegetable, fish, poultry, or meat salads. They're delicious sprinkled atop roasted red peppers or tomatoey pasta dishes, and they are without peer in stewy, spicy fish dishes.

Estratto di Pomodoro (also known as *astrattu* or *la salsa secca*): Six times the strength of tomato paste, *astrattu* is a dark, clay-textured paste of salted tomato purée that has been spread out on large wooden boards to dry in the scorching summer sun until nearly all of the moisture has evaporated. Preserved under a layer of olive oil, it keeps in the fridge for several weeks and is usually sold from big bowls by the spoonful. Its strong, concentrated flavor can wake up the humble ingredients of *cucina povera:* the pasta, beans, eggs, bits of fish, and seasonal vegetables. Add *astrattu* to lentil dishes or braised meat or chicken; spread a thin layer onto bruschetta, then top with a basil leaf; or stir a dab into *pasta con le sarde.*

Patience Gray, in *Honey from a Weed*, describes how tomato sauce is dried by smearing it onto plates, then taking it out onto the rooftop during a particularly hot day. By nightfall the sauce hardens into a brownish red mixture to be rolled into balls and preserved in olive oil for the winter.

Fava beans: Either fresh or dried, fava beans play a large role in Mediterranean diets, including the dishes of the Italian islands.

Dried, they might be boiled and sold as a snack, or simmered into simple rustic soups. Cook as you would other dried beans, but you will need to slip off their tough skins once the beans are tender and cool enough to handle.

Fresh fava beans are one of the ingredients that capture the flavor of the region. Pale green, favas have a mild soft flavor somewhat like limas. When very young, their tough skins have not yet formed and you can eat them raw or lightly blanched, nibbled as an antipasto, along with oil-cured olives, cubed mortadella, fresh milky mozzarella, and wedges of garden tomatoes.

Generally, however, fresh favas need to be both blanched and peeled. For 2 cups shelled fava beans, begin with 2 pounds favas in the pod. Shell, then toss into about 4 cups boiling water. Simmer uncovered until the beans are just tender, 2 to 3 minutes. Drain and let cool until you can handle them.

To peel, use your fingernails or a paring knife and make a little slit across one of the sides and slide the bean right out of its skin. Discard the skins.

For fava bean puree, delicious as a base for soups and minestrones, don't bother to remove the covering membranes. Simply puree the cooked beans with enough liquid to facilitate the process; if the consistency is too rough, strain the mixture and discard the skin and fiber bits that are left behind.

Must: The jellylike grape residue left from winemaking. Must is the basis for a wide variety of sweets in Sardinia and Sicily, and unfortunately there is no substitute for either its texture or flavor.

Olive oil: Gnarled silver-leaved olive trees have covered the hills of Mediterranean islands for millennia, and the flavor of olive oil is the flavor of local cuisine.

In Sicily especially, olive oil is the heart of the cookery. Come harvest time, as most people have at least one or two olive trees, the pressing is a personal tradition. Family presses work overtime, pressing and grinding, separating the solids from the liquid, then putting it all into a centrifuge that produces the oil. This oil is strongly flavored, at its best drizzled over hot bread and sprinkled with salt.

Olive oil is eaten throughout the islands, often homemade. Butter is seldom eaten since there is little room for cows to graze on the rocky landscapes or seafronts. Extra-virgin olive oil is the first trickling of oil, cold-pressed from the olive, and despite the fact that it is more expensive, I always prefer its fragrant, full flavor for cooking as well as salads. Olive oil labeled "pure" is a second or third pressing, inferior in terms of aroma and olive flavor.

With the huge array of oils available, use flavor, aroma, and price as a guide. Olive oils are imported from regions of Italy, Greece, Spain, and France as well as produced in California.

Olives: To detail the olives available, one would need to visit every field, every grove, every tree, since the olives from each tree taste different. Wind and rain, sun and the minerals of the soil—even, legend has it, the disposition of those who tend the trees—affect the flavor of the olives.

Most olives fall into the category of brined (the black Gaeta, Greek, Niçoise, Kalamata, and most of the green olives); oil-cured (often found in Italy and especially in Sicily); and olives spiced with aromatics and marinades. An excellent way of familiarizing yourself with a wide variety of olives is to frequent delis or shops that have a large assortment, and taste your way through.

Olive paste is made from crushed olives, olive oil, and sometimes seasonings such as garlic and herbs. Available in either black or green, it is also sold imported from France as tapenade and from Greece as well. Use as a spread atop buttered bread or a sauce for pasta. A spoonful mixed with mayonnaise is magnificent.

Porcini mushrooms (funghi): Porcini mushrooms taste of the forest— earthy, perfumed, slightly woodsy. They taste like nothing else, are absolutely delicious—and very expensive. I have found a less expensive Argentinian dried mushroom, a cousin to the Italian porcini, which has a stronger, more forceful taste than the elegant porcini but is wonderful in its own right. Since it is so reasonably priced, I can toss it into anything without compunction. The Napa Valley Olive Oil Co. on McCorquadale Drive, in St. Helena, California, sells these marvelous mushrooms by mail order.

European mushrooms include cepes and morels, and I have found the the Japanese shiitake mushroom is often wonderful in Italian pasta dishes or stews.

To rehydrate dried mushrooms: Place mushrooms in a bowl and pour hot water or broth over them. Cover and let sit for about 30 minutes or until mushrooms are softened and liquid is cool enough to touch. Remove mushrooms from liquid and squeeze well, letting the juices from the mushrooms drip back into the soaking liquid. Squeeze them really well, then save the liquid. Since most dried mushrooms are quite sandy, you then need to place the squeezed mushrooms in a bowl of cold water, let them sit a minute or two, then remove and squeeze once again. Discard this water. The rehydrated mushrooms are now ready for use, and the soaking liquid makes one of the best possible additions or bases for sauces or soups. Since the sand sinks to the bottom, you can simply pour off the soaking liquid and leave behind the last few spoonfuls in which the grit has settled. Alternatively, you can strain the liquid through a cheesecloth to be sure no sand escapes into your saucepan.

Sausages, salami, and cured meats: The selection of sausages and salami available throughout Italy and the islands remains intensely regional. Few varieties are available in the United States; the more easily found ones include a pork sausage scented with fennel or with hot peppers. Italian-style air-dried salami is produced in San Francisco and is excellent.

Pancetta is an Italian bacon, salted instead of smoked, and often it is sold rolled into a sausage shape, then sliced. Pancetta may or may not be forcefully spiced with black pepper. Do not use smoked bacon in place of pancetta as its flavor is too pronouncedly smoky.

Prosciutto is salted, air-dried ham, served thinly sliced in a variety of ways, or diced and added to soups and sauces for extra flavor. Italian prosciutto has a sweet, farmyard haylike aroma and is exorbitantly priced; domestic prosciutto is terribly salty but affordable. Bresaola is similar to prosciutto and is eaten in the same ways, but is made from beef instead of pig.

Sun-dried tomatoes: Ripe sweet Roma tomatoes, dried in the sun to an almost leathery or crisp state. One may buy them from either Italy or California, dried or rehydrated and marinated in olive oil and seasonings.

To rehydrate them: Pour boiling water over the dried tomatoes in a bowl and cover. Let sit for 30 minutes or until they plump up and soften. Alternatively, they may be simmered for about 10 minutes until they soften.

Drain, saving the soaking liquid for soup or sauce. Place the warm drained tomatoes in a bowl, season generously with chopped garlic, a sprinkling of salt (if dried tomatoes have not been salted), a tablespoon or two of red wine vinegar and/or balsamic vinegar, and a few sprinkles of crumbled thyme, rosemary, herbes de Provence, or basil to taste, then add olive oil to coat it all. Let sit and marinate for at least an hour, or cover and refrigerate for up to a week.

ITALIAN CHEESES

Throughout the islands there are many local cheeses as well as cheeses that are exported to the rest of the country and beyond. Goat and sheep cheeses are eaten in Sardinia and Sicily; occasionally one finds Italian goat cheese, *formaggio di caprina,* or a fresh pecorino made from sheep's milk, much like feta but less salty. More easily found goat cheese from France and California may be used instead.

Caciocavallo: Sicilian cheese with a mild to pungent flavor that gets chewy—rather than stringy like mozzarella—as it heats. A typical Sicilian dish is fried or grilled in a pan with garlic, splashed with a bit of vinegar and a handful of herbs, then eaten with hunks of crusty bread.

Pecorino: Made from sheep's milk, pecorino may be eaten fresh when it is somewhat like a less salty feta or Mexican queso fresco. Most often, though, pecorino is available dried as a grating cheese.

It can be quite salty, and doesn't melt quite as evenly as Parmesan, but pecorino has a piquant scent of sheep's milk that makes it a distinctive, highly flavorful grating cheese.

Pecorino Romano is made in the central part of Italy while pecorino Sardo comes from Sardinia. If it is labeled plain pecorino, it comes from the south of Italy.

TOMATO PASSATA, PUREE, AND SAUCE

Tomato passata is the pure sieved tomato and some of its juices, usually sold unseasoned and in a waxed cardboard container or glass bottle so that the tomatoes don't pick up the metallic taste of the can.

Tomato puree is a thick passatalike mixture, though seasoned with salt; canned tomato sauce is to my mind very acidic and overly seasoned with salt and other flavors such as onion, garlic, and so forth.

During tomato season, when tomatoes are abundant and flavorful, fresh is your best choice. In the cold months, I prefer tomato passata.

PASTA

Pasta is no more than a simple paste of flour and water, rolled or stretched into a myriad of shapes, then boiled. The delight comes not only in the flavor and texture—tender, chewy, satisfying—but also in the nearly endless variety of shapes from the hollow tubes such as bucatini, the chewy twists known as cavatelli (or cavateppi, or gemelli), the ruffly shapes called chifferini, to the wide flat noodles pappardelle. There is a pasta for every taste and a sauce for every pasta.

Thin pastas such as vermicelli or capellini are best with lively, zesty little sauces, while tiny pastina such as stelline, acini de pepe, or semone de melone are best in soup or even as a pilaf-type accompaniment. Flat pasta is good with strongly flavored sauces, and shell macaroni is best with full-flavored sauces and bits of vegetables, meats, and/or seafoods that can get deliciously trapped inside their hollows. Thicker, sturdier pastas are usually the best for saucing and baking: lasagna, penne, macaroni, pappardelle. Sometimes, however, smaller pastas are delicious sauced and layered or stuffed into vegetables, then baked.

Any delicate pasta, such as a thin flat noodle or fresh pasta, shows off a light, subtle, or cream sauce, and stuffed pastas are best sauced simply, as their filling is almost like a sauce, flavor-wise.

Pasta may be cooked by boiling until just tender, then draining. Or it may be cooked the following way: Add to rapidly boiling salted water, boil for 2 minutes, then cover pan and let sit, off the heat. The heat of the water slowly cooks the pasta, giving a more tender, supple result. The time needed after your initial 2-minute boil will vary; for spaghetti, you will generally need between 6 to 8 minutes of steeping in the hot water. A thinner pasta will take a shorter time, and a thicker one slightly longer.

INDEX